FORTY YEARS IN SOCIAL WORK

REFLECTIONS ON PRACTICE AND THEORY

CHRISTOPHER RHOADES DŸKEMA

NASW PRESS

National Association of Social Workers
Washington, DC

Jeane W. Anastas, PhD, LMSW, *President*
Elizabeth J. Clark, PhD, ACSW, MPH, *Executive Director*

Cheryl Y. Bradley, *Publisher*
Sarah Lowman, *Project Manager*
Rebecca Tippets, *Proofreader*
Karen Schmitt, *Indexer*

Edited by Joel Blau
Cover by Metadog Design Group
Interior design and composition by Electronic Quill Publishing Services
Printed and bound by Victor Graphics, Inc.

First impression: January 2013

© 2013 by the NASW Press

All rights reserved. No part of this book may be reproduced or transmitted in any form or by any means, electronic or mechanical, including photocopying, recording, or by any information storage and retrieval system, without permission in writing from the publisher.

Library of Congress Cataloging-in-Publication Data

Dÿkema, Christopher Rhoades, 1944–2008.
   Forty years in social work : reflections on practice and theory / Christopher Rhoades Dÿkema.
      pages cm
   Includes bibliographical references and index.
   ISBN 978-0-87101-443-6
   1. Dÿkema, Christopher Rhoades, 1944–2008. 2. Social workers—United States—Biography. 3. Social service—United States—History. I. Title.
   HV40.32.D95D95 2012
   361.3092—dc23
   [B]
                         2012039731

Printed in the United States of America

TABLE OF CONTENTS

INTRODUCTION
Christopher Dÿkema: A Short Biography ∽ V
Joel Blau

CHAPTER 1
Becoming a Social Worker (1966–1970) ∽ 1

CHAPTER 2
Starting in Child Welfare (1970–1975) ∽ 15

CHAPTER 3
The Search for Theory in Social Work: Graduate School
(1975–1977) ∽ 43

CHAPTER 4
A Group Home in the Bronx (1977–1979) ∽ 49

CHAPTER 5
On (Not) Getting a Doctorate (1979–1984) ∽ 63

CHAPTER 6
Beyond Ethnicity: A Hospital Social Worker
Tries to Understand His Clients (1984–1988) ∽ 67

CHAPTER 7
Changes in the Emergency Room: Toward Better
Psychosocial Assessments (1989–1999) ∽ 97

CHAPTER 8
A Theory for Social Work Practice? (1999–2007) ～ 129

AFTERWORD
Social Work: Forty Years of Change ～ 147
Joel Blau

Endnotes ～ 153

Index ～ 175

INTRODUCTION
CHRISTOPHER DŸKEMA: A SHORT BIOGRAPHY
Joel Blau

CHRISTOPHER DŸKEMA WAS probably not supposed to become a social worker. Christopher's parents were both academics at Youngstown University; Christopher had gone to high school in nearby Canfield, topped off by a year of prep school in Switzerland, and then enrolled at Columbia University, from which he graduated in 1966. His family expected him to return to Ohio, where he was supposed to select an appropriate graduate school and launch an academic career. Instead, he declined an offer to study Japanese at Harvard to become a caseworker at the New York City Department of Social Services.

Rural Ohio in the 1950s was not a very hospitable place for the son of local academics: most high school students prized sports and venerated football. Christopher not only excelled in class and disliked football, but grew up in a home where, from an early age, an interest in language, culture, and ideas was assumed. For Christopher, the legacy of this experience was a lifelong sense of himself as an outsider. At the same time, however, it also imbued him with a passionate interest in the differences among and between diverse groups of people. As a matter of both experience and sensibility, he was an observer, but as his work shifted from casework to child protective services and, ultimately, to pediatric social work in the Bronx's Montefiore Hospital emergency room, his observations acquired an increasingly coherent purpose: they would be put in the service of his effort to blend the psychosocial and the political/economic into a more comprehensive social work theory.

This professional memoir, then, links accounts of his interaction with clients to a wide-ranging effort to place his practice experience in the broadest possible context. The stories are funny, tragic, and poignant, but they are always distinguished by Christopher Dÿkema's pursuit of the theory or theories that would best explain what he had just experienced. The result is a book of many facets: it is a record of one man's career in social work, a testament to his commitment to the profession's need for theory building, and a history of social welfare over the past 40 years.

Of course, none of these achievements would have been possible without the love and support of a family he cherished dearly: his wife Ellen, also a social worker, to whom he was married for 33 years and with whom he often discussed the theories in this book, and his two sons, Michael and Daniel, who share their father's engagement with ideas and his concern for social justice. Christopher's family both grounded and sustained him. When he died in 2008, he left an admirable legacy: his family and this professional memoir.

CHAPTER ONE
BECOMING A SOCIAL WORKER (1966–1970)

I WORKED IN the social work field for 40 years. Now I am retired because of ill health, and I want to look back on my experiences and the thoughts I developed on the profession, its theory, and practice.

I worked in a number of agencies and did many kinds of work. All of it was fairly conventional social work practice—public assistance, child welfare, and medical social work in an emergency room and in home care. All of it was interesting, despite the frequent frustrations of working within the American social welfare and health care systems.

I entered the field almost by accident. In 1966 I graduated from college in New York City and needed a job. I was a bit unusual in this respect—87 percent of my graduating class went on to some form of advanced education. This was only partly a consequence of the broad love of learning. Many wanted simply to avoid the draft, and the Vietnam War. I, however, had a six-month medical deferment, which I hoped would persist. I was free, as it were, to embark on full adulthood.

I did not want to work in business, and I took a series of civil service examinations. The results came in rather slowly, but then I received an indirect hint from my family that I return to the Midwest. I was in therapy at the time, and the thought of leaving treatment and returning to a place where I had never been very happy galvanized me into taking what I knew to be the most accessible civil service job—the New York City Department of Welfare's caseworker position.

Having passed the not-very-challenging examination, I reported to Personnel, where they processed me at breakneck speed. At the time, the department was opening a new center every few weeks, to cope with the swelling caseload. They told me to report to a training center in Manhattan.

The training lasted a few weeks and introduced us to the basics of public assistance as it existed at the time. I learned that there were several categories. Most of my clients would be receiving Aid to Dependent Children and would be single mothers with one or more offspring. Then there were other federal categories, partially subsidized from Washington, DC, including Aid to the Disabled, Aid to the Blind, and Old Age Assistance. This latter category was for people who had not been included in the earlier formulations of social security—domestic and farm workers and self-employed people. I even had a client so old that he had retired before the first social security check went out in 1940.

Then there was Home Relief, a local expense. It included a variety of people in miscellaneous situations, mostly single, low-functioning adults. There also were a few two-parent families in which the earned income was below the level of eligibility.

The trainer, Mr. Weinstein[1], tried to convey some of the emphasis on services that the most recent amendments to the Social Security Act had established. Congress, we learned, hoped that the services we would provide would help clients become more functional and enter the workforce. Hence, at the end of our dictation of each recertification visit, we had to write a "social study," to summarize the family's situation and "individualize the children." Mr. Weinstein also introduced us to some of the hundreds or thousands of forms we would be using.

He also outlined some rudiments of interviewing and the way we should conduct ourselves on home visits. The last week or so of training alternated between the classroom and our training units in our assigned centers. I recall sitting in the Central Park Zoo at lunch with a fellow trainee, whom I dated for a while, and comparing notes.

∽ • ∽ • ∽

MY ASSIGNMENT WAS to the Kingsbridge Welfare Center at 260 East 161st Street, in the Bronx. This was at the eastern edge of the neighborhood surrounding Yankee Stadium, in a former telephone company building overlooking the New York Central Railroad's Mott Haven Yards.

The immediate neighborhood was "changing"—a loaded word at the time—but still mostly Jewish, especially closer to the Grand Concourse. To the east was Morrisania, an area that had become substantially African American even in the 1930s. In some ways, its atmosphere was like parts of Harlem. To the west, by the Harlem River, was the still Irish area of Highbridge. The center's territory ran from about One Hundred Sixty First Street up to One Hundred Seventieth Street, and from Stebbins Avenue (now partly renamed Reverend James A. Polite Avenue) on the east, over to the Harlem River. It also included all of Manhattan above 115th Street, comprising a little of upper Harlem, Washington Heights, and Inwood. These were very diverse areas.

My supervisor, Lucius Nickerson, was experienced, serious, and conscientious; he worked very hard to help me and the other four trainees learn how to handle a caseload. "Controls" was his watchword. We needed to develop our own controls to keep track of the innumerable tasks. I later became very good at this kind of thing but was slow, at first, to pick it up. Perhaps it was because my strongest initial interest was in the new experience of encountering my clients.

I received 15 ongoing cases and was told to read the narratives. They dated back years and followed the families' lives through many vicissitudes. They were human documents, reflecting both the clients and the many workers' idiosyncrasies. I read them with fascination, and even today, opening and reading a case record or chart is an exciting experience.

After a few days, in late September 1966, I made my first visit, to a woman whose case had been active most of the time since her first application at the age of 13 or 14, in the year before my birth. She was in her mid-thirties and had seven or eight children. The record did seem to indicate some impulsivity and weakness of judgment, particularly in her relationships with men.

She lived in a shabby building to the east of the center. I went to see her, wearing the white shirt, tie, and jacket that I still thought was necessary, though I could have seen that most of the workers dressed more casually. One of the children admitted me and directed me to the living room, where I sat primly on the davenport. The client came, smelling slightly of alcohol, and sat beside me, rather invading my personal space, and clutched my wrist, asking my age. I admitted to being 22, and she exclaimed: "Now I have to tell my son that I finally got an investigator that's younger than he is!" This made me feel properly put in my place, but we went on to discuss the usual business of a recertification visit. I never met this son, who had moved out on his own. However, he has become a notably constructive community activist in a certain New York neighborhood.

As I met more clients, I discovered that most of them were sounder than the first, some of them impressively so. One, for example, who had eight or nine children, lived in a meticulously clean apartment in an otherwise shabby building. Once, when I was there, I saw her executive skill in action. She noticed a barely perceptible bit of dirt or disorder in the living room, but did not clean it up herself. Nor did she tell one of the kids to clean it up. No, she called an older boy to supervise his little brother in cleaning it up. Evidently, a rigorous staffing pattern prevailed. I am sure her children must have gone on to be effective members of society.

I decided that the primary problem most of my clients faced was lack of money, and I tried to distribute as much of it as I could. This was a complex process, because money for more than the basic "food, rent, and other," that is, for clothing, furniture, and other necessities, required specific, detailed grants, with individual approvals at various levels of supervision. These approvals followed complicated formulas that balanced the amount of the grant and the time since the last grant. At first, I was not very good at this, and many of the clients may have felt I was the pleasant fellow who did not come through with the money as fast as would have been desired.

Most of these women had lots of children. Quite normal mothers had six, seven, or eight. Why? At least in part because caseworkers were forbidden, on pain of dismissal, to discuss birth control with them. But this changed. In 1967, we received a memorandum allowing us to respond to clients' requests for information, and the following year we were instructed to initiate and document such discussion. Luker (1992), in *Dubious Conceptions*, detailed the evolving social policy that let this happen. I saw this happen on the ground. With family planning available, the birth rate plummeted among poor women. After about 1970, most women with large broods of children either were members of idiosyncratic religious sects like the Chassidim or the Black Hebrew Israelite Nation or were personally dysfunctional.

I found field visiting exhilarating, not only because of the contact with clients, but also because of the experience of getting to know the several diverse neighborhoods where I worked.

I tried to engage my clients in discussion about their lives, so as to know them better, of course, but also because I found their experiences fascinating. Gradually, I developed a sort of receptivity that prompted people to talk freely, with me asking only a few questions. I already had a fairly good historical and sociological sense and tried to see the clients as part of the human social process, though I did not consciously think of it that way at the time. This was the beginning of what became one of my great professional concerns—the application of social theory to social work practice. Many of my clients responded to my interest, and our conversations became comfortable.

ANOTHER NEW EXPERIENCE was the Social Service Employees Union, which represented caseworkers and some other titles. It had won a representation election, replacing Local 371 of the American Federation of State, County, and Municipal Employees, which still represented our supervisors. It had then gone on to win a strike the previous year, with emphasis on professionalization of the caseworker function, somewhat in line with the service amendments to the Social Security Act. The union was militant, its membership mostly young and single, and it operated on a very participatory basis. There were frequent membership meetings, and leaflets and the union newspaper appeared on our desks every few days. I became an active participant, went to all the meetings, and got to know the delegates and activists in the center. There were intense arguments and disputes, partly involving the various left sectarian groups that had joined the union. These, I found interesting, but I found their pseudo-populist appeals to suspicion and paranoia about our leadership difficult to take seriously.

We struck again in the summer of 1967, for six weeks, and with little success. I was arrested once, when the woman walking in front of me on the picket line said "Shame on you David!" to a scab walking into the building. We happened to be at a gap between the police sawhorses. David, whom I didn't know, lunged down and pushed her, and me too, because I was so close to her. All of us got arrested. The officers took us to the Forty First Precinct, where we were booked. I helped my arresting officer, Jim Fenton, with the paperwork, and he was quite grateful. After some hours in a cell, they loaded me into a paddy wagon, picked up other prisoners from other precincts, and took us to the Tombs, where I got into a conversation with a man who was there for stealing some dresses. I was reading a then very popular book, Kenneth Keniston's *The Uncommitted: A Study of Alienated Youth in American Society,* and he asked:

"Is that a socialistic book?"

"Not exactly. Are you a socialist?"

He said he hadn't really thought about it.

The strike was an emotional high for a while, and then a letdown, but, for me, at least, not a complete one. After the strike, I became more active and participated in a secondary way in the effort to rebuild.

Another new experience was my first participation in a left organization, Students for a Democratic Society (SDS). In college, I had been sympathetic to the civil rights and then the anti-war movements but too diffident to actively participate. In January 1967, however, one of my coworkers invited me to an SDS meeting. I went, and I found that it was the New York At Large Chapter, anomalous because it was not based on a campus. Its leaders were among the founders of the national organization, having been much of the New York delegation to the SDS founding convention at Port Huron, Michigan, a few years before. They were what I learned were called "red-diaper babies," meaning they were from old left families. One, in fact, was the child of parents who had been prominent Communist Party officials until Nikita Khrushchev's revelations about Stalinism in 1956.

The chapter functioned mostly as a discussion group. At first, we read several of Lenin's books. The discussions mostly had to do with the difficulties in applying his thought to contemporary American reality. Though I came to think Lenin had been a leader of genius and principle, I thought these difficulties insuperable. Of the books, the only one that seemed very relevant was *Left-Wing Communism, an Infantile Disorder,* mostly because it made an essentially psychological argument about a sort of mindless militancy that I was already seeing in the union. Ironically, I perceived it especially in those groups which professed a Leninist orientation—the Progressive Labor Party and the bitterly divided Trotskyite Workers League and Spartacist League.

Thus, Leninism never attracted me. I began to read Marx just a bit later and found his theory much more broadly illuminating, of course. Even so, it always seemed doubtful to call myself a Marxist or to see any particular theorist as the one source of enlightenment. In 1968, or so, when I gave some thought to calling myself a Marxist, I encountered that remark of Marx himself, who told one of his sons-in-law that he wasn't one—"*Ce q'il-y-a de certain, c'est que moi, je ne suis pas marxiste.*" (One thing that is certain is that I am not a Marxist.)

As time went on, our readings became more eclectic. At my suggestion, we read Trotsky's *History of the Russian Revolution,* a book still well worth anyone's attention. The At-Large Chapter lasted until the dissolution of SDS in the fall of 1969, but I retained contact with some of the members. We helped found the New American Movement in New York, in 1973.

A FEW MONTHS after I started working at the center, I had an encounter with the Selective Service that made me think of parallels between my own life and my clients'. My first physical examination in May or June of 1966 had resulted in a deferment, but I had only been lucky. I came equipped with a letter from my psychiatrist and presented it to the army's psychiatrist, an elderly man with a middle-European accent, who looked at it and merely wrote: "Letter from Dr. Lerner noted," on my forms. Another doctor deferred me because I also had hearing loss and labyrinthitis.

About six months later, I got another call for a physical. I had no confidence that the same fortunate result would come out of my ear problem for a second time. After all, it hadn't kept me from working at a job. I had determined that I would not participate in a criminal war of aggression, and I decided I had to make the psychiatric letter work this time.

I reflected on my previous experience and the way I, the other examinees, and the staff had behaved. I thought about this in relation to what I now knew, from my brief experience in the welfare center about people with severe psychiatric illness. One was a woman who had decompensated after her second semester at a respected school of social work. I found her difficult because at first I tried to reason with her, never having met anybody with formal thought disorder before. I knew I could not convincingly imitate her, and then thought about other clients who mostly seemed sad, depressed, and ineffectual.

I also thought about my earlier encounter at the induction station in the light of a book I had just read, Erving Goffman's *Asylums,* a valuable work, unfortunately now mostly forgotten.

Goffman was a sociologist, and his book rests on participant-observation research at Saint Elizabeth's Hospital in the District of Columbia, supplemented by wide research into literature on other total institutions, including boarding schools, religious orders, concentration camps, prisons, and so forth. This is how he defined a total institution:

> A total institution may be defined as a place of residence and work where a large number of like-situated individuals, cut off from the wider society for an appreciable period of time, together lead an enclosed, formally administered round of life. (Goffman, 1961, p. xiii)

Obviously, the armed forces fit this definition. Goffman (1961) also described the process of entry into a total institution:

> The recruit comes into the establishment with a conception of himself made possible by certain stable social arrangements in his home world. Upon entrance, he is immediately stripped of the support provided by these arrangements. In the accurate language of some of our oldest total institutions, he begins a series of abasements, degradations, and profanations of self. (Goffman, 1961, p. 14)

This too, was an apt description of my experience the first time I went to the Induction Station at 39 Whitehall Street, at the bottom of Manhattan. After my first, unsatisfactory, meeting with the psychiatrist, I had spent the day stripped to my underwear, my shoes untied, and, carrying my shirt and trousers, following shouted orders to go from one place to another. As I recall, the climax of this undignified process came in two rooms, the first with lines painted on the floor defining a central walkway and with stalls, so to speak, to the sides. We had to stand in these spaces and face the wall, put our outerwear on the floor, drop our underpants, while an official shouted: "Awright, bend over, spread the cheeksa yer ass apart!" A medical team then went along examining the many rectums for hemorrhoids.

The second room, for the hernia examination, was similarly humiliating. We stood in single file along a wall, and a doctor went along, seized our testicles, and told us to cough. He did not use gloves or wash his hands. His appearance and bearing contrasted with most of the doctors in the station, who were young men just out of medical school. He, however, seemed to be a lifer with the army. He was older, fat, slatternly, looked like he drank. The choice of this unappealing character for this particular assignment seemed hardly fortuitous.

Goffman's (1961) book answered many questions about the way the induction station treated us. I reviewed my reaction to the experience and remembered that I had joked nervously with my fellow victims in a mutual effort to bond and allay our anxiety. Goffman described this kind of camaraderie as one of several typical responses. It occurred to me that this was quite normal behavior, but that now, when I wanted not to look normal, I must behave in a radically different manner.

I arrived at the induction station dressed more or less conventionally except that my blue corduroy shirt was very old and its collar conspicuously frayed. I carried a book, on the advice of someone who had taken a Latin–English dictionary. I surveyed my library and chose Martin Heidegger's *Unterwegs zur Sprache*, an extremely obscure book I thought I might expound on to anyone that asked. Nobody did.

I maintained a fixed, unemotional facial expression, a flattened effect. I slumped when I sat, spoke to none of my fellows, and gave muted, mostly monosyllabic responses to questions from officials. When seated I kept my right hand in my crotch, as if guarding my genitalia; standing, I kept it more or less in front of my fly.

My first stop was with the psychiatrist, a new one this time. I had filled out the questionnaire claiming night sweats, enuresis, homosexuality, and perhaps other negative features. He read it and looked at me sharply: "Are you actively a homosexual?" I winced, and, in a strained, but still muted voice, said "Well . . . No." For some reason, he wanted to check my reflexes. I allowed him to take my right arm, but then, when he was done, it went back into my crotch.

The psychiatrist decided I wasn't military material and told me to go. I didn't even have to undress. They sent me to a person, a social worker, perhaps, who asked me what I was doing to rehabilitate myself. I mentioned my therapy. I left the induction station elated but maintained my flattened effect for at least 10 blocks' walk. I had a nice lunch at an Italian restaurant on Broadway near the old police headquarters and then took the subway home.

This experience made me identify, in some ways, with my clients, in their relationship with the welfare system. True, the welfare center was not a total institution, but the client confronted it at an extreme disadvantage. I had felt frustrated at not knowing just what went in on the thinking and procedures of the Selective Service and had had to proceed on guesswork, aided by some discussions with people who conveyed folkloric knowledge of uncertain reliability and, of course, my readings of Goffman.

I determined that it was the soundest ethical stance to be as forthcoming as possible with clients about the reasons for the center's decisions and the laws and procedures that applied. Since then, in all the places I have worked, I have tried to follow this general precept.

∼ • ∼ • ∼

FOR THE FIRST year that I worked at the center, I found the paperwork of the caseworker job onerous and difficult. Mr. Nickerson was supportive, as was his successor, Mr. Henry. My third supervisor was not. He was an Israeli immigrant, with a college degree, if I recall, in agronomy, depressed because his wife was dying and leaving him with a small daughter. He was quite impatient with my failure to get all the forms right, and I developed an intense resentment of him. There must have been some pretty strong transferential elements in this, though I do not recall all this too clearly. I recall discussing my anger at him a lot in therapy. However, in the fall of 1967, something seemed to come together, and I suddenly found these tasks easy, familiar, and comfortable. My relationship with my supervisor became harmonious, and we traded questions about the more arcane forms. I looked in old case records to find obsolete ones to ask him about.

"Mr. Dÿkema, what's a W654?" He chuckled to himself with slight smirk in anticipation of my ignorance.

"Mr. Kashdan, the W654 is a form maintained in the Control Units of non-EDP centers to record each disbursement." (Ours was one of a few centers in which Electronic Data Processing, a primitive form of computerization, prevailed.) "But Mr. Kashdan, what's a PA15?"

He didn't know.

So: "It is a form that became obsolete in 1951, and was the predecessor of the W664." (The W664 was another form our center didn't use.)

Resolving my issues with the unfortunate Mr. Kashdan was probably central to my improved adaptation, but there was also an intellectual and theoretical component that has stuck with me ever since—an attitude toward bureaucracy that sets me apart from most social workers. I began to look at the workings of the center in a different way and try to understand how my work intersected with the clerical units' operations. My relations with those workers improved too, as I took an interest in their work. And this led to a significant theoretical development.

At some point in this period, I picked up Max Weber's essay on bureaucracy in Gerth and Mills's *From Max Weber* (Gerth & Mills, 1958; Weber, 1972). I had read this piece in college, and now its soundness seemed unassailable. Basically, Weber argued that bureaucracy is an example of the triumph of bourgeois legality and justice. It operates according to written and fixed rules that are known. It follows precedent, so that its actions are predictable. It maintains records so that its acts are verifiable. And it works with a qualified professional staff.

Obviously Weber describes an ideal here, an ideal honored often in the breach. But I found that success in advocating for my clients often depended on appeals to what I now understood as the ideals of bureaucracy.

It is true, however, that the ideal Weber (1972) described is more of a European than an American phenomenon. In fact, the aspects of bureaucracy that most social workers, and other Americans, deplore are an American problem, one that social workers need to see as a central issue confronting us as a profession trying to address social needs. Mills (1953) commented that dominance of the business model corrupts government bureaucracy in the United States:

> Most of the waste and inefficiency associated in popular imagery with 'bureaucracy' is, in fact a lack of strict and complete bureaucratization. The 'mess,' and certainly the graft, . . . are more often a result of a persistence of the entrepreneurial outlook among its personnel than of any bureaucratic tendencies as such. Descriptively, bureaucracy refers to a hierarchy of offices or bureaus, each with an assigned area of operation, each employing a staff having specialized qualifications. So defined bureaucracy is the most efficient type of social organization yet devised. . . . Government bureaucracies are, in large part, a public consequence of private bureaucratic developments, which by centralizing property and equipment have been the pace setter of the bureaucratic trend. The very size of modern business, housing the technological motors and financial say-so, compels the rise of centralizing organizations of formal rule and rational subdivisions in all sectors of society, most especially in government. (p. 78)

Since then I have always thought of bureaucracy as an ambiguous ally, sometimes on my side and sometimes not, but always with at least some tendency toward what is appropriate.

This was probably my first really important theoretical insight about my work. Much later, when I supervised students, I encouraged them to read Weber's essay before starting their field placements with me.

The part of Weber's conception that least affected me at the time was the notion of a professional staff. This was characteristic of the time. Like many progressive people affected by new left ideas, I was suspicious of what we saw as elitism. The more positive side of professionalism was not so easy to see. But the problem was not just with my limited thinking. There were attitudes from people in authority that tended to reinforce this populist kind of thinking. An event that influenced me for some time came one day when I came to work to find a union leaflet on my desk describing an incident of professional consciousness at its least attractive.

A caseworker, it appeared, had gotten robbed on payday and found himself temporarily destitute. As was his right, he went to the Emergency Assistance Welfare Center and applied for one-time public assistance so that he could sustain himself. The director of the center where he worked found out and tried to pressure him into resigning on grounds of "unprofessional conduct." Obviously, the director's notion of professionalism depended primarily on maintaining a boundary between worker and client. This was not a professionalism I could respect, as I wanted to recognize but not fetishize the differences between myself and my clients. It took some time until I could see the elements of skill and accountability that legitimately go into professionalism. Partly, too, this was because the graduate social workers I met at times seemed to have little to suggest that would help me with my day-to-day work. Moreover, they often were patronizing in annoying ways.

To be sure, the casework counseling model of practice that prevailed at the time did not easily adapt itself to other areas of social service activity. Later, when I was a child protection worker, the occasional trainings we received from people with master's degrees tended to be diluted versions of beginning casework classes, as casework had been understood when they were in school. The basic theoretical orientation, which I only half understood at the time, was psychodynamic but, of course, did not incorporate some of the insights of such people like Kernberg, Jacobson, and other object relations theorists whose notions of limits-setting and use of authority might have been more relevant. These theoretical developments lay in the future.

∼ • ∼ • ∼

IN MAY AND June of 1968, the famous client demonstrations began at most, or all, welfare centers. Clients, by the hundreds, came to the centers asking for clothing and furniture grants. This, of course, came after urban riots in many cities, some of them only a month or so after Martin Luther King's murder. Some prominent figures in the social work profession had contributed to the thinking behind the demonstrations, and some of the organizers were from Volunteers in Service to America or were workers in other parts of the poverty program, then at its height.

The city responded to the demonstrations by devoting all efforts in the centers to documenting the needs for the clothing and furniture requested and issuing checks on the spot. In effect, the demonstrations expedited a process that ordinarily was laborious and time consuming. The needs were real and legitimate, and there was no reason not to make the grants. Many caseworkers, including myself, called clients and suggested they come to the center immediately.

However, though many poor people got many benefits, the demonstrations generally failed in their goal of reforming the welfare system. In fact, the reorganization of welfare, separating services from income maintenance, which came a few years later, was a clearly regressive step.[2] Also, the hope of some, that clients would feel their collective power in a self-affirmative way, and that this would lead to a gain in consciousness, turned out ambiguously, at least. I found, in the succeeding years, that many people I encountered in the Bronx remembered the events fondly but thought "a rich lady" had donated the money distributed. There were variations in this folkloric misunderstanding. Some thought it applied only to their own center. Others thought she had given the money only to people in the Bronx. Perhaps the most outlandish variant was that the rich lady in question was none other than Jacqueline Kennedy Onassis.

∾ . ∾ . ∾

ANOTHER EVENT THAT profoundly affected me was the student strike at Columbia University in April and May of 1968. I had graduated two years before but still lived nearby. There were many such events in that tumultuous year, and nearly all of them concerned some combination of issues of the war against the Vietnamese, and, as at Columbia, some local issues. Columbia was heavily implicated in the war and could not pretend otherwise. I knew many of the strike participants and did what I could to support it.

∾ . ∾ . ∾

BY THE SPRING of 1968, I was doing very well at work and worked doubly hard in response to client demonstrations. I accumulated so much overtime that when I took another job I continued to receive checks until September. Thus my tenure at the welfare center, even after I had physically left, made up a total of two years.

Early that summer I allowed a friend to convince me that I ought to get a job more in keeping with my literary education. I took a pay cut and worked for five and a half months as a copy editor for Appleton Century Crofts, a company with a distinguished history that had degenerated into textbook publishing; mostly business books, which, as the biggest sellers, got the most editing. The textbooks were trivial to the point of inanity, and I had so little respect for them that I knew I was doing a bad job. Also, I learned that the route to a better position in publishing was through sales and not through copyediting, which was a female-dominated occupation, a modest step up from secretarial work. I decided to quit before I got fired; I left just before Christmas, intending to return to the Department of Welfare. I delayed just a few days too long, however, and found that there was an indefinite hiring freeze.

I had money saved, lived frugally, and paid low rent. I decided to take it easy for a while. In February or March of 1969, the same friend and I began to write a novel, entirely epistolary, set in a helicopter company. We told people it was about racism, imperialism, and sex. Completing it took most of the year, and we tried, unsuccessfully, to sell it.

In December 1969, having nothing to do and needing money, I worked for a few days on shape-up for the Conboy Trucking Company on West 25th Street. My friend, having actually been fired from Appleton Century Crofts, went to work there too. This was my only experience of hard and hazardous manual labor, and any romantic illusions I might have entertained about this vanished. Fortunately, at the end of the month, the hiring freeze ended. I received a letter inviting me to apply for reinstatement, and I did so immediately.

References

Dÿkema, C. R. (1977, January–March). The political economy of social welfare: A perspective. *Journal of Sociology and Social Welfare, 4,* 439–469.

Gerth, H., & Mills, C. W. (1958). *From Max Weber: Essays in sociology.* New York: Oxford University Press.

Goffman, E. (1961). *Asylums: Essays on the social situation of mental patients and other inmates.* Garden City, NY: Anchor—Doubleday.

Keniston, K. (1965). *The uncommitted: Alienated youth in American society.* New York: Harcourt, Brace & World.

Luker, K. (1992). Dubious conceptions: The controversy over teen pregnancy. In J. H. Skolnick & A. Skolnick (Eds.), *Family in transition: Rethinking marriage, sexuality, child rearing, and family organization* (7th ed., pp. 160–172). New York: HarperCollins.

Mills, C. W. (1953). *White collar: The American middle classes.* New York: Oxford University Press.

Weber, M. (1972). Wirtschaft und Gesellschaft: Grundriss der Verstehenden Soziologie. Johannes Winckelmann. Tübingen: J.C.B. Mohr [Paul Siebeck])

Chapter Two

Starting in Child Welfare (1970–1975)

I HAD EXPECTED assignment to a welfare center, either Kingsbridge again or, perhaps, another just then opening at 174th Street and Southern Boulevard. Instead, Personnel sent me to the Bronx field office of the Bureau of Child Welfare (BCW).

The BCW was on two or three floors of the Melrose Building, which also housed the Kingsbridge Welfare Center, and another, called Melrose. On February 10, 1970, the office moved to a building at 192 East 151st Street, just west of the Grand Concourse.

I knew little about the BCW. In training, Mr. Weinstein had told us a little about it, and I had gotten to know some of the workers from the strike in 1967, but otherwise had only vague notions of what it did. What I also did not know was that its function was rapidly changing.

In the late 1960s, a consciousness of child abuse had grown and taken legislative form with funding for child protection. Moreover, in New York state in 1969, there had been a major scandal that aroused much concern about abuse. A little girl, Roxanne Felumero, was found dead in the East River. It transpired that her mother and stepfather, Marie and George Poplis, had beaten her to death over a period of several days. When they found she was dead, they dressed her in a snow suit, put her in a stroller, and stuffed rocks into her clothes. Then they threw the corpse into the East River.

The resulting public outrage became more intense when it came out that the family had been before the Family Court a few months before, and the judge had discharged Roxanne from foster care with the New York Foundling Hospital to the mother and stepfather, who thus reclaimed her after she had been in foster care since age 10 months. This led to a searching examination of the Family Court's functioning, and an effort at reform.

When I arrived at the field office, I met with the director, Nathan Breslauer, who told me I would be working in one of the four protective units that then existed. These units were fairly new, and the "Intake" section, which was responsible for more traditional voluntary requests for placement and other services, was still more than twice as large. There was also a day care section, later split off into a separate agency, and some units that handled problems of resources to pay for care of children already in care, and other specialized functions.

Then I met Rachel Kronberger, the senior supervisor in charge of protective units. Both she and Mr. Breslauer had worked in child welfare for decades, in his case, at least, since before the second World War. Rachel introduced me to my case supervisor, and my unit supervisor, whose name I forget, as she was pregnant and soon went on maternity leave. She did, however, give me a valuable thought, which has stayed with me ever since—that I should try to find something to like about any client I encountered. I worked under her successor, Gillian Bramwell, however, for two or three years.

I soon began to get cases, the first being a single father who had beaten his son. The second, however, was my first experience of finding a suspicious injury to have a completely accidental explanation. The baby, who was not quite a year old, had a second degree burn in a stripe, beginning above his hairline and continuing down his face to a point on his chest. The mother, who impressed me rather favorably, explained that she had bathed him in the tub, drained all the water out, and left him in it as she turned to get a towel. The baby chose this moment for his first venture in pulling himself upright by grasping something above him. Unfortunately, he chose the hot water faucet, which opened and let water cascade onto him. The water was, indeed, boiling as it came from the spigot. I was happy to close her case as "unfounded."

Then there were many cases of what we called "withdrawal babies," born addicted to heroin. This was the period of the great heroin epidemic, which I found flourishing when I arrived at the BCW. This was a significant change that had occurred just in the time since I had left the welfare center.

I had had public assistance clients who were heroin addicts, but they were part of a fairly discrete addict subculture. They had a distinctive accent, for instance, and tended to sound alike, no matter what their racial or ethnic origins might be. The Puerto Rican ones, too, tended to speak quite good English, better than average for the Puerto Rican population in the Bronx at the time.

But a marked change had occurred in the year and a half that I had been away. By January 1970, the substance abuse population among our child protective clients included great numbers of young adults, mostly African American and Puerto Rican, who came from families that often functioned normally. Young women would give birth, and the infants, at first appearing normal and healthy, would become irritable and then show signs of withdrawal. Tests of their urine would be positive for heroin. Then they received treatment with paregoric, from which they were gradually weaned.

There was a rule, almost absolute, that we could not permit an active heroin user to be responsible for an infant. There were good reasons for this, as much experience and research showed the children of substance abusers to be at great risk of serious neglect. I remember my first such case, in which I experienced, for the first time, that primitive defense called splitting. The mother was a little younger than I was, and had a sweet, inoffensive manner. I interviewed her on a bench in a hall at the old Lincoln Hospital at 141st Street and Concord Avenue. I recall being very conscious that I was carefully maintaining objectivity despite her being attractive, dressed in a dainty nightgown, and having pretty feet. What I could not resist was her seeming sincerity when she told me that she had learned her lesson and would never use drugs again.

I went back to the office and told my supervisor that whatever might be the case with others, this young woman had convinced me that she was a reformed character. Gillian Bramwell was gentle and patient with my credulity. She explained the risks of an untreated substance abuser caring for an infant and told me to go back and ask the mother if she could propose a caretaker for the baby from her family or other associates. This might avert the need for foster care placement. If she wanted to regain custody, she would have to enter a rehabilitation program that we could help her find. I want people to like me as much as anybody else, and anticipated a painfully angry response, but the mother was compliant when I told her we could not let her have the baby. In the end, though, it proved impossible to interest the mother in treatment. We placed the baby with her father and stepmother.

I thought about this encounter and concluded that I had believed this mother not just because I was inexperienced, but also because she had firmly believed in what she was saying just as she was saying it. At the time, I had only minimal psychodynamic understanding but was beginning to pick up some of the rudiments, from everyday experience and also from my own therapy.

~ . ~ . ~

I FOUND MYSELF enjoying this work and could see that much of it was valuable and constructive. I saw many children who would have been in danger without the BCW's intervention. At the same time, I also wondered how this could fit in with my general political outlook, which was critical of the class and power relations in American society. This then widespread, generally "new left" outlook also tended to see poor people, and especially people of color, as victims, and government activity vis-à-vis them as presumptively oppressive. There seemed to be many instances in which this was true. Was it true of the government activity in which I was working?

One question was this: How did the communities I worked in respond to BCW intervention? There were times when I met people who complained in general terms about what we were doing. At the same time, I noticed little disapproval among the spectators who gathered when some of my more public and conspicuous interventions were happening.

For example, in the summer and fall of 1970, I had a case of a 12-year-old girl with cerebral palsy, who also was mentally challenged. Her mother was abusive toward her and exuded rage whenever we met. I was careful not to turn my back to her.

Eventually, we took her to court. She did not appear, though we had informed her of the hearing. The judge issued a removal order, and, with another worker, I went to the home with a police escort. The building was small, with two apartments on each floor. I believe the girl and her mother lived on the third floor, looking out to the front over an expressway. We knocked. The girl, whom I will call Marilyn, answered, saying her mother was not there. She was alone, and I made a mental note to amend the court petition to include this form of neglect. After all, in the event of a fire, Marilyn would have been finished.

The mother had impressed Marilyn that she must, on no account, open the door. No amount of wheedling would influence her. I looked at the police and pointed out that we really had to enter the apartment and remove the child. They looked at the door, which was fireproof and metallic and said that if they were able to break it down they would then have to secure the apartment. We went and looked at the fire escape, which, of course, was out of our reach. However, after a moment's thought I knocked on the door of the apartment below. The pleasant elderly lady, Mrs. B, admitted me and one of the officers. She and I sat on a love seat in her small parlor. I explained who I was, told her I was serving a court order to remove Marilyn, and said: "I'm sure you know what's been going on upstairs."

Mrs. B's facial expression, though discreet, indicated that she did. In a building like that, it seemed unlikely that the mother's rages at Marilyn could have gone unnoticed. I explained that Marilyn was afraid to open the door, and asked: "Now if the officers and I just happened to walk through your apartment and out the window onto the fire escape, you wouldn't notice it, would you?" Mrs. B smiled and guessed she wouldn't.

The police went up the fire escape first and used their nightsticks to lever the window open. Because Marilyn knew me, I went in first. She was in the kitchen washing dishes, and she looked around as if people entering her home through the window was quite normal. We let the other worker in through the front door.

"Hi, Marilyn."

"Hi."

"Where's your mom?"

"She's with Willie."

We talked for a bit, then—

"Want to go for a ride, Marilyn?"

She looked nervous—"My mom'll get mad."

But one of the officers assured her that the mother had called his sergeant and said it was all right. She came without complaint. I left a summons from the court on the mother's pillow.

As we went down the stairs, most of the neighbors were standing by their doors watching. I wondered how they would react, but one middle-aged woman stepped forward, seized my hand:

"O, God bless you, sir!"

This part of the community, at least, endorsed what we were doing. Later, when I did many removals, I usually found that neighbors, as far as I could tell, had a fair idea of our clients' parental deficiencies. Certainly, they did not comment.

Gradually, the issue of my role as an agent of the state seemed more and more complicated. Around this time I read two articles by James O'Connor in the then excellent journal *Socialist Revolution*: "The Fiscal Crisis of the State," and "Inflation, Fiscal Crisis, and the Working Class." O'Connor later elaborated on them in an influential book, also called the *Fiscal Crisis of the State* (O'Connor, 1973). It was a complex analysis of state expenditures and showed how they fell into several categories, some of which involved compromises between the needs of the dominant classes and everybody else's. Though every act by a government official manifested elements of both sets of needs, and thus had a compromised character, it was possible for me, as a child protective worker, to apply an ethical consciousness to my work, informed by a theoretical understanding of the complex nature of the state. Thus, I could somewhat escape the unfortunate aspects of my role as an agent of the state.

This was the beginning of my efforts to develop a more sophisticated understanding of where my work in child protection and, really, all social work practice, could fit into a progressive critique of the society. Another thought-provoking experience came a few months later, in January 1971.

Late one afternoon, a pending case arrived and got assigned to my colleague Lester. It presented as a sex abuse case and required an immediate visit. The supervisor directed me to accompany and assist him.

A 12-year-old girl, whom I will call Noemí Cuevas, had told a school aide of her stepfather's having sexually molested her. The report also vaguely mentioned something about photography. In fact, without knowing it, we were stumbling into a child pornography operation.

We arrived at the apartment, which was the second floor of a two-family house. The family consisted of Arnaldo Araújo and Sonia Nieves, each of whom had brought five children, from other partners, to the relationship. They had an infant in common, making a total of 11 children. The apartment was large and comfortable, and the living room, the kitchen, and the parents' bedroom were lavishly furnished; but the children's rooms were bare and hardly furnished.

Ms. Nieves lurked apprehensively in the kitchen. She was pale and looked intimidated. Mr. Araújo was formidably large and muscular, suave in a disquieting way, extremely articulate in English, and dressed, anomalously, in a tweed jacket, gray slacks, and the kind of loafers then called "weejuns." In 1971, this was more typical of an ivy-league college student with conventional aspirations than a man of Puerto Rican origin.

We explained the purpose of our visit, without saying that Noemí was the source. Mr. Araújo denied everything, treating the allegations as an absurdity. We explained that the procedure we followed was to ask him to leave the household during the investigation, which we were beginning.

He demurred at first, but then said, "Well, I don't want you to lose your job over this" and suggested he would leave and wait across the street while we interviewed the rest of the family—he insisted this must happen in the vestibule at the bottom of the stairs—and he left it implicit that we would then leave, that he would return, and that we would let the matter slide. In effect, he was attempting both to intimidate and corrupt us.

We accepted his offer to leave and began to speak to Noemí in the vestibule. She soon told us of the photography and, to our greater concern, said a man named "Gene" who lived someplace else, was the photographer. Lester asked if we could see one of the pictures. She said Mr. Araújo had told Ms. Nieves and the children to destroy them. In fact, they disobeyed him on this point. She ran upstairs and brought a snapshot of herself.

I remember this photograph very vividly, for its combination of skill and perversity. It showed the child standing and nude. The photographer had positioned himself somewhere near her right foot and shot upward. But he also had placed a light behind her left shoulder. The effect was that the light caused her small breasts to cast a bit of shadow and look more prominent, just as the camera angle showed that she had no pubic hair. This created a combined impression of femaleness and juvenility that I found particularly pedophilic in a repellent way. Lester put the photograph in his notebook. Noemí was alarmed and said her stepfather would be angry if it was missing.

We went back up to the apartment, locked and bolted the door, and called the office to report to the supervisor, emphasizing that we needed police assistance as soon as possible. She asked me to call back in a few minutes after she had called the police. While I was talking with her, there was a thumping on the door. Mr. Araújo was back. When we did not open the door, he shouldered his way through it, turning it into matchwood. As he entered through the fragments, I said,

"The police are on their way. We called them."

Abruptly his demeanor changed from murderous to aggrieved:

"Why did you do that?"

Lester said, "It is his house. Maybe we should leave."

We went down to the street. The three of us talked.

"Why did you do that? I wanted to settle this a nice way."

I said, "We needed to be sure."

"So what's gonna happen?"

Lester said, "The police are coming. If you're here you'll probably be arrested."

"So what should I do?"

I said that was up to him, and he turned and walked away.

We waited on the sidewalk for a few minutes, until two officers arrived. We showed them the photograph. They reacted with horror. With them, we drove around for a while looking for Mr. Araújo, who must have taken cover. Then we returned to the apartment. Ms. Nieves looked even more frightened and bewildered. The children were excited and started bringing us more photographs. Most were commercial pornography, but in a manila envelope were two artistic eight-by-ten black and white photographs of Noemí. She was nude and sitting, with her hands gripping her flexed knees, her legs thus spread, exposing her genitalia. The photograph also showed her face. She looked frightened and stricken, her eyes dilated with fear, shame, and humiliation. I have never forgotten her expression.

Perhaps the artist had given them to Mr. Araújo because they were not his best from the commercial point of view. Evidently, he had not been able to make her pretend to enjoy what was happening to her. Two tickets to the upcoming prize fight between Muhammed Ali and Joe Frazier were also in the envelope.

A sergeant and his driver joined the two original officers. They too looked at all the photographs. A little later, Noemí, after discussion with her mother, asked me: "Where are the fight tickets?"

I said, "Aren't they with the pictures?"

But they weren't. I looked at the sergeant, who asked blandly: "What fight tickets?"

I hadn't taken them, and I knew Lester, sitting right beside me, hadn't taken them. I couldn't repress a look of disgust that the police must have stolen them, to which the sergeant responded by suggesting I help myself to any of the family's possessions.

I turned to Ms. Nieves, asking her if she would be willing to go to the precinct and press charges against Mr. Araújo. She said over and over again that she could do nothing against him—"*No puedo hacer nada contra él.*" Eventually, we removed all 11 children and petitioned Family Court the following day. As we went downstairs, the next youngest child, one of Mr. Araújo's own sons, thanked me with relief. He told us later, with fear and revulsion, that his father had been grooming him to participate with Noemí in some form of filmed sexual activity.

In the taxi taking Noemí to the foster care placement, I tried to learn more about Gene—his surname, where he lived, and so forth. She was forthcoming enough, but knew little. Gene's wife was nice. You got to their house by driving past some water and trees.

A few months later, however, the newspapers reported that one Eugene Abrams, an unemployed aerospace engineer living in Nassau County, had been indicted for conducting a million dollar yearly business in child pornography. When inspected, his stock included photographs of Noemí. Some of them also showed her stepfather molesting her. He had been careful not to show his face but forgot to remove a distinctive ring from his finger. Also his body was pretty distinctive in itself. He was convicted of sodomy in the second degree.

This incident raised the issues of oppression in the society that I had been struggling with—I, as a representative of the government was intervening in people's lives in an authoritative way—but raised them in a complex and somewhat confusing way. Many political people I knew would have seen my role as at least presumptively questionable. But much of the conventional progressive attitude mostly saw government as the prime instrument of oppression and, implicitly, accepted the conventional notion that the family is presumptively an area that should be free of official interference. But how could any suspicion of government intervention justify leaving Noemí Cuevas unprotected?

At the same time, there was another part of the left that put forward an alternative and more complex view. This was feminism, which had originated in the dissatisfactions of women in the civil rights and antiwar movements with male leadership. Feminism was only just beginning to have a broader impact, but it included a critique, however implicit and not very developed, of the family as an institution, and it was in the structure of the family that Noemí's oppression had occurred. Moreover, it was clear that the family's apparent prosperity came from her work. Mr. Araújo and Ms. Nieves were not employed, yet they lived in greater comfort than most of their neighbors. As I thought about Noemí's experience as labor, the notion of alienation, which comes, of course, from Hegel and Marx, began to seem especially relevant. Certainly, Noemí's expression in the photographs seemed to sum up alienation.

I also began to have questions about the conventional presumption that the family, unless proved otherwise in specific instances, is essentially benign. In addition, it began to occur to me that the family and the individual can be in conflict in ways with broad implications. In a democratic society, the individual may need protection against the family, and that protection can come only from organized society. What did this insight lead to?

My questions were not yet well formed, but I began to learn a little about the history of the family and understand that the institution, as we know it, is the product of development over much time, in contrast to the common ideological view that it has been the constellation of father, mother, and children that is normative today.[1] Later, family history was a topic I studied in detail. I have always been interested in history and had always, beginning in my time at the welfare center, applied historical knowledge to forming assessments of my clients. I understood that some issues of assessment are more, and some less, susceptible to a broadly social and historical understanding, as opposed to a more purely psychological one.

I also began to notice, as I became more skillful at interviewing, how broader social data about a client would emerge and then contribute to the later stages of the interview and the eventual assessment. This frequently happened in initial visits to child protective clients, when I would present the fact that the BCW had received a report containing specific information about the parents' behavior. There would then be a discussion of the allegations. As this proceeded, the parents would often attempt to divert the discussion to other areas. I found that when I allowed them to do this and we digressed into seemingly more tangential and general topics, I learned things about them that I could apply to a renewed discussion of the circumstances of the report, when I brought the discussion back there. These more general topics often included data about where they had lived, what kind of work they had done, and what sort of social origins they came from, where their family members lived and what they were about, and so forth.

I also found that I learned general information about far-off places and social contexts. I found I had to compare what my clients told me about their native countries and towns with other information but there was a fresh vividness about what people told me that had its own importance. Thus my stock of social knowledge could increase with each encounter.

~ . ~ . ~

THESE EXPERIENCES AND thoughts made me more comfortable with my work. I had always enjoyed it but now had fewer qualms about the use of authority. As I thought about this, I began to think about the more clearly authoritative aspects of the job, such as removals with the help of the police. Many of my colleagues, more ambivalent, perhaps, than I had become, did not like to do this. I decided to develop techniques to achieve removal as peacefully as possible and with the least traumatization of the child.

By this time, I had done a number of removals and had learned some lessons, most of all from the first. This was a bit unusual, as it did not involve a court order for removal. Instead, it was an involuntary psychiatric hospitalization of a child.

The boy was 12 years of age, but he looked younger. I will call him Joey. Joey carried a diagnosis of "pseudo-psychopathic schizophrenia" and was one of the two or three most-frightening children I have ever encountered. I met with his guidance counselor, who showed me a semester's record of his violent outbreaks, culminating in an incident where Joey noticed that a classmate had put his fingers in the crack at the hinge side of an open door. Joey slammed the door, severing some of the fingers. He picked one up and ran to the guidance counselor saying, "This is part of William's hand. It came off in the door."

They sent him to a special school called "The Achievement Academy for Uninterrupted Education." He lasted there a week, when he threw another child down a flight of stairs. A psychiatric examination had recommended hospital admission, but this somehow did not happen, probably because the mother did not cooperate. I visited the mother, who was obviously psychotic and delusional, and as she rambled on, said, "Sometimes I think I could hurt the children past all forgiveness. . . ."

Child protection was so new that no one told me how to conduct a removal. I went with another worker, and two police officers escorted us. I had seen too many movies and told the officers to come in after us if we did not come out with the child within a certain time. I did not realize how unwise this was—I later learned that it was important to keep the police constantly in view in case they showed signs of losing interest and drifting away.

We entered the apartment, finding Joey, his mother, and the grandmother, who was at least as psychotic as the mother. We explained that Joey needed to go to the hospital. All vociferously resisted this thought, the grandmother repeating over and over: "I'm a policeman and a nurse and I say he ain't going!"

We were getting nowhere, but then the police knocked and entered. The sight of these emblems of constituted authority changed the whole dynamic of the situation. The mother became cooperative and helped one of the officers take a hammer away from Joey. We took Joey away in the police car, and, later, Bellevue Hospital admitted him.

From this, I learned that keeping the police visible, but in the background, was a key to success. It was better not to let them do the talking, as their attitudes tended either toward ambivalence about the removal, which they often did not understand or else toward overly heavy-handed interventions. Their presence, however, made it clear that there was no alternative to cooperation with the BCW worker.

The procedure I developed usually followed these lines. It began with enlisting the police in such a manner that they would assist reliably without creating difficulties. One of the tasks of the other assisting child protective worker was to help the police understand the events as they occurred.

Establishing my legitimacy with the police was the first step in any removal. I had noticed that plain-clothes officers identified themselves to one another by flashing their shields. Hence, I put my agency identification card in my wallet so that I could reach into my pocket, briskly pull out my wallet, and exhibit the card with a flourish. (In those days it was not the custom for most people to wear visible identification.)[2]

I began by going personally to the precinct, walking in with a vigorous stride, flashing my ID, and saying, "We are caseworkers from the Bureau of Child Welfare, representing the commissioner of social services of the city of New York, and requesting police assistance in removing a child from parental custody under Article 10 of the Family Court Act." When we were serving a court order, I would present it, but when we were acting on the presumption that the children were at imminent risk and had not time to get an order, I would explain the legality of this under the Family Court Act.

In the 1970s, this was sometimes an unfamiliar request. If the officers at the desk looked puzzled, I would refer them to the relevant reference in the *Police Patrol Manual*, which I had memorized. This was an enormous tome that they sometimes pored over. I would ask that, if possible, the car with the officers responsible for the sector where we were going come to the precinct to rendezvous with us and receive instructions from the sergeant.

Once at the home, I and the other worker would enter first, with the police following. I made a point of speaking in a low monotone, which, I found, kept my own voice from rising, and tended to keep the conversation more peaceable. I explained that our purpose was to remove the children and would give a clear, brief, and straightforward explanation of the reasons. The parents would try to argue, but

I explained that this was not the time for that. If this was an ongoing case, I would refer to previous interviews. I also told the parents of their right to appear in court and to legal representation.

The argument was usually somewhat lengthy, but I politely declined further discussion of the merits of the removal. Mostly, after a little time, some tears from the parents would indicate that they understood there was no alternative. After allowing the parents to grieve for a few minutes, I would gently suggest packing up the child's possessions, including, for children of relevant age, transitional objects (Winnicott, 1971). Then we would leave.

I participated in many removals. Some involved my own cases and, in some others, I assisted colleagues. With two exceptions, there was no violence. In one case, the grandmother was clasping the girl to her chest, and the police had to open her arms for me to take the child. In the other, the judge had insisted I remove a child I did not think it appropriate to remove at that time. This precipitated a violent scene that played out in the large lobby of an apartment building.

In one case, for example, I removed five children of a mother reported by a pediatrician. One of the children, a girl of 10 years, had petit mal seizures. Regular phenobarbital was supposed to control the seizures, but they persisted. The family lived around the corner from the pediatrician's clinic, and he had observed the mother obviously under the influence of some drug. She was intoxicated when I interviewed her and admitted that she had taken her daughter's medicine. The children, who were the youngest of a total of 17 offspring, were not really distressed when we came for them. The eldest, about 12 or 13 years of age, at first thought she would remain because she had stayed in the home the last time her siblings were removed. She affected a distancing amusement and made clever comments. When I told her she was coming too, she was a little surprised but went off to pack her things with a pretense of good humor.

We left the mother with an elder daughter, in her twenties and developmentally delayed. A few weeks later, the mother died of a heroin overdose. Later still, in another context, I met the 10-year-old again. She had learned from television how bad drugs were and had mobilized her siblings to throw her mother's drugs away, to make her get up and walk when she overdosed, and generally to maintain her life. With the child gone, there was nobody to do this, and when the mentally challenged daughter tried to attract the neighbors' attention, they ignored her until it was too late.

Some removals followed a different course, though. In one case I helped recover a baby from his father and return him to the mother. I will call the couple Samuel Delgado and Ramona Flores. They lived in the South Bronx, had the one infant in common, and Ms. Flores had a four-year-old daughter from a previous relationship. One day Mr. Delgado became angry when the girl dirtied her pajamas. He beat her so badly that she required hospital admission. The worker who received the resulting report found Ms. Flores cooperative, and so petitioned the court only against Mr. Delgado.

Neighbors were indignant at what Mr. Delgado had done and, fearing vigilante justice, he fled. Unfortunately, he took the baby along.

Ms. Flores told the worker that Mr. Delgado had probably gone to the home of his brother and sister-in-law. They lived in Inwood, at the northern tip of Manhattan. The judge issued a Warrant to Produce the Child, which was an order for Mr. Delgado's arrest that directed him to hand over the baby. This was a more emphatic form of court order than the usual removal order. Unfortunately, the warrant did not specify the apartment number, and the police, therefore, could not forcibly enter the dwelling. The worker went to the address, but the sister-in-law angrily denied that the baby and his father were there.

It was decided that another attempt be made. The worker on the case was absent, and another worker in the unit received this task. He seemed anxious, and I offered to help.

I met with Ms. Flores, who said the apartment was on the top floor and that the man and woman were prosperous, being burglars by trade. She thought Mr. Delgado had hidden in the bathroom and gone out the window and up the fire escape when the other worker and the police had come to the door. I thought that if he had done this once he might do it again.

We left Ms. Flores at the station house on Audubon Avenue in Washington Heights and went with two officers to the address. I outlined the situation and said I hoped to make enough commotion at the door that Mr. Delgado would again go out the bathroom window. One of the officers, on the roof looking down, could then apprehend him. The lead officer was a little reluctant but agreed when I insinuated he was afraid of heights.

We found the apartment and waited for the officer to assume his position up above. Then I knocked, and when the sister-in-law opened the door, I took a step into the doorway to keep it open. She again denied that the people we sought were there and became vociferously angry. I replied in kind, raising my voice, and kept this up for what felt like some time. Finally, though, through the apartment, we heard the officer shout: "Hey! C'mon up!" The woman deflated, stopped trying to close the door, and we waited a few minutes. Mr. Delgado came down the stairs from the roof, his hands in the air, with the officer covering him with his gun. They handcuffed and arrested him.

Now his brother the burglar appeared from inside the apartment. He and his wife became effusively cordial and invited us in to see that the baby was not there. I told them bluntly that I knew they knew where the baby was and that they would be in more trouble than they knew what to do with if they did not hand him over. They exchanged glances and took us down the hall to an unsuspecting elderly woman who had been babysitting. We took the baby, his clothes and Pampers, and left with the police and Mr. Delgado.

At the precinct, we returned the baby to Ms. Flores and then took her home. Her joy made this a great satisfaction.

The coda, so to speak, of most removals, was between me and the child, or children. I tried to keep the children with me in the office as we made placement arrangements and tried to help them understand what had happened and where they were going. This continued in the taxi, during the sometimes lengthy trip to the placement. If the children were young, I often sang or recited poetry. At the foster home or agency, I waited for a while so that the children could have a sense of continuity in a major change in their circumstances.

∼ • ∼ • ∼

OF COURSE, REMOVALS were a small proportion of my work at the BCW, but I have described them at length, in part because they were exciting and satisfying when I was able to do them well and, also, because they exemplify the complexities of the authoritative role in their clearest form. It is worth noting that child protection, among the arenas of social work practice, is the only one in which workers exercise constituted authority in a purely social agency and not a host agency like probation, parole, and so forth. Yet it is clear that social work practice in most settings has elements of authority. Later in my career, for example, as a medical social worker, I was a mandated reporter. This is an authoritative role too, and there were many other parts of my work that patients experienced as the exercise of authority. Thus, the lessons of child removal have a relevance beyond their immediate scope.

I also found that authoritative intervention, despite what many would think, did not necessarily destroy my relationship with the parents and the family. This is quite comprehensible, of course, in light of the insights we find in the object relations psychoanalytic theorists. Many clients responded positively to what, in object relations terms, would be limits setting. In the personality that splits, there are often elements that want to do better, and these elements fear what they might do to their children if not controlled.

At the same time, some interventions were not dramatic in the way removals were, but were, nonetheless, authoritative. Sometimes they involved forbearance rather than its opposite. For example, I remember a woman that a hospital reported for hitting her young son's face with a belt when he would not eat. When I interviewed her, she was intensely remorseful. As I listened further, she told me of her relationship with the father, who had impregnated her after they had met at a dance hall. He lived with his mother at the time and did nothing to establish a home, though he had a good job as a mover. She herself was an immigrant, worked as a waitress, and lived in a furnished room. Because the mother had no proper home, the first baby went, initially, into foster care. Eventually, the mother accumulated enough money to rent an apartment and create a home. The father whom she had subsequently married was willing to move in, but proved unfaithful and sometimes abusive.

I was impressed with the mother's sincere concern for her children; when I met the father, I found him unwilling to engage in discussion of the problems they faced. He explicitly disavowed any responsibility for helping his wife with the children. We let the child go home, and I monitored the situation for a few months. There were no further injuries, and the two boys seemed well.

Eventually, the mother confided that she had a plan. Her husband, despite his gross faults, did earn a fairly good living, and, probably in a spirit of grandiosity, gave her a bit more money than she really needed to run the household. She was depositing this money in a bank account that only she knew about and had decided that when she had enough for an airline ticket she would fly with the children back to her parents' farm in Ireland. Eventually, I received a postcard from County Monaghan, or wherever it was, where they were doing well.

There were other cases in which the use of authority involved getting the parent out of trouble rather than into it. One of my earlier cases was of a fatality, a four-year-old girl who died of a ruptured liver. The report came from the hospital emergency room where she died. The social worker asked the mother: "Did you beat the children?" The mother said she had, because she had, indeed, physically punished them. On the basis of this probably inadequate interview, she was arrested, and I had to place the several surviving children.

In the taxi on the way to the foster care agency, however, I heard the children talking among themselves and about how a boy in the house had kicked their dead sister in the belly. It turned out that this was the mother's brother, age 10. She had taken him from her own physically abusive mother to protect him. According to the children, he had been lying down, and the four-year-old tickled him. He lashed out with his foot, and his toe hit her abdomen, inflicting the fatal injury. I was able to make this account of the injury known to the proper authorities. The mother was exonerated, released from jail, and reunited with her children.

I should also describe a case in which I made a serious mistake. Just before Christmas in 1972, we received another report of a withdrawal baby. The report arrived fairly late in the afternoon, partly, I think, because the Application Unit had been thorough and taken some time to search out the family's previous case record. It dated from a year or more before and recorded another worker's work in response to a report that the infant's elder sister, too, had gone into heroin withdrawal after birth.

By procedure, we had to respond within 24 hours. I hurried out to the address, which was at 165th Street and Bryant Avenue. I arrived at about 4:00 in the afternoon, but it was cloudy and getting dark. The building, when I arrived, seemed shabby even though there were signs it had been renovated.[3] I entered to look for the client's apartment and mounted the stairs, finding nothing promising. I was feeling abstracted, for some reason, and it was only on the fifth floor landing that I realized I had seen no sign of human habitation, that all the apartment doors swung open. I was on the top floor of an abandoned building. Appalled at my foolishness and inattention, I became intensely alert. In those days, I carried a knife called a 007. I opened it and held it as I started down the stairs. One or two floors below, I saw a women with grocery bags coming up and put the knife away. She told me my client was in an apartment behind the staircase on the ground floor.

This was an unfortunate beginning. The mother was at home with a man and her three elder children, the former withdrawal baby, and two brothers ages four or five. The apartment was dark, as there was no electricity in the building, but the tenants did still have gas and heated the place from the oven, blowing warm air around with a window fan they ran off current pirated from a street light outside.

Despite the extreme squalor of her home, the mother's appearance was altogether presentable. She was clean, wore attractive and rather expensive clothes, and was quite pretty. She showed no overt signs of substance abuse.

The discussion usual in such circumstances took place. I told her we could not leave the children with her and that the new baby, once ready for discharge from the hospital, could not go from the hospital to her care. And, of course, I asked if she could propose a friend or relative as caretaker. She and the man were hostile, but she agreed to explore the possibility of her mother assuming responsibility. We agreed to further discussion after the holiday, because the baby was still in the hospital, being withdrawn from her addiction.

I became ill, with a high fever, after Christmas, stayed home for a few days, sleeping almost all the time. Then my supervisor called, said the baby was now ready for discharge, and could I come to work to resolve the situation. I did not want to saddle my overburdened colleagues with my own work, so the next day I came in and located the mother, who took me to the grandmother's home.

I do not know how much my perceptions were clouded by illness and debilitation. The grandmother's building was run-down but did seem to be inhabited. The grandmother herself swore faithfully that she would take care of all four children, along with her own younger ones, and that on no account would she give them to the mother. On this basis, I called the hospital and authorized the discharge.

One thing I do recall with clarity. When I visited the grandmother's home the first time, the front stoop was intact and I used these steps to enter the building. However, when I returned for a follow-up visit three or four weeks later, they had collapsed, and I had to pick my way up a pile of rubble.

The apartment proved to be in ruinous condition, with heaps of plaster on the floor, which had fallen off the walls. The grandmother was in bed, moaning with pain from a migraine. The children, who were filthy, were running around unsupervised and, much to my consternation, only the two eldest children of my client, the boys, were present. The infant and the previous years' withdrawal baby were absent.

"Where's the baby?" I asked the grandmother. "She's with Saaaandy," she whimpered. "But you promised you wouldn't let her have the children." The grandmother groaned again.

I returned the following day with a case aide and removed my client's children. To my surprise, the one-year-old had returned. The grandmother explained that Sandy, the mother, had left her there the previous evening. The baby, however, remained with the mother, and the grandmother had no idea where she was staying, because they had had to move out of the apartment on Bryant Avenue.

During the next week or two, I made great efforts to locate the mother and the baby. The homeless shelter system was in its infancy then, and there was no coherent way to locate anybody in it. However, the mother showed up in the BCW office. I interviewed her in the service section. She was clean and dressed, as usual, in attractive and fairly expensive garments. We discussed the basis of the removal, and at one point she mentioned that she had the baby with her and had left her in our small nursery. I excused myself and found the welfare patrolman, explaining that we were taking the child into custody. I looked at the baby, who looked clean and properly dressed. After some further discussion, the mother signed a voluntary commitment, giving her children's custody to the commissioner of social services.

A little later, the nursery staff called me. "Mr. Dÿkema, you have to *see* this child." They had changed her diaper and showed me a diaper rash more advanced than any I have ever seen. Her whole diaper area was inflamed. Parts were bleached white by contact with feces, and there were areas where the skin had broken down and were oozing blood. We looked more closely and found caked grime that the mother had missed when she cleaned her baby up for the visit to the BCW worker.

Later, when I began to supervise students, I always cited this as an example of how much damage you can do when you make decisions when sick. I should have acknowledged that I was too sick to work, when I acceded to the mother's plan.

Why didn't I do this? Because I wanted to be conscientious and a good colleague. These are virtues, but they can have their dark side. What distressed me the most was that the infant, who must have been in pain, did not cry. Most likely she had cried at the pain initially but gave up when she got no response. It is possible that she had been alone for long periods of time. I suppose it could have been worse. I hope she is all right now.

FOR MUCH OF the last two or three years that I worked at the field office, my supervisor was a man I will call Sergei Stravinsky. The office had expanded its staff, and some of us who were experienced and tested moved into new units under supervisors transferred from welfare centers.

My first impression of Sergei was uncertain. He seemed constantly jittery and nervous and spoke loudly in a high and accented voice. But I found that he was intelligent and knew more about psychodynamic issues than most of the supervisors I had had. Eventually, I found that, under real pressure, his almost hysterical manner gave way to a sober, judicious calm.

Some of Sergei's behavior crossed the boundary that defines acceptability. Although his sexism lacked the typical sadistic quality, it was vocal and often spilled over into what we would now call sexual harassment. Curiously, though, the women he targeted were not usually timid and lacking in assertiveness. Some of the women immediately groped him back. One, I recall, had grabbed Sergei's crotch when he touched her breast, then went around the office telling all who listened that his testicles were "so small and spongy."

Sergei was Russian, but his parents, after the Bolshevik Revolution, had left the Soviet Union. He explained that his paternal grandfather owned a small railroad and his maternal grandfather was an Orthodox Priest, who had been Lenin's theology teacher at the *gymnasium* at Simbirsk,[4] and later became a bishop. They moved to Poland, where Sergei was born in the later 1920s. He grew up in Warsaw.

Sergei was an adolescent during World War II and had hair-raising tales to tell. In one, he had stolen some gestapo letterhead stationery and wrote letters to isolated German outposts to hand over weapons to Sergei. He would then load them on his bicycle, concealed in firewood, and pedal off to a camp of the Polish partisans, who bought them. Once, when he was in their camp, the Germans attacked, and Sergei, whose survival skills must have been superior, managed to escape.

Another time, someone killed a German soldier and the Germans, in reprisal, rounded up, at random, a number of people and held them in the courtyard of what had been Sergei's school.[5] He escaped with the help of the custodian.

Nearer the end of the war, Sergei was in a labor camp in Hamburg or Bremen where his fellow prisoners frequently died of dysentery. He explained that his survival was "because I was aware of zee kyewrateef propairties of charcoal," which he took from the supply for the steam engines that powered the equipment in the camp.

Sergei had a sense of humor, he could laugh at himself, and this made his eccentricities and sometimes reprehensible behavior more tolerable. One day I challenged his noisy excitability. On a visit to Barnes and Noble—then comprising only one store, the original one at 18th Street and 5th Avenue[6]—I had picked out some books and joined the line to the cash register. I noticed, by the register, a rack of Berlitz phrase books in several languages. I glanced through the Russian one and bought it too.

I kept the book in my desk drawer, certain phrases marked with paper clips. A few mornings later, I was working quietly at my desk when Sergei sprang to his feet and called loudly:

Meestair Dÿkema, vat is happening mit zee Smeeth case?

I pulled out the phrase book, and replied: "*Ya nyervnii!*" which, according to Berlitz, meant "I am having a nervous breakdown!" I turned to the next phrase, which had something to do with my malfunctioning carburetor. There were two or three others. This brought Sergei to a stop. He asked why I had this book. I said, "I have to communicate with my supervisor, don't I?" When I left for graduate school a few months later, I gave the phrase book to a case aide,[7] a middle-aged woman who was fond of Sergei and also liked to tease him.

Sergei had some facility with languages, though always with a pronounced Slavic accent. He had at least a smattering of German, which helped me carry out a difficult removal.

A woman addicted to heroin brought her infant to the father's sister, asked if she would mind the baby for a while, and promised to be back soon. In fact, she vanished for some days. The aunt reported the situation, because she herself was in the last stages of pregnancy. I visited, and we arranged for the paternal grandparents—who lived in a small housing project on Manhattan's Lower West Side—to keep the baby at least until we were able to locate the mother. The grandparents promised me they would not let the mother take the child.

With nothing to go on, I could not find the mother. About two weeks later, another of the father's sisters called to say she was at the grandparents' home, the mother had showed up, and the grandfather was going to let her take the baby. He feared that holding the baby would cause disturbance that could exacerbate his wife's cardiac condition. I told her I would be there as soon as possible.

When I asked for a backup worker to accompany me, our case supervisor said no one could be spared. She offered me a WEP (Work Experience Program) worker, a man I knew to be less than useless, and who, under WEP's rules, could not be asked to work overtime.[8]

I took a taxi downtown and arrived to find a somewhat tense atmosphere. The mother, who I met for the first time, was surly and free-floatingly hostile and angry. The grandfather had a sour expression. All seemed a little afraid of the mother. I needed the police to help but knew that the mother, if she knew they were coming, would take the baby and leave. After some discussion, I asked to use the telephone, called my unit, and asked for Sergei. I had to send one of my coworkers to find him and bring him to the telephone. I said,

"*Sergei, ich brauche die männer im blau.*" (Sergei, I need the men in blue.)

"*Die männer im blau? Die polizei.* The police?" (I had avoided using the word *polizei*, because the mother might have figured it out.)

"*Ja.*"

We confirmed the address. With the mother, who had been standing at my elbow, I returned to the living room and sat on a davenport. I did not want the mother to get bored and leave, so I tried to be just provocative enough to keep her engaged, and mild enough that she would not leave the apartment with the baby, or else hit me.

After 10 or 15 minutes' wait, the doorbell rang. I ran to open the door and said, "Come in officer! I am Christopher Dÿkema from the Bureau of Child Welfare, and this is the child who is being taken into protective custody."

After some explanation, the police helped me remove the baby, and we placed him in foster care. The mother was irate but could do nothing. The rest of the family showed varying degrees of ambivalence. Later, when we decided to place him in the home of yet another of the father's sisters, I visited her home. She explained that the local police had shot and killed a member of the extended family not long before. Hence, they were not very welcome. I expressed regret that this had happened but pointed out that the baby was obviously not safe with the mother and that this was the only way I could get him away from her. She acknowledged that this was true.

~ . ~ . ~

DURING THE YEARS from 1970 to 1975, when I worked at the Bronx field office of the BCW, I became more active in the union. On my return to the Department of Social Services, I found a changed situation. In the 18 months I had been out of the department, the Social Service Employees Union (SSEU) had merged with Local 371 of the American Federation of State, County, and Municipal Employees (AFSCME). Also, although we did not know it at the time, these years were the period leading up to the fiscal crisis and near bankruptcy of New York City (NYC) in 1975. Moreover, on a national level, a more restrictive policy in social services, particularly public assistance, was creating pressures for repeated reorganization of the agency. Hence, the union confronted mounting external problems and had to adapt its internal processes to be effective in representing the members.

In the union there were many conflicting tendencies. A significant black nationalist impulse, and an appeal to white guilt, led to Stanley Hill becoming union president in 1970, defeating Martin Morgenstern, whose supporters gradually reorganized into a caucus to oppose him. But that came a little later. There also were caucuses composed of members of Leninist groups, in particular, the Trotskyite Workers League and Spartacist League, who were bitterly hostile to each other and, too, the Progressive Labor Party. At one point, too, we had a small group of splinter de Leonites.[9]

As the membership had become older, it had become less participatory. Fewer people attended membership meetings, and the need for a representative structure was more and more apparent.

Another problem was that there were too many officers and employees working at the union office. This was a result of the merger. To achieve it, positions for prominent activists on all sides had had to be found. When Stanley Hill took office, many of his supporters took these positions, though several Morgenstern supporters also continued in office.

In the late 1990s when Hill was executive director of AFSCME District Council 37, massive corruption and vote fraud discredited his leadership, though not Hill personally. All of us who knew him saw him as an honest, but weak, leader, unable to restrain his more unsavory associates. It was the same in the two years he was president of SSEU/371.

The union's response to the then commissioner of social services, Jule Sugarman's, reorganization of the department, was halting and confused. Eventually, the opposing caucus, led by another union vice president, Barton Cohen, took the lead in formulating policy responses that protected the staff.

I had voted for Stanley Hill. I knew him as a very congenial man and, vaguely, thought it would be good to have a black president. As time went on, however, I found more and more frustration in his leadership. Also, the plethora of officers and employees, which was a drain on the union's treasury, seemed less and less defensible, especially when it became more and more clear that many of Hill's supporters among them did little or nothing. Moreover, there were increasingly credible stories of their misusing union funds.

In the Bronx field office, I became close to Gary, a man about 10 years older than myself, who also was becoming active in the union as an alternate delegate. I became grievance chairman in the spring of 1970. The following year he and I, with others, ousted the person who had been senior delegate for some time. We saw her as ineffectual and confused, motivated by suspicion of leadership, fitfully attracted to some of the Trotskyites, even as she was an ardent Zionist. At about the same time, I followed Gary into what formally called itself the Cohen Caucus. In 1972, the caucus took the lead in a constitutional reform to reduce the number of officers and then defeated Hill for the presidency.

I vividly recall the night after the election, with the count of the ballots at the American Arbitration Association (AAA). Our caucus had a room nearby with refreshments. The Hill supporters had to sit around the AAA's premises looking more and more depressed as the results came in. Cohen won overwhelmingly. It was clear that a majority of African American members had supported him. Patrick Knight, who was treasurer of the union and of the caucus, explained that he had rented all the available space, leaving the Hillites nowhere to go to hide their misery. In the morning, I volunteered to go with Patrick to change the locks on the union office so that the defeated party could do no damage.

I also served on the Contract Negotiating Committee in 1972 and 1974, an experience from which I learned very much about not only the mechanics of negotiations, but also the administrative issues of a large agency. I also became secretary of the BCW chapter in the union. In 1974, too, the caucus offered me any of some minor union offices, and, out of curiosity, I chose to be a delegate to the NYC City Central Labor Council (CLC).

I found the CLC a nearly somnolent body, so much so that the president, Harry van Arsdale, not infrequently called from the podium: "Brother Smith, wake up! Brother Jones, wake up!" It met in a hall on East 16th Street, just off Union Square.

Van Arsdale himself was a historical artifact I am glad to have encountered. He was the last New Yorker I ever heard with the accent that referred to "Toity Toid Street," and "the terlet." The CLC generally reflected the utterly insular outlook of conservative construction workers and began with a pledge to the flag, as if we were in school. Van Arsdale saluted with his hand on his heart, like everybody else, but also with his other hand raised and extended toward the national banner. Someone once told me this feature had been eliminated in the 1940s because it too much resembled the Nazi salute. Also, because the flag, according to proper and legally defined practice, was on its own right on the stage, and because van Arsdale would not face away from the audience, he put his left hand on the right side of his chest.

The discussions were on a sophomoric level, dealing with extraordinary trivia. Once in a long while, someone, usually a union official who usually did not attend, would come to put forward information about something important. I remember this happening once with Victor Gotbaum, the executive director of AFSCME District Council 37, and another time with Sandra Feldman, of the United Federation of Teachers. The usual crowd would listen respectfully and then return to business, such as it was, as usual.

As a CLC delegate, I attended the New York state conventions of the American Federation of Labor-Congress of Industrial Organizations in 1974 and 1976. This event was at the Concord Hotel in Kiamesha Lake, New York. The Concord, now defunct, was itself part of a nearly vanished slice of life, the Jewish Catskill resort. It had everything—indoor swimming; outdoor swimming; another body of water in which we could paddle about in little foot-operated boats, seated in comfortable chairs; indoor and outdoor tennis; ping pong; and large rooms full of slot machines, pinball machines, and table football tables. Also, separately for men and women, were hot rooms, where, nude, you could sit and sweat. One room was dry heat; the other, steam. Then there was a pool to cool off in. I sat and looked at my fellow delegates, most of them middle-aged, fat, and flabby. "The wasted bodies of the American labor movement," I thought. In the evening there were stand-up comedy acts and, I think, dancing, which some of the wives attended in aristocratic splendor. Several, I noted, wore tiaras.

The food was stupefyingly abundant. There was a menu, but you could order as many of the dishes as you wanted. After serving the orders, the waiters would then put plates of Chinese food—of the chop suey school—in the middle of the table for anyone to grab. All of this was reliably good, and not infrequently better. I have fond memories of a very tasty kippered herring for breakfast and a really superior roast beef for dinner. The whole ambiance was determinedly middlebrow.[10]

The convention's business took up the morning. Its major task—hence the biennial schedule—was discussion and votes as to which candidates for New York state office the labor movement should endorse.

The chair was Ray Corbett, a tall structural ironworker, with white hair and a well-tailored suit, also white, or nearly white. He smiled genially, though he seemed to clench his teeth as he did so. Also, because of an eye ailment, he always wore sunglasses. The effect was unsettling, but not frightening.

The discussion was dishearteningly narrow and parochial. I recall a representative of one of the building trades unions speaking in favor of Luis Nine, a legislator, now dead, from the Bronx. Wilkins Avenue, in his district, was renamed "Luis Nine Boulevard" after him. The speaker called him *Lewis Nine*, as in the numeral. "He stood with us against the environmentalists!" was what recommended Mr. Nine.

There was more than a little bile to some of the discussion, and as a result, the ashtrays on the round tables where we sat were made of disposable cardboard with some kind of noncombustible coating. Someone explained that this was a precautionary measure. At the convention in 1970 or 1972, debate became so heated that delegates hurled the glass ashtrays at one other.

∿ • ∿ • ∿

MUCH MORE IMPORTANT was that for two or three years, I was senior delegate from the field office. I formed the habit of going to my desk in the morning, attending to anything urgent, and then going around the office, meeting the members, and learning of any pressing concerns. In the months when the fiscal crisis was deepening, when there was a panicky fear of layoffs, I established a policy that no one should repeat any rumor without telling me first so that I could verify what was happening. Most of my activity as delegate in the office itself involved efforts to maintain adequate working conditions and control the caseload.

The office was a converted shoe factory, and the air quality was frequently poor. We grieved about this problem over a long period of time, with indifferent results. Recently, I met someone, who, after some 30 years, was my successor as delegate. She was dealing with the same problem. Of course, the office, after 37 years, has moved to another building on Waters Place.

We were more successful with the caseload, though this was a constant struggle. For most of the time I was delegate, we were able to keep the pending rate to one new case a week. That, in itself, was a large workload, and the turnover rate among the staff remained high. It usually took a year for a worker to become comfortable and reasonably competent with the work. Many did not stay that long.

Also, there were issues among staff. One of a delegate's defined responsibilities was to mediate disputes of this sort. Because we represented all levels of nonmanagerial staff, these disagreements happened fairly frequently. I wrote responses to negative evaluations, represented members when they were in trouble, and so forth.

Most of the time I was able to work harmoniously with the director, first Mr. Breslauer, and then with his successor and wife, Mrs. Kronberger. Upon their marriage, after what apparently were lengthy and complex proceedings for divorce from their respective spouses, she reverted to her unmarried name, Miss Werner. The romance between them had been an open secret, mostly because of their rather ostentatious efforts to conceal it. With both, I tried to acknowledge that they were caught between the desire to do the work well and the constraints imposed from above.

As the surrounding fiscal situation deteriorated, the membership became more and more cynical, in ways that were not constructive. They felt frightened and helpless, but impotently resentful. Nietzsche's notion of "ressentiment" goes some way toward explaining this:

> Menschen des Ressentiment, . . . ein ganzes zitterndes Erdreich unterirdischer Rache, unerschöpflich, unersättlich in Ausbrüchen. . . .
> . . . people of ressentiment, . . . a whole quivering world of subterranean impulses towards revenge, inexhaustible, insatiable in outbreaks. (Nietzsche, 1999, p. 370)

Except that there was little outlet for their impulses. The bond market ruled, and we were on the defensive. One expression of this feeling was anger at the union and the union leadership, and there were elements in the union that fed into this feeling.

In the latter years of this period, my co-delegate Denise, a somewhat strange woman, who gave contradictory accounts of her personal and family origins, was a member of the Progressive Labor Party. She was the picture of the sectarian zealot. On one occasion, she asked me quite seriously if I didn't think the most serious problem in the world was "revisionism."[11] I was astounded, and she seemed surprised when I said I thought it was not a high priority. Another time she saw me reading Gramsci's *Prison Notebooks* and made a patronizing comment about how erudite I was. I could not help hearing echoes of the anti-intellectual attitudes prevalent in the little rural corner when I grew up. When I tried to convey to her some of Gramsci's more subtle interpretation of Marxism, she said I sounded like Kautsky. I was sure she had not read Kautsky himself and must have formed her impressions from reading Lenin's secondary tract, *The Proletarian Revolution and the Renegade Kautsky*.[12]

Despite all this, she could be engaging and did mobilize some of the members' dissatisfaction with the way things were going. At the same time, she had only mindless militancy to offer as an alternative, and gave little attention to the everyday issues in the office. Our relations were uneasy and guarded.[13]

One of my roles in the Cohen Caucus, since I actually had an understanding of Leninism, was to help diminish the sectarian caucuses' disruption of meetings and, generally, to help them come across as absurd and ridiculous. I recall one occasion when I was able to do this in the office itself.

One evening, at a delegate assembly, a Progressive Labor Party (PLP) member, not a member of the union, gave out leaflets. The leaflets included a quaint woodcut, probably dating from the 19th century, showing heroic workers on the march. This was so anachronistic that I could only laugh. Clearly, it was part of the propaganda the PLP reserved for students, and some activists, susceptible to romantic fantasies, but not ordinary working people.

But then I had an idea: although, on principle, I would not red-bait, but how would this look to normal people? After all, it was the PLP's own chosen mode of expression. I carefully preserved the leaflet, paid for 150 or so copies, and had a like-thinking delegate from another office get one of his members to put one on each desk at the field office, early in the morning, before anyone had come to work.

Denise saw this and managed to collect some of the leaflets before anyone could see them. She looked alarmed and thanked me nervously for distributing PLP material. I feigned ignorance.

∽ • ∽ • ∽

THE YEARS I spent at Bronx BCW were formative for me professionally, and I learned a lot there that I have never forgotten. Ever since, when I have worked in other settings, a concern for children's safety and well-being was constantly with me. About the child protective agency, in its various changing names, I have been ambivalent. For many years it was underfunded and overwhelmed, its staff poorly trained, and the foster care system quite questionable. The city administration also took an essentially antiprofessional stance toward the workforce. For a decade or two, the agency discontinued the long-time practice of facilitating staff's getting master's degrees. The policy in the 1990s of offering senior staff pension buyouts deprived the agency of much valuable experience.

In recent years, the situation has improved significantly in the field offices. Since the reorganization into the Administration for Children's Services (ACS), and a greater emphasis on professionalism, I have seen a real improvement. Foster care, however, has lagged, with diminishing oversight from ACS. The misguided policy of entrusting it, largely unmonitored, to new community-based agencies with little professional focus and with much politicization mixed with outright fraud, has led to disaster.

Though most of the BCW's inadequacies in the 1970s came from the city's failure to provide sufficient funding and staffing, some were simply the result of a general lack of knowledge in the field, which was broader than the agency itself. We had little idea, for example, how to investigate sexual abuse. I cringe at the incompetence with which I approached many of the comparatively few sex abuse cases I received. Still, this was a formative time, not only for me, but also for child protection as a professional focus. There has been a great gain in knowledge in the past few decades. The social work profession has begun to take more account of child protection in recent years.

This is good, but there should be even more emphasis on the clinical issues it involves. The greater emphasis on counseling and psychotherapy in schools of social work needs to make room for the clinical issues most social workers face in other types of agencies. Object relations theory, in particular, is very applicable to any social work practice that involves an authoritative component, and some rethinking of the old functionalist ideal that the key relationship is between the client and the agency is in order. This rethinking should include some of the considerations, mentioned earlier, about the relation among the worker, the agency, and the state as an arena of conflict between social forces. As a start, the social work profession needs to transcend the notion that social work practice in counseling and psychotherapy is a higher, or the highest, level of clinicality, and that practice outside a counseling context is somehow cruder and less deserving of prestige.[14]

IN 1972, MICHAEL Lerner, now famous as a writer, rabbi, the founding editor of *Tikkun*, and, briefly, a spiritual inspiration to Hillary Rodham Clinton, traveled the United States urging unaffiliated leftists to join in an organization he proposed to call the New American Movement (NAM).[15] I attended a meeting he called and liked the idea. In conception, NAM was a socialist organization, but not Leninist, and open to feminism. Feminism had always attracted me. My mother, even in the 1950s, had been an outspoken feminist, and had always been employed as a college teacher in the same institution as my father. NAM seemed a fresh departure, combining the flexibility and openness to American reality of the new left, with interpretations of theory that drew on traditions of Marxism that both social democracy and Stalinism had suppressed or at least ignored.

I joined with others who were founding a NAM chapter in NYC and was active for a number of years. Then NAM merged with the Democratic Socialist Organizing Committee, an event that coincided with increased family responsibilities that precluded much of my previous activity. NAM was active in other cities and had an impact. In NYC it proved difficult to move beyond a small group of activists, though some of our actions were significant.

IN THE SPRING of 1975, I applied to the Hunter College School of Social Work, was accepted, and began my formal professional training in the fall of that year.

References

Deutscher, I. (1970). *Lenin's childhood.* New York and Toronto: Oxford University Press.

Gans, H. J. (1974). *Popular culture and high culture: An analysis and evaluation of taste.* New York: Basic Books.

Hermand, J. (1997). *A Hitler youth in Poland: The Nazis' program for evacuating children during World War II* (M. B. Dembo, Trans.). Evanston, IL: Northwestern University Press.

Herreshoff, D. (1973). *The origins of American Marxism: From the transcendentalists to De Leon.* New York: Monad Press for the Anchor Foundation, Inc.

Hillquit, M. (1971). *History of socialism in the United States.* New York: Dover Books. (Original published 1903)

Nietzsche, F. (1999). Zur genealogie der moral (On the genealogy of morality). In *Kritische studienausgabe 5* (pp. 247–412). München: Deutscher Taschenbuch Verlag, GMBH.

O'Connor, J. (1973). *The fiscal crisis of the state.* New York: St. Martin's Press.

Winnicott, D. W. (1971). Transitional objects and transitional phenomena. In *Playing and reality* (pp. 1–26). London and New York: Tavistock Publications in Association with Methuen.

Questions for Discussion

1. The author says that child protective social work makes the social worker an agent of the state, who has the authority to remove children and break up families. How is this role different from other roles that social workers have? To what extent do social workers usually function as state agents?

2. The residents of poor communities often seem to welcome the removal of at-risk children. What has been the response of the people in the community to the kind of social work that you do?

To what do you attribute the differences and similarities?

3. Discuss the methods the author used to deal with cases of sexual abuse? Is there anything that you would have done differently?

4. The author admits that once when he got sick, he erred in accepting a grandmother's promise that she would keep the children away from their mother. What is the biggest mistake that you have made as a social worker, and how could it have been avoided?

5. In addition to his union activities, the author was also involved in various kinds of progressive politics. What do you see as the key political issues for social workers to be involved in today? Have they changed much since the period the author describes?

CHAPTER THREE

THE SEARCH FOR THEORY IN SOCIAL WORK: GRADUATE SCHOOL (1975–1977)

I STARTED GRADUATE school with some uncertainty. Some of my previous experiences with graduate social workers had not been pleasant. Many were patronizing to me as a child protective worker, even as they seemed naive about the realities of my clients' lives and about the legal implications of children being in danger. One of my colleagues was the first child protective worker I knew who became expert in cases of sexual abuse. Among his first cases was one the Jewish Board of Family and Children's Services (JBFCS) reported of an outwardly respectable and middle-class family in which the father regularly molested his daughter. Once my colleague had investigated and needed some information from JBFCS to facilitate removal, that agency's representatives did not want to cooperate, and wanted to leave the child in the home while they continued to work with the family. Apparently, they thought the child protective agency would follow their bidding in a secondary role. They explained that they were aware of the ongoing abuse and had reported the situation to the State Central Registry to "put some bite" in their therapy. Eventually, our supervisor threatened to involve the District Attorney of Bronx County. Also, occasionally, training at the BCW was conducted by staff who were graduates. These experiences also had seemed rather distant from what we confronted in the field. I remember a colleague commenting that the trainers were giving us a brief and diluted version of what they themselves had gotten in their first casework classes. At the same time, I knew the MSW would be a valuable professional credential, and I was open to the idea that the content of the training might be more substantial than some said.

Soon after beginning the semester, however, I was finding much of the experience interesting and stimulating. My policy class coincided with my interest in history, and with some of my experiences in the union, particularly in the fiscal crisis just then at its peak. I wrote a paper on public assistance which, in the summer of 1976, I expanded into an article published in the *Journal of Sociology and Social Welfare* (Dÿkema, 1977).

But much more new and crucial for me was the class in Human Behavior and the Social Environment, with an excellent teacher, Florence Vigilante. This was my first formal encounter with psychoanalytic theory, though I had picked up some bits and pieces from working at the BCW and also through my own personal therapy. The psychodynamic point of view attracted me because of its clear basis in material experience—it views the human personality as developing out of the body's encounters with the surrounding world. Also, the psychoanalytic approach is historical, in that it deals with the personal history of the individual. The psychoanalytic tradition continues to develop, and parts of it have been superseded. One does not have to accept all of Freud's original formulations,[1] or adhere to any particular psychoanalytic school to recognize that this is a fundamentally valuable way to understand the human personality. It remains an indispensable conceptual tool.

At the same time, the course discussed human behavior at length and gave little emphasis to the social environment. This seemed to be a problem, compounded in the second semester, which of course, was about psychopathology. This course too was extremely valuable, but, at least as I experienced it at the time, had few points of contact with social theory.

I was so fortunate to take this course with Eda Goldstein, then an adjunct professor, and not yet the author of the books in use in so many graduate schools. Her lectures were models of clarity and thorough exposition. Moreover, she introduced us in depth to the concept of borderline personality and told us that she had been working with other analysts who were developing the theory that underlay it. She did not mention that Otto Kernberg was among them. Without knowing it, I was on the periphery of the milieu in which this crucial adaptation of psychoanalytic theory was occurring. However, I began to see that this was a valuable tool for understanding many clients and patients I had encountered. Later, I came to see a potential sociological dimension in some of Kernberg's writings, though once when I encountered him at a conference and said so, he seemed very surprised.

In my last semester at Hunter, however, I took a course in various schools of personality and psychotherapy. I did a presentation on the encounter between Marxism and psychoanalysis. There is a rich tradition in this area, despite the opposition from powerful elements in both camps. Psychoanalysis had a conservative character in the United States in the 1950s and 1960s, and still does, to an extent. In addition, Stalinist Marxism took a crudely antipsychological stance.[2] I discovered, however, that there were competing traditions in both psychoanalysis and in Marxism. These included the Frankfurt School, which I began to explore, and other bodies of theory.

Somewhat independent of my course work, I also began to learn about the history of the family as an institution and its link to personality. Social work's emphasis on the family and work with it was familiar, of course. That had been the focus in child protective work, and it certainly was the focus in graduate school. But discussions of family structure and functioning on the level of practice, and the theory of practice, in my classes, both in my practice classes and in a family therapy course, were fairly narrow. I began to think and read more broadly about this fundamental social institution. In November 1976 I read Zaretsky's (1976) *Capitalism, the Family, and Personal Life*. This slim volume gives a brief introduction to some of the basic history of the forms of family that are in the heritage of the prevailing culture in Europe and North America. It shows how they have shaped a variety of forms of personality. Zaretsky begins:

> The following book examines the division between the private and public, or inner and outer worlds of our society. It explains this division in terms of the impact of capitalism upon the family: on one hand, the decline of the traditional patriarchal family, based upon private productive property; or the other, the rise of a new emphasis on personal life experienced as something outside work and society. (p. 9)

This seemed immediately relevant to social work practice, inasmuch as the social worker comes from the public sphere to intervene in the private life of the client.

Zaretsky (1976) also provided a brief introduction to those forms of family life that have prevailed under the increasing influence of relationships between people mediated through money and literacy—that is, through the institutions of capitalism and the day-to-day experience of living under them. First among these was the early bourgeois family, in which the family was a productive unit in itself, with all members working in the domestic enterprise. There was a time when this was the scene of most economic production in the society.

Later, the late bourgeois family became the normative—though not numerically dominant—form as the market expanded and new modes of production developed. In the late bourgeois family, production had moved outside the home, as the father went to work in his enterprise.

For those who lived in late bourgeois families, the economic sphere, belonging to men, was profane. They experience the home, by contrast, as a refuge from the crudities of the economic world. The home was also the sphere of women. Women, most of all the sainted mother of the middle-class family—celebrated by authors like John Ruskin (1871/1981)[3]—dominated it and symbolized its almost sacerdotal character.

In the 19th century, the late bourgeois family, with its trappings, was the norm in England, much of the rest of western Europe, and North America. But this was not the only experience. Majorities of the populations belonged to the still numerically dominant peasant populations, or else worked for money.

Zaretsky (1976) discussed employees who worked for wages and salaries as examples of proletarianization, the process by which people come to sustain themselves materially by getting paid for work they do for someone else instead of working in their own or their family's enterprise. This, in fact, is, for Zaretsky:

> the underlying thesis of the book.... that the rise of industrial capitalism, while destroying the traditional form of family life, gave rise to a new search for personal identity which takes place outside of the division of labour. In a phrase: proletarianization gave rise to subjectivity. (p. 9)

Obviously, a large part of what social work is about is the subjectivity, the feelings, of human responses to experience. And the patterns of these responses are what I had learned in Human Behavior. This applies to the relations between mothers and infants, the oedipal situation, the rivalry of siblings and much more. And all this reflects the diversity of family forms.

On a social level, too, the subjectivity arising out of proletarianization gives increasing importance to the individual and to the individual apart from and often opposed to the family. The ongoing historical development of democratic values is part of the same process. Noemí Cuevas' desire to free herself from her stepfather's exploitation was, in a small sphere, a democratic struggle for her subjective individuality. The child protective agency's intervention to help her exemplified the ambiguities of government in the way that O'Connor had helped me understand, but now, as he called the unchanging validity of family institutions into question, Zaretsky pointed toward a more refined understanding of the issues.

This thinking resonated not only with what I had learned in class, but also with what I was encountering in the field. In my first year, I worked at a project of the Community Service Society, which had just decided to shift its focus from casework counseling to community organization projects. Project ACCESS was an effort to advocate for clients for the local welfare center in East Harlem. The work was somewhat interesting, but did tend to resemble what I had done at Kingsbridge.

My second-year placement, however, was at the Abraham Jacobi Hospital of Bronx Municipal Hospital Center, in the child and adolescent outpatient psychiatric clinic, then directed by the late Paulina Kernberg. The atmosphere was intense, my supervisor was extremely demanding and rigorous, and the orientation strongly psychoanalytic with an inclination toward the object relations school.

The patients—Italian, African, and Jewish American, with a few Hispanics—were a cross-section of the population of the northeast Bronx at the time.

At Jacobi, I learned a great many lessons that have stayed with me ever since. The emphasis on borderline personality was strong, as one would expect with Dr. Kernberg as the director of Child Psychiatry. The theory of borderlines was especially valuable in fitting in with my experiences in child protection. I did not quite understand this at the time, but, over the years it has become clear to me that social workers, in particular, end up with the clients who more closely approximate this range of pathology.

At the same time, some of my original doubts about social work training persisted, though in a more developed form. It struck me that the excellent course in Human Behavior, with its advanced and coherent basis in a psychological theory, had no parallel counterpart in the theory of the society in which human beings live.

Zaretsky (1976), for example, after pointing out that "proletarianization gave rise to subjectivity," went on to show the limitations of psychoanalysis, which were the same limitations I was perceiving in formal social work training:

> Psychoanalysis has no theory of how the family is itself socially determined—instead it explains the family in terms of itself. As a result, psychoanalysis cannot distinguish what is universal in the family (a biological unit after all as well as a social one) from what is specific to the family of a particular mode of production. It cannot distinguish what in the human condition is subject to historical transformation and what should be seen as 'civilization and its discontents'. (p. 128)

The closest to a course in the area of social theory parallel to Human Behavior was one called "Social Work in the Urban Environment." It was interesting, but mostly provided data on the then current state of material life for the typical social work clientele in New York City at the time. There was no theory about it to speak of. Also, unlike the course in Human Behavior, it was largely ahistorical. Its value was only as durable as the conditions it discussed.

Social work as a profession seemed to have as little historical sensibility as most Americans. Already, in child protective work, I had found that understanding the sociological and historical aspect of clients' lives helped me form a diagnostic understanding. This was the social analogue of knowing a client's developmental history in psychodynamic terms. Having read Zaretsky, I found also that the various family forms he described had left discernible traces both in the society and in the behavior of many people I knew, both as clients and otherwise. For example, many people who work for wages or a salary try to behave in the family sphere as if they were small business people. Fathers, for example, sometimes try to assert a kind of authority that is more consistent with that of the independent entrepreneur. Some of the aspirations and expectations that many bring to family life are inconsistent with their live circumstances. The resulting conflicts within the family are frequent occasions for social work intervention.

But what to do with this insight? As valuable as it was, my professional training offered no guidance in this area. Though my initial uncertainty about the intrinsic value of graduate training was gone, I did see this theoretical deficiency as a central problem, both for me and for the social work profession. Social work, it seemed to me, needed a social theory on a comparable level of sophistication to the personality theory offered in Human Behavior.

After all, personality theory is not specific to social work. We share it with psychology and psychiatry. A social theory, by contrast, would be social work's own, and potentially would serve as a basis on which the social work profession could respond to its detractors. In the following years, this deficiency seemed all the more problematic as social work went on the defensive against right-wing attacks on social services and the value of professional skill.

I graduated from the Hunter College School of Social Work in the spring of 1977 and returned to the New York City Department of Social Services, but to a different part of what by now was called Special Services for Children, the Division of Group Homes.

References

Dÿkema, C. R. (1977, January–March). The political economy of social welfare: A perspective. *Journal of Sociology and Social Welfare, 4,* 439–469.
Ruskin, J. (1981). Lecture II: Of queens' gardens. In *Sesame and lilies.* New York: A. L. Burt. (Original work published 1871)
Zaretsky, E. (1976). *Capitalism, the family, & personal life.* New York: Harper & Row.

Questions for Discussion

1. To what extent have the courses in social work school helped you understand what you actually do as a social worker?

2. How has the family changed? What kind of family did you grow up in, and how accurately does the author's summary of the different kinds of family life describe the roles in your family?

3. Do you agree with the author that social work lacks better theories? Does it need them? If so, why?

CHAPTER FOUR
A GROUP HOME IN THE BRONX (1977–1979)

THE GROUP HOME program was a small part of Special Services for Children, the Bureau of Institutions and Facilities. It comprised six or eight group homes of 12 residents, each in various parts of New York City. There also was a division of Group Residences, institutions that had more residents; a non-secure detention program for juveniles awaiting court hearings on delinquency petitions, who were thought not to need confinement in the Spofford Juvenile Center; and a group of diagnostic reception centers, where adolescents just accepted into care underwent evaluation. And, of course, there was a foster family care program.

My assignment was to a home on Saint Lawrence Avenue between Lacombe and Patterson Avenues in the Soundview section of the Bronx. Twelve girls lived there. After I had been working at the program for most of a year, one of my colleagues quit, and I had to take over, in addition, half of the boys in another group home on Marolla Place in the far Northeast Bronx, just off the Boston Post Road.

In each house, there was a senior houseparent, a male and a female houseparent, and the house homemaker. The child care staff members lived in the home for most of the week and were required to maintain a real personal residence elsewhere. It was an open secret that they often just rented a room to occupy on their days off, when they were required to absent themselves from the home. At Saint Lawrence Avenue, the senior houseparent was a middle-aged African American woman, widowed young, who had presided over the house for several years. Generally, her sense of the residents was accurate, and she was able to maintain order most of the time with a group of quite challenging adolescents. The female houseparent was a native of one of the West Indian Islands, a little older than her supervisor. She was less dynamic, but the girls generally found her warm and accessible.

The house homemaker was a younger African American woman, known for the quality of her cooking, which was a fairly conventional Southern cuisine. I put on a bit of weight, as it was expected that I would take several meals in a week with the girls.

There was also a male houseparent, Mr. Bolton, a young African American man with energy and, sometimes, more enterprise than judgment. One of his efforts led to a grotesque incident.

One day he decided that the group home should subscribe to a newspaper. Not a bad idea, but which? The *New York Times* he rightly thought too heavy. The *New York Post* and the *New York Daily News* were too sensational. He considered the *Amsterdam News*, but apparently thought it too parochial. *Newsday*, which might have been an acceptable compromise, was still mostly a Long Island paper. Eventually, he decided on the *New York Daily News World*. This paper is probably defunct now, but in 1978 it had some presence in the city. The previous year there had been a newspaper strike, and the *News World* was the only daily available. Some people bought it for the local coverage, which was fairly adequate, and a diminishing number continued to buy it, even though much of its coverage showed that it was an organ of the Reverend Sun Myung Moon's Unification Church.

Some days later, Mr. Bolton told me that two church missionaries had visited the group home and had plied him with religious tracts, and with a tape cassette on which a man with an affectedly mellifluous voice expounded on Moon's doctrines.

I was immediately concerned. Though I thought most of our residents would regard the missionaries as ridiculous, there were some—more fragile, more psychiatrically compromised— who might have been vulnerable. Certainly, our residents did not need the Moonies attempting to involve them.

Then Mr. Bolton told me the missionaries very much desired a meeting with me. Perhaps they thought I was in charge. Perhaps they thought I was important because mine was the only white face. I agreed immediately and, in preparation, listened to the tape, which gave a summary of the creation and everything important that had happened since then.

God, it seemed, had created the universe much as in *Genesis*, but then with the fall of the angels, Satan had gained the upper hand. He could not destroy god, but god had skulked around ever since, trying to mount a counteroffensive. He had tried once, with Jesus, but this failed because Jesus died before marrying and having a family. The Jews, of course, bore much of the blame for this failure. Now god was trying again, through Reverend Moon. The speaker did not quite say Moon was the messiah.

The appointed hour arrived. I met with them, a man and a woman, a German and an Austrian. There were many such in the New York Streets that year. In previous years, Moon's proselytizers had been nearly incomprehensible Koreans and Japanese, who wandered the streets of East Harlem, in particular, wearing colonial American costumes. But in 1978, Moon must have decided to send people who could actually speak English.

We met in the group home living room. It was on the second floor and got little use, as the girls mostly socialized in the television room, the dining room, and the kitchen, downstairs. They lugged a television and a videocassette recorder (VCR) with them. VCRs were very new in 1978 and were about the size of a substantial suitcase. They plugged this system into the wall, connected the components, and then, to their confusion, it did not work.

Then they tried to convert me. I have always enjoyed talking to street evangelists, and their strategy was familiar. On the one hand, they appealed to the latent generally Christian patriarchal monotheism that is part of most Americans' thinking, even if they are not observant or even actively religious. Then they tried to link this to any existential anxiety, fear, or guilt I might be experiencing.

I responded to their arguments with very basic, innocently stated, questions. I made them spend a long time explaining how to define god, how he himself originated, whether god was masculine or feminine, and so forth. Then there was a long discussion of the ever-fascinating theodicy question.[1]

The missionaries' frustration grew, and they began to confer in their native language before responding to my seemingly guileless questions. I listened to their colloquies and guided my new questions accordingly. After several such go-rounds, they talked with each other again, with mounting anxiety and frustration. This time I joined their conversation, speaking in German myself. The man replied and then said something to his partner. I made another comment, again in German, and then the man suddenly realized that something had gone terribly wrong. He and the woman hurriedly packed up their equipment and left. I followed them down the stairs, continuing our theological discussion, and thanked them for expressing their interesting views. They never came back.

AT THE MAROLLA group home, the senior houseparent was a relative of the woman at Saint Lawrence but always left me with an equivocal impression, though we were able to get along. His assistants were a shifting group, though one was a conscientious man who, though he never said so, seemed dubious about his boss.

The residents themselves ranged in age from about 13 to 20 years. They could remain in the group home after age 18 if they were in some form of education or training. Several had been in the home for a number of years and had really grown up there.

I started to work in the foster care system at a point in its history that coincided with one of the recurrent waves of concern that too many children were lingering in care too long. A push for adoption was the result. However, the girls at the group home were among that part of the long-term foster care population not considered likely candidates for adoption. They were too old and had been in care too long. Many were not appealing to the usual potential adoptive parent. Some of them had been in foster family homes which rejected them when they began to experience the turmoil of puberty and early adolescence. One, who I will call Daria, had gone through this demoralizing experience. Her early life had been with a mother who apparently was extremely neglectful, with a penchant for compulsive sexual promiscuity. Daria had many siblings and half-siblings and had little contact with most of them. She was in a foster home for some years, but apparently the foster parents rejected her when she was about 12 years of age. From there she went to the care of an aunt, then she stayed for a time in a residence for teenagers run by SERA, a substance abuse program that later foundered on financial mismanagement and corruption. From it, she ran away and spent some time living in the catch-as-catch-can residential arrangements available to members of a street gang. Some minor offense landed her in Non-Secure Detention, from which, after adjustment of the charges against her, the group home program recruited her. When I met her, she was 14 and had been in the home a number of months. Later, she told me that she had figured out that running with a gang was not wise or prudent. At first she would not speak to me, though this changed gradually. I had noted in reading her case record, that one of the psychologists gave her a performance IQ score in the 90s; her verbal IQ was 106. Allowing for the cultural inappropriateness of the test, this seemed to indicate a high level of effective intelligence. She was constantly challenging, and I had to work very hard with her, often over the opposition of the child care staff, who did not like her, in large part because she was much smarter than they were.

Others of the long-term residents had had even more damaging early lives, frequently involving sexual abuse. One—I will call her Janice—had spent her first eight or nine years with an alcoholic and extremely neglectful mother who did nothing to prevent a boyfriend from molesting her. After a brief and unsuccessful stay in a foster home, she came to the group home when she was about 11 years of age and it was just opening.

Still another, "Wanda," was the child of an addict who had used her as a lookout in burglaries when she was 10 years of age. I read the case records of two others, who were cousins, and discovered that one of my friends from the field office had removed the two sibling groups from the home of a pair of addicted sisters.

Similarly, the addicted mother of "Annie" had left her at age three, in the care of a four-year-old boy who chose to throw her out a window. Fortunately, the apartment was on the first floor, but it was in the rear of the building and overlooked a courtyard that was a story lower. Annie's jaw was smashed and she spent two years with it wired. She had some facial scarring but was so pretty that male attention somewhat made up for the disfigurement. Others of the residents had obvious organic defects and significant psychiatric illness.

Some of these girls were more damaged than others. One of the cousins, for example, had been a successful student and was in college, studying nursing. So too was Wanda, though she was unable to complete college. Of the boys, several were impaired, though there was one who we recognized as talented. He has gone on to be a successful actor. I will not name him, of course, but he has spoken to the mass media of his time at Marolla. One boy had a long history of arson. He was not among my particular charges, but his social worker described driving him through the Bronx as he casually pointed out a number of buildings he had burned down. He went by the name "Wise," though he had a different real name. This was because he was a *Five Percenter*, a member of a group that claimed a kind of religious ideology in justification of antisociality. He sometimes read from the Five Percenters' sacred text. He left it around, and I once read most of it. It was a looseleaf binder with several pages of penciled and barely literate writing.

Each group home had an office, which I used to interview residents somewhat privately, and also, in the mornings, and early afternoons, to do some of the mountainous paperwork. The one at Marolla was especially pleasant. It was on the top floor, and sitting at the desk, I looked out across Marolla Place to Seton Hill Park, a large undeveloped tract with the ruins of 19th century gristmills and, just across the street, a pond with green algae in which ducks paddled back and forth.

The days I was not at the group homes I spent at the office, which was at 80 Lafayette Street, in lower Manhattan. The area was pleasant, close to Canal Street, Chinatown, and Little Italy. There were six social work positions, not all of them filled at one time. My colleagues were congenial for the most part, and one was a man with whom I had become quite friendly during the 1967 strike when he was a charismatic delegate at the Melrose Welfare Center. Unfortunately, he had become chronically schizophrenic and had to leave. There was a unit supervisor, a position not always filled, and a case supervisor, who was the director of Social Service for the program. She was pleasant and supportive, but she frequently drank heavily and embarrassingly. Eventually, she suffered a serious injury and went on extended medical leave.

When I began, the director of the program was a mild and rather bland man with a background as a child care worker. He reported to another administrator who was astute and reliably sound. After a few months, however, this director was replaced by another, "Mr. Smith," who, according to people who claimed to know, had insinuated himself into the graces of higher levels of administration while providing training in our program on cultural issues. He had then moved into our directorship, displacing his predecessor.

Whether or not this was true, I have never worked under a more clearly psychopathic administrator. Among his more destructive characteristics was a propensity for unannounced visits to the group homes with his administrative assistant (AA), "Robert," whom I knew from the field office. There he had a well-deserved reputation for well-intentioned stupidity. Once, one of the senior houseparents asked me what Robert was really about. This was after he had conducted himself in a spectacularly maladroit manner in a staff meeting. I explained that whereas most people learn many lessons from experience, Robert had learned only two: that you advance in life by hanging around people more important than yourself and that you try very hard at whatever you are doing. The problem with this was that many things Robert found himself doing made little sense.

On his impromptu visits to the group homes, Mr. Smith would gather the residents around him for genial and rather loose conversation. Because the residents had learned that you only get things in life by asking for them insistently and repeatedly, they would present him with all their various desires. He then made offhand promises, which the social workers found difficult to keep. On occasion, too, his remarks to the female residents were somewhat sexually inappropriate.

He also decided the program should have an open intake, meaning we would accept any child referred. Because the group homes were located in rather ordinary residential communities, and used community schools, we had to assume a certain minimal capacity for appropriate behavior among the residents. When I saw the referral materials we received on some of the potential residents, I was appalled and knew that if we accepted them the results would be disastrous. They really belonged in residential treatment.

With one or two of the other social workers, I was able to keep out the most unsuitable girls by recruiting new residents through a personal contact with the social worker at the Hegeman Diagnostic Reception Center in East New York. When a vacancy seemed to be coming up, I would call him and arrange to interview girls at the center to fill it. Mr. Smith did not know we were doing this, and it worked reasonably well.

One of the other social workers, however, had to accept a number of residents who were so disruptive that the group home could not contain them. Moreover, Mr. Smith himself lived only a few blocks away, and this home had had the most exposure to his unsettling influence. Eventually, there was a riot at the house, with several thousand dollars of damage. The house had to be closed for repairs and the remaining residents dispersed.

This disastrous event occurred a few weeks after the social work staff had decided to expose one of Mr. Smith's more egregious acts. In a rather paranoid manner, he had attempted to set the child care staff to spy on the social workers. They, however, distrusted him so much that they told us of this. Two or three of us discussed this over lunch, by a fortuitous chance, at a restaurant at the bend on Doyers Street in Chinatown, which Herbert Asbury, in *Gangs of New York*, says was called "the bloody angle" because of frequent ambushes there in the Tong Wars of the 19th century. We met with the other social workers and decided to write a memorandum, ostensibly to our director of social service, politely requesting clarification of this change in procedure. I was delegated to compose the memorandum, which we all signed. Then we were able to hand it to Mr. Smith's superior just before a scheduled meeting between them. Smith returned from the meeting visibly shaken, and with his AA. They had apparently figured out that I was the author of the memorandum and were rather obsequious.

The riot led to Mr. Smith's banishment and replacement by a woman of eminent sense and judgment. This was just as I was going on leave from the job. He returned to his civil service rank and went to the Bronx field office as a supervisor II or III. However, a few weeks later he was found sitting in his car with a bullet hole behind his ear.

I was struck by the unanimity with which all who commented took it as a matter of course that the manner of his death reflected badly on his life. There were no expressions of distress or sympathy. Nor were there the usual bewailings of the violence of the society or the insecurity of life in the city then becoming a mass obsession among New Yorkers. Instead, people speculated as to whether it was an aggrieved spouse, of one sex or the other, who had killed him, or if he had been involved in something even more nefarious.

Despite the obvious obstacles to effective work, and the burden of covering half of the boys' house, I generally enjoyed the experience and thought our achievements with the residents were fairly creditable. Successful work in the program, as in many other parts of the social services, depended on a creative approach to the paperwork. As I have said, the push to move children out of care was largely irrelevant to the needs of most of our residents, but it did result in a huge burden of documentation of efforts to define discharge goals and work toward them. With some residents, it was actually realistic to think of their return to their families, as the turmoil of early adolescence gave way to greater maturity and the parents, with some work from me, were better able to accept their children. Most of our residents, however, were not candidates for return home, if only because they had no homes to return to.

I found, however, that the key to doing the paperwork rapidly and making it possible to have time for real work was to do the quarterly reports as mechanically as possible in a manner that differed as little as possible from resident to resident. Writing the same words over and over took a lot less time. Also, I discovered that it was easier to do this when the projected discharge was far in the future. Hence, I learned to define all residents' discharge goals as "discharge to his/her own responsibility upon the attainment of his/her majority." There were more than a few residents who really needed just to live apart from their families so all could work on their relationship issues without having to cope with the everyday conflicts of domestic life. But for them, too, I defined their goals far into the future and used the time I otherwise would have had to devote to documentation for actual intervention with the people involved. When we really did discharge them, at age 15 or 16, I noticed that nobody questioned me about the disparity between the defined goal and the actual outcome. Clearly, nobody paid much attention to the reports I created.

This led me to wonder if anything I wrote—apart from the narrative portion of the record—really mattered. I experimented with a form we had to include whenever we accepted a new resident, addressed to the State Board of Social Welfare, a body whose nature and function was never made clear. We had to sign the name of the commissioner of social services to this form. At the time, he was one J. Henry Smith, a retired dress manufacturer put in the position on the assumption, popular in some political circles at the time, that the way to get positive results out of the social services was to put businessmen in charge. What did the "J" stand for? I took to completing the initial. First it was "John Henry Smith." Then "Jasper Henry Smith." Eventually, I settled on "Joachim Henry Smith." This too attracted no notice.

AT FIRST, A number of the girls, especially Daria and Annie, were angry and challenging toward me, but this changed over time. I won Annie's confidence later in the summer of 1977, when I helped her get out of a fair amount of trouble. Annie had a younger sister, who lived with an aunt. One day she visited, found fault with the way the aunt was caring for the child, and called the group home to ask if she could bring the sister to stay with her. The senior houseparent, of course, told her this was not permissible. Annie, angry, started home and, while waiting for the train at the Hub, 149th Street and 3rd Avenue, came upon a man, apparently drunk, passed out on the platform. Some cash was visible on his person. Annie reached out and took it. The man then woke up, and his colleagues, the other plain-clothes police, arrested her. "Damn!," she said later, "I might have known a white man drunk in that station would be a cop!"

I went to the Family Court with Annie and found out that the probation officer was someone I knew from my frequent court appearances while I had worked at the field office. We agreed that Annie's conduct was wrong but that the police had more or less entrapped her. We then helped her understand that stealing was not a useful way to express her anger. The probation officer let her go with a warning.

When I started in the program, my supervisor told me one of my tasks was to discourage pregnancy and encourage contraception. Somewhat later, we had training with SIECUS, the Sexuality Information and Education Council of the United States, in which one of the trainers made the point that people who work with adolescents frequently do not accept their sexuality as valid and feel free to treat it as presumptively and primarily problematic in a way that they would consider impolite with adults.

I realized this was true of the way I had been approaching the issue with the girls, even though I thought of myself as enlightened. When the girls came to tell me of their amatory involvements, which happened fairly often, I would quickly start to talk about contraception. I realized that this irritated them and began, instead, to listen more sympathetically to the feelings, sometimes ambivalent, that they had for the boys in question. With this basis, a later discussion of contraception became easier, and I was able to refer many girls to an adolescent clinic at Mount Sinai Hospital that apparently followed a similarly accepting approach. The clinic eventually became so popular among our residents that it became a form of group amusement to vie with one another in calling and making appointments for pelvic examinations.

Daria, however, was different. She was pregnant in the fall of 1977, miscarried, and set about becoming pregnant again. She was successful about a year later. Her partner was a boy who lived down the street and whose sister was friendly with some of our girls. I will call him Shorty. He was stereotypically handsome, seemed in love mostly with himself, and was strikingly less intelligent than Daria. He also had an annoying habit of sneaking over the roofs and entering the room Daria shared with Annie. While they copulated, Annie went out on the fire escape. When found in the group home, he was surly to the staff. Eventually, I put a stop to this when some of the other girls told me that Shorty was no longer living with his family down the block but was in some kind of institution. This was because he had hit a police officer in the Four Train. This sounded unmistakably like the New York Division for Youth (DFY), which houses juveniles adjudged delinquent.[2]

The other girls were unsympathetic to Shorty because they liked Daria and knew of Shorty's infidelities with a girl, Janey, who briefly stayed in the group home until we decided she was too disturbed and uncontrollable for our setting and sent her to a Group Residence. The other girls were scornful of Janey, who they thought was stupid and utterly lacking in common sense. They were right. Annie, in particular, who had a real comic gift, created great hilarity by imitating how she imagined Shorty would walk if Janey infected him with gonorrhea—another issue they had accurately assessed.

Some hours of telephoning yielded the location of the group home where Shorty was living. I went there immediately and spoke with the very cooperative director. He assured me that he would tell Shorty that if there were any further complaints about his trespassing in the group home the DFY would transfer him to another facility. Because it was a state agency, that might mean a location hundreds of miles away. The problem did stop, and a few weeks later, when I ran into Shorty on the street, he was exaggeratedly deferential.

Daria was delighted to be pregnant, and we spent months working out a plan for her and the baby. We explored mother–child programs of various sorts. Daria was constantly ambivalent, but eventually she insisted that another of Shorty's elder sisters, who also lived nearby, become the guardian. I foresaw that, over time, they would not agree and insisted that they sign an agreement setting forth ground rules for their relationship and the baby's care. When the inevitable anger between them emerged, Daria was able to acknowledge that she had made an error in judgment.

Through all this, the child care staff were unremittingly hostile toward Daria and angry at me for not taking her to court. They refused to believe that there was nothing I could realistically allege against her under the Family Court Act. Eventually, Daria agreed to voluntarily place her baby in foster care. Mr. Bolton, for example, had complained bitterly about Shorty's nocturnal visits to Daria, whose room was just above his. However, when I told him that I had solved his problem, he was annoyed with me. I thought I detected some identification with Shorty, and an unacknowledged attraction to Daria, who was quite attractive.

∿ . ∿ . ∿

I KNOW LITTLE of the eventual outcomes for most of the residents. Around 1990, when working in the Montefiore Medical Center emergency room, I met Janice, who, though under outpatient psychiatric care, held a modestly important job with the New York City Transit Authority and seemed to be doing reasonably well. I had also met Wanda on the street in 1984 or so, and Janice told me she had since died of cancer.

In graduate school, I had written a paper in which I suggested the strong possibility that some children in foster care would do better in group care, specifically because it is not a family setting. Zaretsky's historical view showed that the family structure that we in the United States consider normative is only one among many family forms that have existed. It is relatively small, delimited, and more or less isolated. Earlier family forms had been more inclusive and had offered developing children a wider range of relationships with adults and a less intense and charged parent–child relationship. Though frankly dysfunctional and pathological families, like those of the group home residents, were clearly exceptional, it occurred to me that the general norm of family life tended to create a particular risk of dysfunction, especially given the weak and laggard development of family support in the form of the kind of social services that exist in other advanced countries.

It seemed to me that for those children who had grown up in pathological families, a group home setting would provide a set of adult–child relationships that would have less emotional charge and thus would be more supportable. Despite its stigmatization, and other obvious drawbacks, being raised by a bureaucracy rather than a foster family might have certain inherent advantages.

My two years in the Division of Group Homes generally confirmed my speculation. Though there must have been transferential elements in the conflicts between residents and staff, it also was true that the residents knew that the individual adults involved were important but were only individuals among other individuals in the administration of the agency. Those who had lived in the program for some years had a finely developed sense of bureaucratic functioning.

Part of the stigma on group care comes from the efforts of the child welfare system to follow the conventions of the society which privilege the nuclear family as a preferred form and views group care as an unfortunate last resort. In fact, this is an example of the constant historical tendency in child welfare policy to assume that there is always only one truly sound way to address its stated tasks. This kind of thinking embodies an implicitly antiprofessional thrust. The alternative, and sounder, approach would be a primary assumption that decisions as to which of the range of alternatives is the appropriate placement for each child should come from individualized assessment by a competent person. Of course, that would be much more expensive than the existing way of doing things. Perhaps just as challenging to conventional thinking would be that true professionalization of the foster care process demands an admission that the problems it addresses are much more than just marginal exceptions to a basically sound family institution.

More and more, it seemed to me that the social work profession and the presuppositions of social work practice need to take a systematic and critical view of the family as an institution.

IN LATE 1977 and 1978, in addition to continued work in the New American Movement, I joined with others to form a collective to publish *Catalyst, A Socialist Journal of the Social Services*. This was an exciting project that resulted in a publication of generally high quality. It survives today as the *Journal of Progressive Human Services*. The collective was a working group, but it also made a serious effort to advance the members' theoretical level. There were periodic retreats, with readings and discussion. On a few occasions I contributed internal theoretical documents and also wrote articles for the journal (Dÿkema, 1978). In general, we were critical of the weakness, passivity, and intellectual superficiality of the social work profession in the face of what clearly were mounting threats.

In these years, too, I belonged to a small group that read and discussed the first volume of Karl Marx's *Das Kapital*. As with most people who actually undertake this study, I found that Marx's actual thought is markedly different than the common myths would have us believe. For example, his initial discussion of what a commodity is presents an interpretation of the relations involved that has an essentially psychological dimension. This insight illuminates many issues we confront in social work practice. The alienation I saw in Noemí Cuevas's expression in that unforgettable photograph was many things, but one was her sense that she had become, in the crudest way, a commodity.

My general interest in developing social theory to inform social work's conceptualization and practice, became, now, a conscious project that I have continued over the years. I read more on the history of the family and other aspects of the social reality of the clients I was encountering. Zaretsky's formulation, I found, though accurate and sound as far as it went, mostly dealt with those parts of society that had been literate and capable of influencing the prevalent expectations of family life. It only barely touched on others, in particular the vast rural populations that, until recently, comprised the majority of the human species. Many social work clients, and many social workers themselves, are very close to the peasant heritage.

My first introduction to this subject was the chapter on peasant immigrants to the United States in Oscar Handlin's the *Uprooted* (Handlin, 1951). Handlin introduced me to European peasant culture in its 19th century form.[3] Though Handlin's treatment of peasant culture is brief and somewhat superficial, it was my first encounter with a provocative and useful idea. Handlin described European peasants as substantially pagan, with only an overlay of the Christian version of patriarchal monotheism. Later, in 1980, I read Mark Poster's *Critical Theory of the Family* (Poster, 1978),[4] which treats Zaretsky's material in much more detail. Poster looked at the peasant populations of the past as an important family form and showed what kind of personality characteristics would have been typical in the peasant village. Other historical works, much more detailed and scholarly than Handlin's,[5] show peasant culture as essentially pagan. The religions that presume a single father-god—patriarchal monotheism—were an overlay only partly integrated with older forms of belief. To a considerable extent, patriarchal monotheism was a fairly new intrusion from urban areas, as were secular ideologies.

The implications of this are vast. The transition from peasant life to modernity forms much of the cultural field in which social work practice takes place. This is a large issue, which I have encountered in various forms over the years and will discuss in detail later.

At the same time, I found it difficult to formulate a comprehensive theory, though I was beginning to assemble some of its components.

IN 1979, MICHAEL, my elder son was born, followed by his brother Daniel in 1981. I went on paternity leave in the fall of 1979.

References

Devlin, J. (1987). *The superstitious mind: French peasants and the supernatural in the nineteenth century.* New Haven: Yale University Press.
Dÿkema, C. R. (1978). Towards a new age of social services: Lessons to be learned from our history. *Catalyst: A Socialist Journal of the Social Services, 1,* 57–75.
Handlin, O. (1951). *The uprooted: The epic story of the great migrations that made the American people.* Boston: Little, Brown.
Poster, M. (1978). *Critical theory of the family: A continuum book.* New York: Seabury Press.
Redfield, R. (1953). *The primitive world and its transformations.* Ithaca, NY: Cornell University Press.
Redfield, R. (1956). *Peasant society and culture.* Chicago: University of Chicago Press.
Thomas, W. I., & Znaniecki, F. (1958). *The Polish peasant in Europe and America.* New York: Dover Publications.
Tönnies, F. (1935). Gemeinschaft und gesellschaft: Grundbegriffe der reinen soziologie (Community and society: Basic terms of pure sociology). Darmstadt: Wissenschaftliche Buchgesellschaft.
Weber, E. (1976). *Peasants into Frenchmen: The modernization of rural France, 1870–1914.* Stanford: Stanford University Press

Questions for Discussions

1. Many of the residents of the group home were at first reluctant to accept the author's help. Why did they gradually warm to him? Are there other actions he could have taken?

2. Why did the author change his response to the female residents of the group home when they confided in him about their sexual activities? What does this change suggest about how social workers might talk to adolescents about sex?

3. The author contends that a bureaucracy like a group home might be preferable to their family for some damaged adolescents. Why does the author make this statement? Do you agree or disagree?

4. What does the author mean when he says that we tend to stress only one true way to think about child welfare. By contrast, what does he mean about the need to "professionalize" it?

5. In his efforts to develop a theory about the family, the author becomes increasingly interested in families that have recently emigrated from peasant (as opposed to industrial) societies. Have you had clients from such a background? If so, how do you think their background influences their values and behavior?

CHAPTER FIVE
ON (NOT) GETTING A DOCTORATE (1979–1984)

I WAS A full-time parent for a year, starting in the fall of 1979. In January 1980, I applied to the doctoral program at the Columbia University School of Social Work and began my course work in the fall of that year.

I took an advanced social policy course with Alfred Kahn, a practice course with Carol Meyer, and research with David Fanshel. All were exciting and interesting, as was my advisor, Brenda McGowan. I felt I was learning a lot. At the same time, I felt a twinge of doubt at an initial meeting with incoming doctoral students when I learned that much of the emphasis of the program would be on research. I should have paid more attention to this sensation.

I did not know that I was entering the doctoral program just at the beginning of the period when decisive elements of the social work profession, in the chronic seeking for acceptance and legitimacy, turned toward hypothesis-testing research. I had always been dubious about this. I had read C. Wright Mills's (1967) criticism of this tendency in sociology, calling it "abstracted empiricism." As I took more research methods courses, my doubts increased rather than diminished. I found myself thinking that the methods of measurement had far too strong a tendency to determine the focus of investigation and to restrict research to what was measurable, rather than what was important or intrinsically interesting.

Perhaps I should have focused on social policy, in which I could have found a doable dissertation topic and brought it to a successful conclusion. But I did not want to do this. I felt that I had already written what I wanted to write about social policy, and although it continued to interest me, I now wanted to work on the theoretical basis of social work practice. But everybody I spoke with thought a theoretical dissertation was a terrible idea. When I discussed the question with other students and the faculty, they told me this was something I should leave until after I had achieved the degree, that it would bog me down and that, instead, I should find a sharply delimited area to explore and do what many called a "quick and dirty" hypothesis-testing study. I read the dissertations of some who had actually done this and convinced myself, against my better judgment, that I could emulate them.

The topic I eventually chose was an effort to measure a variable I called "interventive appropriateness" among child protective workers. In an effort to define this, I wrote a proposal in the form of a lengthy paper, drawing on several bodies of theory. The faculty seemed unsure how to relate to this. The proposal eventually accepted was brief and ended with a mathematical equation that I understood at the time, though it seemed to represent reification of a useless sort.

Other variables, which either encouraged or threatened interventive appropriateness, were tolerance of ambiguity, and authoritarianism. I read widely in the literature of authoritarianism research, which I really wanted to incorporate into what I was doing. In particular, I studied the Frankfurt School's earlier work on authoritarianism, published mostly in German (Fromm, 1932a, 1932b, 1936, 1984; Horkheimer, 1936, 1949). It antedated, by several years, the better known *Authoritarian Personality* (Adorno, Frenkel-Brunswik, Levinson, & Sanford, 1950) published in English, and a report of research in the United States. I found it more applicable because it discussed the theoretical basis of their research approach, whereas the *Authoritarian Personality* mostly leaves the theoretical foundation implicit and presents empirical information dating from the 1940s. Of course, the Frankfurt School's critical theory was quite opposed to the positivist–empiricist approach to which I was trying to conform (Jay, 1973), but I had hoped to work around this and satisfy the requirements of the doctoral program.

I wrote vignettes depicting abuse and neglect incidents of various kinds and asked the subjects to choose among several interventions. These I hoped to correlate with other measures of authoritarianism, tolerance of ambiguity, and other variables. Unfortunately, when I tested it on small groups, it proved impossible to keep the instrument from discriminating either too much or too little. I felt the question I was investigating was relevant and important but that the issue of measurement was becoming insuperable.

In the end, I spent many years on this endeavor, revising, over and over, the instruments and the conceptualization. I must have done two or three times the work people usually do when they actually complete a dissertation.

I must accept most of the blame for this fiasco. If I had been more confident of my ability to stick with what I saw as valuable and really wanted to do, the results would have been better.

I HAD VARIOUS brief jobs in this period. One, in the summer of 1981, was at the Cornell University Cooperative Extension, in its Family Life Development Center, and in the Child Protective Services Training Institute. The Family Life Development Center was a resource for community groups trying to set up services, and generally offered thought and guidance to people who needed it. I maintained a library of relevant literature and successfully begged donations of books from publishers. I spent more time in the Training Institute, where I took part in writing curriculum for Child Protective Supervisors' training.

In the following summer, I was one of David Fanshel's case record readers in his evaluation study of the Casey Family Program and, in the following year, worked a day or two each week for the Foster Care Monitoring Committee, which was attempting to determine the degree to which Special Services for Children was meeting the recommendations of a committee that had studied its functioning.

These experiences were pleasant and interesting, but temporary.

References

Adorno, T. W., Frenkel-Brunswik, E., Levinson, D. J., & Sanford, R. N. (1950). *The authoritarian personality* (Studies in prejudice). New York: Harper and Brothers.

Fromm, E. (1932a). Die psychoanalytische charakterologie und ihre bedeutung für die sozialpsychologie (The psychoanalytic characterology and their significance for social psychology). *Zeitschrift für Sozialforschung, 1,* 253–277.

Fromm, E. (1932b). Über methode und aufgabe einer analytischen sozialpsychologie (About an analytic method and task of social psychology). *Zeitschrift für Sozialforschung, 1,* 29–54.

Fromm, E. (1936). *Sozialpsychologischer: Teil Schriften Des Instituts Für Sozialforschung Studien Über Autorität und Familie: Forschungsberichte Aus dem Institut Für Sozialforschung (Social psychological: Some writings from the Institute for Social Research Studies on Authority and Family: Reports from the Institute for Social Research)* (Vol. 5). Paris: Librairie Félix Alcan.

Fromm, E. (1984). *The working class in Weimar Germany: A psychological and sociological study.* Cambridge, MA: Harvard University Press.

Horkheimer, M. (1936). *Allgemeiner: Teil Schriften des Instituts Für Sozialforschung Studien Über Autorität und Familie: Forschungsberichte aus dem Institut für Sozialforschung (Some writings from the Institute for Social Research Studies on Authority and the Family: Research reports from the Institute for Social Research)* (Vol. 5). Paris: Librairie Félix Alcan.

Horkheimer, M. (1949). Authoritarianism and the family. In R. N. Anshen (Ed.), *The family: Its function and destiny* (pp. 381–398). New York: Harper and Brothers.

Jay, M. (1973). *The dialectical imagination: A history of the Frankfurt School and the Institute of Social Research, 1923–1950.* Boston: Little, Brown.

Mills, C. W. (1967). *The sociological imagination.* New York: Oxford University Press.

Questions for Discussion

1. Why didn't the author succeed in getting a doctorate? Do you think he accepts enough of the responsibility for his failure?

2. What conflicts have you encountered in your own social work education, and how have you overcome them?

3. Define C. Wright Mills's concept of "abstracted empiricism." Is the author right when he cites Mills's critique about the risk that an emphasis on numbers defines what will and will not be explored?

4. What does the author mean when he relates the increased emphasis on quantification in social work to the profession's pursuit of legitimacy?

Chapter Six

Beyond Ethnicity: A Hospital Social Worker Tries to Understand His Clients (1984–1988)

IN THE SUMMER of 1984, I went back to work full-time, as the emergency room (ER) social worker at Montefiore Medical Center. I gradually replaced my predecessor, who had had the job since the early 1970s. I knew him from the Bureau of Child Welfare (BCW), which he had left for the ER. He was ill, gradually became unable to work, and died the following year.

Montefiore Medical Center is a large teaching hospital located in the Northwest Bronx. It is affiliated with the Albert Einstein College of Medicine and, a few years ago, merged with the Hospital of the Albert Einstein College of Medicine (HAECOM) in the Northeast Bronx. Now the former HAECOM is called the Weiler Division, and the original Montefiore Medical Center is the Moses Division.

Shortly after I started, the ER moved to a new, but temporary location, while a new building under construction replaced the one where it had been. The temporary ER was a prefabricated building in a yard beside the main entrance to the institution. It was larger and had a separate, partitioned-off area for the pediatric ER, which now was open all the time. You entered from the street into a small lobby. To the left was a waiting area and registration. To the right were double doors into the adult ER, and the triage nurse sat just to the side of these doors. Behind her was a small partition, and behind it was my office and a door into the pediatric area.

When I went to look at the new quarters before we moved in, I encountered, for the first, but by no means the last time, the issue of Spanish-language signage. The doors to the adult area bore a sign:

SEE THE NURSE AT THE TRIAGE DESK BEFORE ENTERING

VEA LA ENFERMA EN EL ESCRITORIO DE TRIAGE ANTES DE ENTRAR

I found the unit manager and pointed out that the Spanish version actually meant: "Look at the sick woman, at the triage desk, etc." This was at the least confusing and certainly would expose us to ridicule and annoyance. The sign-makers were able to add a syllable to form *"enfermera."* I also pointed out that the Spanish *"ver,"* means more restrictedly to visually appreciate, whereas the English "see" can also connote interpersonal interaction. On this point, however, I did not prevail.

The temporary ER, though larger than the one it replaced, was still small. This meant that there were incongruous juxtapositions of functions. In the rear of the large central room, there were several smaller rooms dedicated to various disparate purposes. There was the asthma room, where people received treatment. A little farther on was the staff lounge, and some small offices were behind it. Next to the staff lounge was the psychiatric observation room, which locked securely. Next was the surgery room, and to its right, two or three other rooms for various miscellaneous purposes. One had a bathtub, for washing up the derelicts who sometimes came to the ER. It had a cover, a plywood sheet with a mattress on top that made the tub into a bed.

The psychiatric isolation room was too small to contain all of the psychiatric patients all the time. Others sat around this corner of the ER on chairs, along with other patients, many of them waiting for the orthopedic surgeons. Sometimes the psychiatric patients would help those with broken bones, pushing them around in their chairs.

Once, a woman arrived in the ER with her children, ages five and 10. She had picked them up from school and come seeking treatment of an agonizing headache. She soon became delirious, because she had encephalitis. While I was locating a caretaker for the children—which took a few hours—the children sat among all the other miscellaneous people. I found them under the supervision of a schizophrenic heroin addict, a pleasant man who had helped them with their homework.

At the time I started, the hospital's immediate neighborhood was what some call a NORC, a naturally occurring retirement community. Ethnically, it was still predominantly Jewish and Irish, with a significant sprinkling of other groups. Black and Hispanic people were moving in and replacing the elderly people as they died off.

Working at the hospital brought me many new experiences. I had never worked in a host setting before, and certainly not in a medical one. This was a complexity that I had to master, and it was all the more complex because the hours I worked, from two in the afternoon until 10 at night, meant that I overlapped with other social workers only in the first three hours. After five, I was the only social worker in the hospital and was responsible for the occasional problems that arose on the inpatient services.

There also were multiple administrative hierarchies around me. There was the hierarchy of the social service department, to which I belonged. Then there were the hierarchies of the doctors and the nurses, and there also was a hierarchy of clericals and their administrators. Once I had this sorted out, I realized that though nurses are technically subordinate to doctors, they form the skeletal structure of a hospital. Eventually, I came to understand that the most basic nursing task is to impose an order on random events. This, of course, is not really possible, so a nurse's work is a continual struggle. It is not surprising that nurses tend to be compulsive and somewhat anxious. These are characteristics that sometimes annoy people, but they are what makes the difference between success and failure.

I also came to understand that my function was to address those categories of problems that are least susceptible to the nursing approach to reality. Some of these are inherent in the situation, such as those parts of the patient's reality that concern his or her life outside the hospital. Hence, I was responsible for ensuring that a patient's discharge was safe. Also, with time, I took on the task of dealing with that minority of patients who would not respond to the standard nursing way of dealing with the recalcitrant patient. This is to be even more giving, more structured, and sometimes more firm. Most people cooperate with nurses when they apply this general technique, but for some, it is the opposite of what will move them.

I recall, for example, one happening on a sort of tableau. The patient was sitting on a stretcher, and the nurse, who was not very tall, was looking up at her, entreating her to accept admission for treatment of cellulitis of her feet. The patient found all sorts of reasons to demur. I took the nurse aside and pointed out that the patient was obviously enjoying the experience of making the nurse dance for her and suggested she leave the patient alone for half an hour or so.

"But I have other patients," she said, apparently feeling she could not leave this patient unresolved before going on to the others. I suggested she go attend to another patient and leave this patient to sit. Very anxiously, the nurse did this, and found, when she came back to the patient, that she was ready and willing to be admitted. Other such recalcitrant patients were the antisocial, often substance-abusing people who would come to the ER and not want to leave. I took responsibility for dealing with them.

Perhaps the most spectacular such patient I ever encountered was a 75-year-old woman who came to the ER from the office of a community agency. She claimed some obscure ailment that proved not to exist and then explained that she was homeless, having just arrived from Puerto Rico. She did, in fact, have a used airline ticket from San Juan to New York, but that was the only verifiable assertion she made. Her English, though accented, was fluent and educated. She claimed to have been a legal secretary in New York in the past. This could have been true. She also denied having any family resources anywhere and said that the office of the Mayor of San Juan had paid for her ticket to New York.

It took only an hour or so to determine that she had no immediate medical needs, though she did walk with a cane because of arthritis. Thus, it became my responsibility to plan her discharge.

At that time, no social worker regularly covered the ER before my arrival in the afternoon. Other social workers took turns being the "Social Worker of the Day" and handled problems that arose in areas of the institution that had no regular social worker. I alerted my supervisor that this matter needed attention in the morning and suggested that a Spanish-speaker should be involved in case any calls to San Juan were necessary. Accordingly, a bilingual secretary of Puerto Rican origin who was studying toward her bachelor's degree in social work interviewed the patient. The patient, clearly with intent, made opprobrious remarks about the secretary's brown complexion. Curiously, the patient herself had a dark complexion and clearly African features, but this did not deter her.

The secretary was so enraged that she could not come to grips with the problem of discharging the patient. It was too late for me to do anything when I arrived, and so the patient gained a day in the ER, receiving three meals a day and the attention of the staff.

During the ensuing days, a succession of Social Workers of the Day worked out diligently conceived discharge plans and offered them to the patient. These included nursing home placement, placement in a shelter for homeless elderly people, and some other alternatives. She rejected all of them, but on a novel ground: she would only go to a place where we could guarantee that there would be no Puerto Ricans.

This has always impressed me as the most ingenious example of psychopathic manipulation that I have ever encountered. Nobody knew what to say in response to this absurdity. In the end, the patient remained in the ER for seven days. I would speak with her in the afternoon and made a point of speaking Spanish, even as she insisted on using English to address me. One day I arrived to find one of our social work administrators ignominiously trying, with mounting frustration, to reason with the patient.

By the fifth or sixth day, I discussed the situation with my supervisor and proposed involving the police to have the patient arrested for trespass. After consultations with lawyers, I was told to offer the patient transportation to the women's shelter, then at the Kingsbridge Armory nearby. If she refused this, I would call the police.

The patient dismissed my offer of the armory. When the police arrived, they were surprised that we were asking them to arrest someone who looked like their grandmothers. The patient threatened to sue but accepted the police's offer of a ride to the armory. A while later, I called the armory—from a pay telephone—and discovered that, at the shelter, she claimed to be unwell. An ambulance brought her to North Central Bronx Hospital, the municipal institution next door, where they proved more manipulable. She spent two months on an inpatient service, though she was quite well.

Afterward, I used to cite this case to those people who spoke of social workers as stereotypically soft and indulgent, and would point out that the essence of social work practice is not the mere mobilization of compassion but is action based on sound assessment.

This patient was anomalous, of course. In fact, she was unique. By contrast, in the 1980s much of my work with elderly people was quite the opposite. Over and over, I advocated for their admission when, frequently, it proved impossible to arrange services to ensure their safety at home. This brought me into fairly frequent conflict with the medical house staff.

Fortunately, much has changed for the better in the past 20 years. But in the early and mid-1980s, the attitudes of the internal medical residents were often unreconstructed. A fair proportion of them came from comfortable suburban backgrounds and were the kind of people who became arbitragers in the early 1990s and dot-com hustlers as we approached the millennium. It was common, as they completed their training, to hear them discussing the luxurious premises of the practices they were joining. I recall in the spring of one year, hearing one third-year resident tell a gaping intern that the practice he was joining in Florida was on the beach, with stairs down to the glistening sand.

They were enthusiastic about admitting patients with complex and challenging medical problems. People who had prosaic ailments or had only fallen and injured themselves to the point of temporary nonfunctionality were not interesting. I recall a resident turning up her nose at this: "Nobody will learn anything from *her.*" The patient was a frail, old woman who clearly could not have fed herself, shopped, or kept herself clean alone at home. Patients, to this way of thinking, existed to meet the educational and professional needs of the house staff. Also, those patients who were crabby and demanding met with the complaint: "She'll just *torture* the house staff on the floor."

At first, I wondered if there was a racial aspect to this harshly narcissistic attitude, but there wasn't. On the contrary, the African American and Hispanic patients were more likely to have available family to care for them at home, so the issue of admitting them arose a bit less frequently. No, it was those patients most ethnically similar to the house staff themselves who could have been their grandmothers,[1] who came in for the bulk of these rejections.

I vividly recall an elderly woman who came to the ER with her son, having fallen twice at home. She was unable to stand. Soon after beginning his workup, the doctor called me to her bedside and said, "This is the X family (mispronouncing their name). Mrs. X will be worked up, probably on an outpatient basis, for weakness," and suggested I try to arrange home services.

It was evening, and arranging services was not feasible. Also, when I looked at the chart and the patient's son, I recognized him as a prominent and well-connected local journalist with a known interest in health care issues. Clearly, the doctor did not know who he was dealing with.

I interviewed the son and his wife in my office and discussed the question of her safety at home, her living circumstances, and her ability to care for herself. Though neither of us mentioned it explicitly, it was clear that I knew who he was. A couple of hours later, the doctor came back and said all the patient's laboratory values were normal, and she did not need admission. The son chuckled and asked me if there was a typewriter handy. I excused myself and took the doctor aside, pointing out that we could not safely discharge the patient, also that it was madness for him to behave in this way, that if he wanted to see his name in the papers with unfavorable comments, all he needed to do was continue what he was doing. I further explained all this to the charge nurse and doctor. We admitted the patient, of course, and the next day an investigator from the New York State Department of Health came to look into the matter.

This was surely a triumph of reason and humanity. However, I couldn't help thinking about the large role power and influence had played in making something happen that should have been a matter of course for any patient. But on the same night, by chance, I received a call from a neighbor of a man discharged from the ER some hours earlier, unbeknownst to me. She described, in detail, how unwell he seemed and how unable he was to care for himself. At my suggestion, she called 911, he returned, and I helped her articulate her concerns to the medical staff. He too was admitted. This seemed to redress the balance.

The elderly patients included many who had come from Europe in the 1920s, 1930s, and 1940s. Some had quite interesting stories to tell. One man, for example, had been in the audience when Freud delivered his introductory lectures on psychoanalysis. He quoted him: "I'm not perfect!"

Another woman had grown up in Petrograd. Her family owned a luxury goods business, and with the Russian Revolution, had moved themselves permanently to its branch in Riga, in the newly independent Latvia. Though she had left the Soviet Union, and presumably was unsympathetic to the Bolsheviks, she spoke with awe at the eloquence of a speech she had heard by Leon Trotsky, even after some 60 years.

Still another woman told me a story that sounded like one of Scholem Aleichem's tales. I appreciated it in particular because I knew the historical background. It took place in the fall of 1914, in the Russian city of Bialystok. At the beginning of World War I, the Russian empire had invaded Germany and met with disastrous defeat at a place called Tannenberg, in East Prussia. The Russian army retreated in disarray into Russia itself, and one of the first cities it came to was Bialystok, a provincial industrial center. The army authorities ordered the civilian population to evacuate eastward, most likely to prevent them from working for the Germans.

The patient's father owned a wagon but no horse. He bought one that had a brand showing it had once belonged to the Russian army. Two officers saw the brand and wanted to shoot her father as a horse thief, but he ran away. The patient and her younger brother were seated in the wagon, the patient holding the reins. She drove away and went to a prearranged rendezvous at the farm of a peasant her father knew. The peasant was absent, but his wife and son told her and her brother to sleep in the hay mow in the barn. The patient had suspicions, however, and was ready when the wife and son came to rob, and probably kill, them in the middle of the night. She and her brother took off again in the wagon and, after more adventures which I do not recall, reunited with her father.

This patient was quite obsequious with me, and it occurred to me that this might be the way she had learned, as a child, to comport herself with gentiles in positions of authority. It made me feel a little like a Cossack, mounted on a horse, holding a knout.

There was a grimmer story of the same period from a woman who was very ill, was facing surgery, and seemed to want to talk about the earlier perils of her life. As a girl, she lived in southern Russia during the Civil War, in an area where Aleksei Maksimovich Kaledin, the leader, or *Ataman,* of the White Russian Cossacks of the Don, was active. One day, his cavalry rode into the patient's village and began a pogrom of all the Jews in sight. She saw her mother sabered to death. A woman she knew, a baker, hid her in an oven until the soldiers had left. Then she had to walk 20 miles to another city under Bolshevik control, where she would be safe.

A very old man told me the story of Pushkin's *Eugene Onegin,* with tears in his eyes. He lived in an apartment in a senior citizens' building and spent his days reading Russian literature. He had emigrated to the United States of America before the World War I to avoid military conscription. At that time, we were just beginning to see the first Central American immigrants with their stories of the hazards of crossing the border. This man's story was remarkably similar. With others, he paid a guide, much like the *coyotes* on the Mexican border, to get him across from the Russian Empire to Austrian territory, with armed border guards shooting.

Many of the patients from European countries were from German-speaking areas, whether Germany itself, Austria, or other places. Many were Jewish refugees, who now and then told me hair-raising stories about how they had escaped the Nazis. Others were not. With these patients, I spoke German quite often in those years. At first, I wondered if the Jewish survivors would be reluctant to do so, but in general they were quite enthusiastic. I was a little surprised, but then I reflected that this was also the language their mothers had used to sing lullabies to them.

The great number of elderly patients meant that bereavement work was a fairly common task. I frequently had my students take this on but did it often enough myself. I discovered there were clear ethnic distinctions in the way survivors grieved. Caribbean Hispanics were quite demonstrative, but gathered, frequently, in large groups, to lend support to the immediate family. Once in a long while, a female survivor would have an actual *ataque*, which is a quite dramatic hysterical episode, in which the person cries out incoherently; launches herself into space; and lands on the floor, crying out and twitching. The first time I had seen this, while working at the BCW, I had mistaken it for a seizure.

African American women would sometimes lose their legs and collapse to the floor, but would remain communicative. African American men would often become free-floatingly angry. They too would sometimes fall to the floor. I recall catching a quite tall young man's arm and bringing it over my shoulders so as to keep him upright. His younger brother had just died of meningitis.

Jews tended to be moderately demonstrative but usually accepting. Partly, this was because the patients had generally been old and their deaths anticipated. This was somewhat true, too, of the Irish and Italians.

On occasion, deaths would bring surprising revelations about the lives people had lived. On one occasion, a man in the prime of life came in by ambulance, with a fatal gunshot wound. Murders were more common in the 1980s. Soon, a young, very attractive woman arrived, grieving quite demonstratively. She was casually but expensively dressed, in designer jeans that showed her off to best advantage. I spent some time with her, helped her grieve, and then she left. Somewhat later, however, the staff called to tell me the patient's "wife" had arrived. This woman, too, was grieving, and I provided similar support to her. She was a little older, was pleasant looking, and dressed casually in an exercise suit. I saw no reason to mention the other woman.

∼ . ∼ . ∼

I FOUND, TOO, that one of my responsibilities was interpreting medical findings to patients and thus promoting what doctors call "compliance" with treatment.

There were obstacles to compliance, some of them arising out of the physicians' use of arcane terminology and some from the premodern outlook of many patients. I recall a very concerned doctor telling a patient's equally worried mother: "She dropped her crit." This meant that the patient's hematocrit level was below normal.[2] I reflected that the doctor not only was using a word the mother was unlikely to understand, but also was implicitly imputing some form of volition to the child, in a way that would be further confusing.

In other instances, I tried to help doctors understand that although medicine rests on the scientific method, with its rational assessment of data, many of our patients saw the process of diagnosis and treatment in more or less shamanistic terms. Hence, when they achieved rapid positive results, I would caution them not to preen themselves too much, but rather, to explain, in simple terms, how they had proceeded and why it had worked. After all, I would say, the next doctor the patient goes to may have to deal with some medical problem less susceptible to rapid relief, and the patient might well think it was a personality defect, or a weakness of inherent powers that caused the doctor to fail.

This applied to patients, in particular, who came from societies that were closer to premodernity, and, frequently, to the peasant heritage, which I was learning more about.

∾ . ∾ . ∾

IN 1986, THE crack epidemic became an omnipresent factor in great numbers of cases. I recall a night when I went home musing that crack had in some way affected all of the six or eight cases I worked on. All this reminded me of the heroin epidemic I had worked through at the BCW, but it was infinitely worse. I began to hear of this new drug, and a patient then explained to me what it was and how it worked. He was a member of a local family, all of whose members were disposed to substance abuse and other forms of delinquency. A look at the New York State Department of Corrections Inmate Population Information Search shows him to be incarcerated even as I write.

A crack addict who stands out in memory after some 20 years was an 18- or 19-year-old girl who came to the ER with a Bartholin cyst. This is an infection in one of two small glands in the external female genitalia. Because of its location, it is extremely painful, often making it uncomfortable to walk. Hers was large—the surgeon who opened and drained it said it was the size of an orange. The pediatricians asked that I see her because she seemed unusually forlorn. When I asked what she did for a living, I was dumbfounded when she explained she had been prostituting herself.

The impact on the addicts' children was the crack epidemic's most distressing aspect. By definition, children had been at risk in the care of a heroin-addicted parent. Heroin had been bad enough, but crack was much worse. For example, during the crack epidemic, I recall a sign in the pediatrician's charting room asking that we look out for an infant whose mother could not remember where she had left the baby while high on crack. In another case, we evaluated a seven-year-old girl who had gone into foster care when a sibling was born with a positive toxicology for cocaine, and child welfare had thus become involved. After some weeks away from her mother, the girl trusted the foster mother enough to confide that her mother had prostituted her for money. She would arrive home from school, and the customers would be waiting. Heroin addicts did bad things, but I can't remember them doing that.

Crack invaded not just the homes of basically low-functioning people, but also affected people who seemed unimpeachably respectable. One evening, the unit manager asked me to see a man whose wife had brought him in because he was using crack. A representative of their quite strict church came along. The manager wondered if I could just refer him to a drug program so that the overburdened medical staff would not have to concern themselves with him. I told her no when I noticed that he was talking to an empty chair as if someone he knew was sitting there. He had a good job as a mechanic in a car dealership. And this pillar of society was a crackhead.

Crack came along just a little later than AIDS and, of course, infinitely helped its spread. I first encountered an AIDS patient when the nursing staff called me to an inpatient service to interview her about a disagreement concerning discharge. I knew as little about AIDS as most people at the time and told the charge nurse that I knew I was asking a probably ridiculous question but inquired about risks to me from being in proximity to the patient. He smiled enigmatically and said, "Only if you have sexual intercourse with her."

I found the patient in her room. She was horrifying to look at, weighed only 60 pounds, and had tuberculosis throughout her body. Also she had oral thrush and, as we spoke, pulled slime off her tongue and wiped her fingers on the sheets.

Before the introduction of antiretrovirals, AIDS struck quickly, and people who seemed well one month would look ashen and emaciated the next. I remember a man who came to the ER with his family and his girlfriend, having suddenly become sick. All were quite presentable people and thunderstruck with the AIDS diagnosis. I tried to help the girlfriend, who was in shock, understand the situation and urged her to be tested.

Also, many who thought they had put the follies of youth, recreational drug use in particular, behind them, now found they were mistaken. I remember, in particular, a woman who had stopped using drugs, had gone to college, and had a respectable job when she got sick. Twice she came to the ER for admission, with her 10-year-old daughter. My task was to arrange care for the girl while the mother was hospitalized. This meant the mother had to accept help from relatives who were nasty to her because of her previous drug use and who disparaged her to the child. The daughter was intelligent and beginning to understand the enormity of what was happening to her. The second time they arrived at the ER, the patient told her something to the effect that all this was only going to get worse. She stepped out of her mother's cubicle with an unforgettable expression of shock, desolation, and desperation.

Another patient with AIDS was an infant. Her aunt, recruited as foster mother, brought the child to the ER because she seemed to be constantly ill. Something about the situation made me suspect what was going on, and I asked about the mother. The aunt described the mother's substance abuse and illness. I pointed this out to the medical staff.

Still other AIDS patients were women who had caught it from men they had trusted. I remember an immigrant from Central America who had married an American, and, I am sure, had aspired to no more than obscure housewifehood. She was unsure of how her husband had been infected, but now she was infected too. Her children were too young to understand what was going on.

∽ . ∽ . ∽

ANOTHER OF MY areas of responsibility was work with victims of domestic violence, obviously women in most cases. This was somewhat familiar to me, because I had had child protective cases in which men also abused the mothers of the children. This has changed over the years, but when I began in the 1980s, a great many battered women were ambivalent about asserting themselves toward the men who had assaulted them. I spent many hours discussing this issue with patients and learned arguments that sometimes were effective. Of these, the best seemed to be my pointing out that children learn from what they see and then asking how the patient would feel in 20 years or so if her daughter came to her with a bruise and said, "Look what he did to me!" For mothers of sons, there was a parallel argument, of a young woman coming to the patient and saying, "Look what your son did to me!"

Many women yielded to this approach. They were willing to accept martyrdom for themselves—perhaps it gave them a sense that this was what a virtuous wife should do—but not to inflict it on others. I also learned that an important question in assessment of the immediate danger to the woman had to do with whether or not the man was drunk or high during the abuse incident. It was much worse if he was sober, because this meant violent aggression was more consistent with his normal state. Sober abusers were more likely to inflict ritualized injuries, to be paranoid, and to be more dangerous. I remember a woman who came to the ER with a fairly minor injury, but when I interviewed her, she told me her husband was intensely jealous and that he also had an obsessive interest in her menstrual flow. He wanted to know all about its frequency, quantity, quality. I pointed out how bizarre this was and urged her to move out and stay with a friend. She told me he drove a school bus, but I couldn't figure out a way to make an issue of that.

I also worked with rape victims. For some years, we also involved volunteer counselors from Bronx Women Against Rape, though it eventually faded away. The counselors were women, which was helpful, because, in those years, many victims were reluctant to speak with a male worker. Many felt shame to a degree greater than more recently.

FOR THE FIRST several years I worked in the ER, we had psychiatric patients, but no psychiatrist regularly present. When somebody needed to see a psychiatrist, the "psych resident on call" came to evaluate. This person was also responsible for psychiatric issues throughout the hospital. Many of them were inexperienced, and much of the initial assessment devolved on me. This was particularly true with the pediatric psychiatric patients, and most of all with those who came to the ER after making suicidal gestures. Unless they showed signs of serious psychiatric illness, they got admitted to the adolescent medical floor, where the social worker and the consulting psychiatrist worked with them. Beginning in the mid-1980s and for six or seven years, a great many adolescent girls came to us after cutting their wrists or, as time went on, overdosing on any available pills.

I noticed some distinctive characteristics of this group of patients. Most of them were girls. Most were Puerto Rican. Most too, were Protestants, and sometimes the family's involvement with churches had some overt role in the issues that brought the patients to the ER. Demographically similar girls who were Catholic came to the ER with other, and somewhat more miscellaneous, kinds of problems. Also, the suicidality was fairly seasonal. I thought of T. S. Eliot's famous line, "April is the cruelest month," because spring, as I came to put it, was suicidal teenager season.

When I interviewed them, these girls tended to describe having begun the school year with aspirations, social, academic, or both, which, by the spring, were turning out either less well or, sometimes, far more complicated than they had anticipated. Quite often, they had hoped to form relationships with boys and were in conflict about the results. Sometimes the problem was simply that the relationships had failed. Alternatively, and quite frequently, the relationships were so successful that they had progressed to sexual intimacy, or the boyfriends might be pressuring the girls for sex. Sometimes, the precipitant for the suicidal gesture came when the girls' parents found out about their sexual relationships and other church members, or pastors, became involved.

For some time, my assessments of these patients were the primary intake material, with the psychiatric assessment being brief. The patients were usually intelligent, often good students, sensitive, and had a considerable emotional range. They were serious about their relationships and also about their religion, which often was fairly new to their families. This was a period when conversion to Protestantism was widespread in the Puerto Rican population.[3] I noticed that the names of sibling groups sometimes could indicate the point at which the family had turned toward the Reformation. The older children would have names like José, María, Juan. Then the younger ones would have such names quarried from the Old Testament as Josué, Isaías, or, in English, Christian.

I recall a girl of 12 years who expressed suicidal intent because she had been shunned on orders from the family's pastor. The pastor's daughter was also her best friend. The pastor had made this rather drastic decree because someone saw the patient entering a bodega that he considered suspect. The parents, of course, felt they had to do as he said.

Certainly, the superego of the typical suicidal girl was often very harsh and seemed to turn against her. The parents too, and often representatives of their churches, were correspondingly angry and recriminatory.

Sometime in the early 1990s, this kind of suicidality became less frequent. I don't recall exactly which year I noticed that suicidal teenager season was not so distinctively marked as it had been. Perhaps this change had something to do with what Max Weber called "the routinization of charisma" (Weber, 1972), in other words that the zeal of the recent convert to a new religion may have settled down to be more quiet and everyday.[4]

∽ · ∽ · ∽

MANY ADOLESCENT PATIENTS came to the ER with problems arising out of sexual misadventures, such as unplanned pregnancy and sexually transmitted diseases (STDs). These were girls more than boys, and I had many discussions with them about relationships with their sexual partners and the patients' feelings, usually quite ambivalent, about them. In the 1980s, it was much more typical then for girls to feel unable to assert their needs in their sexual relationships. I recall being surprised and impressed by a girl of 13 or 14 who, firmly and rather profanely, told me that she unfailingly insisted that her partners use condoms. She was exceptional then.

As in the group home program, I tried to encourage contraception. In the ER, it was easier to bring this topic up, because patients were there, frequently, to get evaluation or treatment for problems that contraception would have prevented or at least ameliorated.

One issue with great potential impact on patients' relationships, that I learned about at this time, involves STDs. Gonorrhea manifests itself, with unpleasant symptoms, quite soon after infection. Chlamydia, by contrast, can remain asymptomatic for at least a year. Thus, if a patient develops pelvic inflammatory disease, the current partner may not be the culprit, or, even if he is, he may also be asymptomatic. I learned to make sure that the medical staff had clarified this matter to patients.

Relationships with parents often entered into these discussions too. I recall, for example, a girl who came to the ER for treatment of an ordinary, though very painful, urinary tract infection. Just before receiving treatment, she called her mother, who harshly accused her of having a shameful, that is, a sexually transmitted infection. I asked why she was crying, and she explained she would have to go home and face her mother. In the end, the doctor and I signed a letter, in which I explained to the mother that her suspicions were mistaken. The letter was rather formal:

> Muy estimada señora . . . .
> Tengo el honor de informarle a Ud. que . . . Attentamente,
> [Much esteemed lady . . . I have the honor of informing you that . . . Sincerely]

∽ • ∽ • ∽

ANOTHER KIND OF case that was fairly frequent in the 1980s was what I came to call "the request for a virginity clearance." A sullen adolescent girl would appear in the ER, accompanied by angry parents who would say: "Check her to see if she's a virgin!" There were many circumstances that would inspire parental suspicion: staying out late, long unexplained absences, rumors reported by neighbors, seeming interest in some particular boy of whom the parents disapproved, and a whole host of others.

The prevailing view of the ER staff was that these requests were inappropriate, and for several reasons. For one, they did not qualify as emergencies. No one's life or health was at stake. For another, the patients had a right to refuse the examination, and their gynecological findings, by law and regulation, were confidential, even with respect to parents. But the most important reason was that verification of virginity is not medically feasible. The condition of the hymen proves nothing definitive.[5]

In one particularly egregious example, a girl of 12 years came to the ER with her father. I will call them Angélica and John García. The patient looked 17 years of age or so, was physically fully developed, and exceptionally attractive. The father, age about 32, with whom she lived alone, was a rather rigid man, who had a steady, responsible, and well-paying job. It was clear that he was a man with all the virtues of sobriety, hard work, and a general conscientiousness. The parents were estranged, and the patient had moved from her mother's home a year before because the mother had too many men around.

Angélica was apparently a good student, and no trouble for her father at home. But sometimes she would get home late. Late, in this case, meant only an hour or two. Mr. García was sure she had been spending her time in sexual activity. While Angélica wept from embarrassment, he told me that he had come home to find her panties soaking in soapy water in the bathroom washbasin. When he reached into the water, and pulled them out, he thought he saw sperm dripping off along with the soap suds.

Angélica denied any sexual activity, claimed to have no boyfriend, and said she was sometimes late because of stopping to play softball.

The father's behavior reminded me of the type of sexual abuser who is jealous of any potential rivals among the daughter's age peers. However, he seemed intelligent enough, that if he had been molesting his daughter, he certainly would not have brought her to the ER, asking for virginity clearance. Very possibly, I thought, when Angélica came to live with him a year before, she had been prepubescent and had become pubescent during the time they had lived together in the same apartment. Clearly, some incestuous impulses would be an entirely normal consequence of living in proximity to this really beautiful child, and I concluded that his almost frantic and inappropriate behavior came from his successful efforts to substitute concern for the values of purity, instead of acting on his real desires, or even, probably, consciously experiencing them.

As in most such cases, I clarified the impossibility of the ER's complying with his request and also pointed out a bit of reality: that even if a physician could give him a definitive and satisfying answer, Angélica, if she wanted to, could change everything the next day. Eventually, I succeeded in getting both to agree to go into counseling together. I also gently suggested that perhaps Mr. García should seek mature female companionship. Perhaps one of the local clergy could introduce him to a fitting person. About this he seemed uncertain.

※ · ※ · ※

WHEN WE MOVED into the temporary ER, I quickly became close with the pediatricians, who, I found, had no coherent approach to child abuse reporting. I began to keep records of all reports, called many of them in myself, and helped the doctors with the reporting forms. I also discovered that we had no procedure to comply with the mandate to photograph inquiries, so I wrote one to meet the deficiency.

I worked closely with the medical staff in assessing children who presented with potential child protective issues, interviewed the parents, and took responsibility for making the report and for dealing with Special Services for Children. Most of the time, this was the Emergency Children's Service, the after-hours, weekends, and holidays branch of the agency.

Physical abuses formed a greater proportion of the child protective task in those days, and much of my time went to assessment and reporting of such cases. More of the parents were oppositional, and we had to use the hospital's security officers to take the children into protective custody. I became more comfortable with confronting anger. Some of the cases were quite extreme.

One, in the late summer of 1985, concerned a three-year-old girl whose stepfather brought her to the triage nurse and said she had a broken leg. When asked how this had happened, he said he had broken it himself, and when further asked why, said: "Because she is a very disobedient child." In fact, she had a spiral fracture of her femur. We also found she had a fractured humerus. The stepfather, with curious poise and self-confidence, pointed out certain marks that he said he had inflicted with his belt buckle.

He explained that the patient was not yet toilet trained, and had defecated on the floor. He had picked her up to put her on the toilet, she had struggled, and her foot went into the bowl, got caught in the drain. He pulled on her leg and, thus, broke it. The mother came along with him and complained that the staff's horrified reaction was "judgmental."

I was able to interview the stepfather only briefly before the police took him away. He seemed to think his conduct appropriate, and he incongruously recited some of his life achievements—being an art student, having been listed in *Who's Who of American High School Students*.

I suspected the stepfather had some kind of ideological rationale for what he had done. Later, when I went to testify in court about the case, I sat in the waiting room near him and the mother, who had since married him, and looked at him, enraptured, as he read and expounded to her from a book by the Reverend Herbert W. Armstrong, founder of the Worldwide Church of God.[6] I also testified at his criminal trial.

Since I had considerable experience with appearing in court, I advised many of the doctors about this part of their work. Many of them were anxious. Every doctor seems to know somebody whose brother-in-law's cousin is a doctor who was harassed unmercifully in court by a lawyer. I helped prepare them to testify, reassured them that nothing terrible would happen to them, and explained that harassment by a parent's lawyer indicated the lawyer's desperation more than anything else.

∼ • ∼ • ∼

ALTHOUGH I HAD informally task-supervised social work students in the group home program, I began, in the spring semester of 1985, to task-supervise three students. Then, in the academic year 1985 to 1986, I task-supervised two more. In the fall of 1986, I took the seminar in field instruction at New York University and was field instructor for one of their students. Since then I have had one, two, three, and, one year, four students every year, with a total of more than 50.

In the first years, I tended to approach the didactic aspect of student supervision in psychoanalytic terms, clarifying clinical issues with reference to sources like Otto Kernberg. For example, my first student worked with a man who had become paraplegic in a failed suicide attempt. I used the concept of borderline personality to clarify his experience. So too, of the relative who was slated to assume responsibility for his care.

At this point in the development of my theoretical understanding, I had a pretty clear notion of the small and the large. Understanding the patient's reality on an individual level drew on psychoanalysis, which I understood rather eclectically, drawing on various psychoanalytic schools, particularly ego psychology and object relations, which I had absorbed in graduate school and in my field placement. I viewed the larger scale aspects of the patient's reality through a combination of a similarly eclectic Marxian outlook and historical knowledge. I knew there were intermediate areas that needed theorization and found there were others exploring some of the same ground.

This was the period when the social work field's interest in ethnicity was at its height. A more general consciousness of ethnicity had begun rather suddenly in the late 1960s with the publication of such books as *Beyond the Melting Pot* (Glazer & Moynihan, 1970) and *The Rise of the Unmeltable Ethnics* (Novak, 1971–1972).

These writers had interested me for a time until I began to notice the high rate of intermarriage among many people I knew who belonged to these allegedly unmeltable groups. Despite the enthusiasm for ethnicity, others had noticed the same phenomenon in a more scholarly way:

> Studies over several decades have found that rates of intermarriage across ethnic lines have been on the upswing. The most recent data are reported in a 1976 study by Richard Alba, based on a 1963 national sample of the Catholic population. Alba found gigantean leaps in the rate of intermarriage between the first and fourth generations of all six European groups in his sample—Irish, Germans, French, Poles, Italians, and Eastern Europeans. In each instance, by the third generation a substantial majority were marrying outside their group, and in the case of the Irish over three-quarters were doing so. These figures raise serious questions concerning the future of these groups as distinct biological and social entities. (Steinberg, 1981, p. 68)

Steinberg goes on to say:

> At a time when between a third and half of the current generation is marrying across ethnic lines, surely it would be a mistake to take the ethnic resurgence at face value. Indeed, the impulse to recapture the ethnic past is itself symptomatic of the ethnic crisis, and a belated realization that ethnicity is rapidly diminishing as a significant factor in American life. Irving Howe is probably right when he suggests that much of the romantic lure of the ethnic past rests on the fact that it is irretrievable. (Steinberg, 1981, p. 73)

In social worker circles, however, enthusiasm for ethnicity was still going strong. I had already read *Ethnic-Sensitive Social Work Practice* (Devore & Schlesinger, 1981) in 1982. I do not know if this work still appears in bibliographies for social work students. In the early 1980s, it could have been a valuable corrective for students coming from fairly narrow social experience, especially if they were disposed toward a primarily intrapsychic focus on clinical issues. The book draws on many of the then-reigning practice models, particularly Lawrence Shulman's excellent introductory practice text, and attempts to infuse a sensitivity to ethnic experience into their methods.

Unfortunately, however, the authors' presentation of ethnicity and class, which they call "ethclass," is largely anecdotal. Ethnic group A has this important characteristic. Ethnic group B has that one. It is important to keep these facts in mind in working with them. But instead of a theory of social development and participation, Devore and Schlesinger (1981) only present data. Mostly, the information is important and helpful, but I found it offered little to bridge the theoretical gap between the large and the small. A particularly significant instance is in their weak treatment of social change from one generation to another among the ethnic groups they discuss. They mention that it happens, and creates issues of importance, but offer no general account of this phenomenon as a process rooted in material experience.[7]

Thus, Devore and Schlesinger's approach is not really dynamic. In fact, it shares basic similarities with the seemingly quite different empirical research trend in social work. Both are essentially empiricist, in love with facts.

Of course, Devore and Schlesinger's facts are rooted in practice, rather than in a fantasy of aping researchers in other fields where hypothesis-testing and experimental and pseudo-experimental studies actually are useful and relevant.[8] But both tendencies fail in a key aspect. Neither one puts forward dynamic concepts as part of a theoretically comprehended process of developing human society. Such concepts would prepare the practitioner to address the diversity of potential client populations. By contrast, courses in human behavior rest on theories of the process of individual development, but no body of theory does the same for the social aspect of psychosocial assessment.

To be fair, it is also true that Devore and Schlesinger's book is in one of social work's better traditions, the effort to be part of increasing democratization and inclusion of people marginalized in the social process. It is true that their book sounds a little dated, because it clearly presupposes that members of the ethnic groups in question are still close to experiences in their countries of origin and that the immigrant generation is still an influence in work with them. Most of that has changed, of course. At the time, however, they were putting forward ideas for practice that were necessary and important.

These same comments apply to the other major book in the social work profession's engagement with ethnicity. In the spring of 1985, I read the first edition of *Ethnicity and Family Therapy* (McGoldrick, Pearce, & Giordano, 1982), which belonged to one of my students. It suffered from the same deficiencies as Devore and Schlesinger's book. Some of the better contributions to the volume offered a fair number of useful facts.[9] At times over the years, I have referred to them, with occasional profit, in the first, and then the second edition. But acknowledging this is to repeat the truism that knowledge is better than ignorance.

In the ER, I had many opportunities to encounter people of the most varied ethnic and national origins, the Bronx being one of the world's most demographically diverse places. I have a retentive memory and have always loved accumulating factual knowledge. As a boy, I was a great reader of encyclopedias. And, too, more recently, I had read a fair amount of anthropological literature and tended to think about the many social practices and beliefs I encountered among patients in an anthropological and an individual way.

It seemed inadequate, however, to see an assemblage of facts as the material that would fill in the theoretical gap between the small and the large. In reading the book, I found that many of the contributions ran together in my head. As I thought more about this, it was clear that the various ethnicities fell into groups whose experiences resembled each other. In studying the history of immigration, I had learned, historically, that most immigrants to the United States fell into three broad groups according to their circumstances in their countries of origin: those who were poor rural people using backward agriculture techniques, those who had been members of the educated middle classes of their countries of origin, and those who were urban industrial workers. This generalization still holds, to a considerable extent.

The initial example of the first group was the Irish who came to the United States during and after the potato famine that began in 1845. Later, peasant immigrants came from Italy, some parts of Germany, and Eastern Europe. The first of the second group were the Germans who came in significant numbers after the failed revolution of 1848. The third group began to come later in the 19th century and in the beginning of the 20th century. They included Germans, English, and Eastern European Jews. Taking the latter group as an example:

> In terms of their eventual adjustment to life in America, what was most significant about the urban background of Eastern European Jews was that they worked in occupations that prepared them for roles in a modern industrial economy. Again, the 1897 Russian census provides indispensable documentation. According to the census, 38 percent of Jews were employed in manufacturing or as artisans and another 32 percent in commerce, making a total of 70 percent. In contrast, only 18 percent of Russia's non-Jewish population were so classified. On the other hand, 61 percent of non-Jews, compared with only 3 percent of Jews, were in agriculture. In a word, Eastern European Jews were not peasants. This simple fact would have far-reaching implications for their destiny in the United States. (Steinberg, 1981, p. 95)

Thus there were three roughly definable common areas of experience among the immigrant forebears of the various ethnic groups that compose much of the white population of the United States. I began to think of these groups using a theory that clarified much of what I found in the patients I encountered.

This was the notion of character structure, a concept derived from psychoanalysis, but which lends itself to a social interpretation. Around this time, I began to read Wilhelm Reich's *Character Analysis* (Reich, 1949).

Some of the sources that I drew on to further my understanding of the social aspects of character were historical and more empirical than theoretical. Though they dealt with events distant in time and space, they did suggest conceptual ways of understanding human adaptation that I could apply to contemporary understanding in the ER.

For example, I had read Steven Marcus's *The Other Victorians* (Marcus, 1964) a few years before and now reread it with a fresh eye. Also in the mid-1980s, I read Barker-Benfield's *Horrors of the Half-Known Life* (Barker-Benfield, 1976), Miller's *Emigrants and Exiles* (Miller, 1985), and Adorno's the *Stars Down to Earth* (Adorno, 1994).

Marcus is a literary scholar, with a specialization in the Victorian novel. In *The Other Victorians*, he ventured into an area usually recognized as allied with his primary academic area of interest. Marcus spent a sabbatical year reading in the vast collection of pornography and other sexual literature of the Kinsey Institute at the University of Indiana. His book compares Victorian pornography, and other popular sexual literature of the period, with the Victorian novel, to draw conclusions about the prevalent personality and character of the time.

Marcus includes chapters on popular pornographic works, and on the medical literature of the period, in particular the work of the physician William Acton. Through study of these texts, and comparison with the Victorian novel, Marcus arrived at a view of the dominant personality of middle-class Victorians, which arose, directly and indirectly, out of the specific pattern of material life of society at the time. In the early and middle 19th century, England was still in what is called the accumulationist stage of the development of capitalism, a period in which the primary accumulation of capital in expanding industry was the dominant economic reality. Marcus showed how the inner lives of Victorians reflected the exigencies of economic life.

Marcus (1964) began his book by calling it

> a study of human fantasies ... I use the word 'fantasy' not in a belittling or deprecatory sense but to describe the quality of thinking or of mind that one meets with in scientific or medical accounts of human sexuality in the English nineteenth century. (p. 1)

All people, including social workers and social work clients, formulate their understandings of the world around them and of the people they encounter on the basis of common fantasies.

Marcus's work was about people fairly distant in time and space, though some of their family ideals are not dead. But his mode of analysis systematically linked intrapsychic and group experience. This seemed to offer guidance to understanding systems of fantasy—and of cultural adaptation—in the contemporary world.

For example, both Marcus (1964) and Barker-Benfield (1976) introduced me to the provocative concept of "spermatic economy," which describes the anxiety about the quantity and quality of sperm that bedeviled many men in the 19th century. One aspect of this was the widespread belief that orgasm, and particularly masturbation, with its loss of sperm, was debilitating, a threat to health, or even to life. Though medical opinion now recognizes masturbation as a nearly universal and harmless source of gratification, I remember some last echoes of this folk belief in my childhood in the American Midwest.[10]

The ideas of spermatic economy rested, of course, on a fantasy that any individual's supply of sperm was limited and that it was dangerous to squander it. The only prudent course was frugality and its judiciously limited expenditure. Of course, we usually think money is what people squander, but middle-class Victorians thought similarly about sperm and money. For example, it is significant that the colloquial word for orgasm until the latter part of the 19th century was "to spend." This expression yielded to the contemporary expression "to come" only as the 20th century came closer and economic life shifted from a primary emphasis on accumulation to consumption.[11]

Fantasies of spermatic economy are, of course, an aspect of anal character. A long time ago Sigmund Freud (1908, 1991), in putting forward the concept of anal character, traced the unconscious connection between money and feces:

> The connections which exist between the two complexes of interest in money and defæcation, which seem so dissimilar, appear to be the most far-reaching. It is well known to any physician who has used psychoanalysis that the most refractory and obdurate cases of so-called chronic constipation in neurotics can be cured by this means. . . . But in psycho-analysis one only attains this result when one deals with the money complex of the persons concerned, and induces them to bring it into consciousness with all its connections. (pp. 28, 49)

He goes on to show that money and feces are connected in the mythologies of various peoples. Victorians who were anxious about waste added sperm to the equation of money and feces. Marcus (1964) cited William Acton:

> The semen "is a highly organized fluid, requiring the expenditure of much vital force in its elaboration and expulsion." The fantasies that are

at work here have to do with economics; the body is regarded as a productive system with only a limited amount of material at its disposal. And the model on which the notion of semen is formed is clearly that of money. (p. 22)

However, Acton was a member of the solid English middle classes. He wrote for people like himself and both reflected and reinforced the kind of personality that prevailed among them. As I read and thought about Marcus's analysis of Acton's work, his concepts linked with the impressions of the late bourgeois family that I had formed in reading Zaretsky and Poster. Here are some of Poster's (1978) descriptions of the late bourgeois family's essential characteristics:

> The bourgeois family by definition is located in urban areas. From the late Middle Ages and early Renaissance until the mid-eighteenth century (for France, but a little earlier for England and later for central Europe), it is not essentially different from contemporaneous family forms. Evidence for a history of the emergence of the bourgeois family is thin. It is known that from 1750 to the present, the bourgeois family's demographic pattern moved progressively toward a pattern of low fertility, low mortality. Family planning on a large scale first began in this group. In everyday life, relations among the members of the bourgeois family took on a distinct pattern of emotional intensity and privacy. Marriage entailed a conflict for this group between the needs of parents, not so much to uphold traditional customs or lineage but to preserve their capital accumulation and the value of individual choice. Selection of partners over the course of the 19th and 20th centuries more and more became the choice of the young themselves, but only as the bourgeoisie was progressively proletarianized into white-collar jobs based on salaried labor. (Poster, p. 168)[12]

Likewise, Barker-Benfield's (1976) *Horrors* covered some of the same ground in a study of several 19th century men's attitudes toward women and sexuality.[13] Some of the notions he and Marcus described seem bizarre to us now:

> They believed that the masturbator's debilitation would be passed on to his children, in exactly the way that drunkards were believed to bequeath their weaknesses. Gardner defined sperm as 'the concentrated powers of [man's] perfected being.' According to him, 'Sperm is the purest extract of the blood, and according to the expression of Feruel, *totus homo semen est*.' (pp. 180–181)

Of course, not all people in 19th century English and American society were like this. In fact, late bourgeois families, and their members, were a minority of the population. They were, however, culturally and politically dominant and established values that still retain some currency.[14] The lower middle and working classes, and the peasantries of rural areas, especially in Ireland, England's first colony, experienced life in different ways. Hence they formed family structures, personalities, and attitudes toward sexuality that were quite different. Moreover, all these groups interacted in complex ways, just as different groups in contemporary American society do.

Marcus also discussed *My Secret Life* (Walter, 1966), a memoir in thousands of pages, recording the erotic life of a Victorian gentleman. This book's pseudonymous author details his thousands of sexual experiences throughout a fairly long life. He was affluent and could afford many sexual experiences, with hundreds or even thousands of partners.[15] As he got older, some of the experiences became more complex and sometimes outré. Though Walter describes some liaisons with women of the middle and even upper classes, most of his partners were prostitutes of varying degrees, casually encountered working class women, and servants, over whose sexuality the men of a bourgeois household had a presumptive claim. He describes these women's bodies in detail and observes their personalities. He also is scrupulous in detailing how much he paid them, or what other outlays—for food, clothes, cheap jewelry, and other things—went into securing their cooperation.

Walter does make desultory references to the concern about loss of sperm, but he was not very worried. Perhaps he had not read Acton's books. Certainly, his sexual partners had not. *My Secret Life*, however, is an invaluable source for understanding the sexual interactions of the classes. Many working class women could not survive on their earnings from work and had to prostitute themselves. Walter, though his interest in these women was primarily sexual, did pay some attention to their personalities, and it is clear that the sexual repression in the service of respectability that we associate with Victorian times did not apply to them.[16]

In the mid-1980s, in addition to Marcus and Barker-Benfield, I read Miller's (1985) *Emigrants and Exiles*, which linked the characterological themes of the two other authors with my developing understanding of the peasant heritage of so many people I encountered in my work. *Emigrants and Exiles* is a history of Irish emigration to North America. In explaining the reasons why so many Irish people emigrated, Miller described, in detail, the social changes in Ireland in the 19th century, as a premodern peasant society changed to modernity, in a brutal and humanly very destructive process.[17]

"Modernity," of course, describes any society in which the predominant relations between people are mediated through money and literacy. He shows how a fairly simple agricultural system, supporting a large population, changed, through a process he calls "commercialization," into one where more modern methods of cultivation prevailed and the "strong farmer" came to dominate among a drastically reduced population. The strong farmer's family structure was more clearly bourgeois than the peasant's and the dominant personality in this new social stratum resembled that of the repressed middle class:

> The strong-farmer family carefully calculated and maximized its economic resources, but at the expense of collateral kin and at the risk of fomenting both sibling rivalry and intergenerational strife. The great emphasis such families placed on acquisitiveness and respectability, and the fact that they could afford to hire needed assistance, inclined them to draw rigid social lines between themselves and less fortunate relations. Strife between parents and children, especially between fathers and noninheriting sons, was harder to contain, but the age gap between husbands and wives—and the loveless nature of many "matches"—often made the mother–son (especially mother–youngest son) relationship exceptionally close: so much so that jealousy between mothers and their son's brides was proverbial. Otherwise, potential rebellion by noninheriting children was usually thwarted by a "process of socialization" which instilled "in them a deep sense of inferiority [and] of submissiveness" and an aversion to premarital sexual escapades which might disgrace the family "name" and upset parents' cautious calculations. (Miller, 1985, p. 57)

Miller's work advanced my understanding of psychosocial assessment issues in two ways. It was an example of the changes peasant populations undergo in moving from a fairly traditional rural culture to an urban and industrial one. And, when Miller describes the mass emigration of rural Irish people to, in large part, the United States of America, he shows the first instance of such a population movement in the formation of the American population. At the time the potato famine, beginning in 1845 (Woodham-Smith, 1989), drove the Irish en masse to the United States, the American economy was expanding very rapidly and becoming industrial. Previously, most people in the United States could look forward to becoming small proprietors, but the decades before the Civil War saw the beginning of a permanent class that worked for wages.

The psychosocial adaptations of peasants in the 1840s as they encountered modernity are essentially similar to those of contemporary displaced rural people. I had already read a bit of the historical and sociological literature of peasant life and culture, and had gone beyond the insights I had gotten from Oscar Handlin's fairly simple treatment (Moberg, 1951; Seton Watson, 1989).

These historical sources gave me a sense of how the concept of character could partially bridge the gap between theories of intrapsychic functioning and theories of society. In the nineteenth century this had mostly to do with the achievement and maintenance of anal character, whether among the middle classes who pioneered it or among populations that circumstance forced to adapt in ways that at least mimicked anality.

My own experience at work showed that such adaptations were often only partial and internally conflicted. Some people could function as fairly integrated anal characters without too much effort. Others were inconsistent, with competing anal and oral features. As I thought about it, too, it was clear that one important way contemporary American society differs from what Marcus and Barker-Benfield described is in placing inconsistent demands on the personality.

I also discovered an interesting theoretical treatment of this issue in Theodor Wiesengrund Adorno's the *Stars Down to Earth* (Adorno, 1975),[18] which I encountered in the course of investigating the literature of authoritarianism that I intended as a basic component of my doctoral dissertation. Adorno described "the biphasic approach," which is anal where this is necessary, as in participation in work. It is also oral in the realm of consumption, which much of the surrounding contemporary culture works to enforce, so that the products of industry will sell, and thus facilitate disposal of surplus that otherwise would be a drag on the economy, creating stagnation (Baran & Sweezy, 1966). The astrology column, as Adorno saw it, was a way to pacify him, or, usually her, and keep her from thinking too much about this constant contradiction.

The authoritarianism literature was a major project of the *Institut für Sozialforschung*, or the Institute for Social Research, founded in Frankfurt, Germany, in 1923 (Jay, 1973; Tar, 1985; Wiggershaus, 1988). The institute developed a distinctive analytic approach, called critical theory, and is often called the Frankfurt School. In the late 1920s, in response to the obvious rise of Nazism, the institute turned to empirical investigation of authoritarianism. At the same time, their studies had a solid theoretical basis.[19] Max Horkheimer, the director of the institute, wrote an introductory essay in which he defined the basis of authoritarianism as arising out of deterioration of the position of the father in what Zaretsky calls the late bourgeois family. Whereas the late bourgeois father in the 19th century was an independent entrepreneur and a figure his children could internalize as a solid, reliable figure, the rise of large industry meant that his son or grandson worked at a salary for a large enterprise. This was the proletarianization Zaretsky discussed, though the incomes involved might still be substantial. Even so, his independence and his autonomy were compromised. Authoritarianism arose in response to the weakening of the paternal role, with the children of such men seeking romantic authority figures they could really admire. The Frankfurt School thus predicted the outcome of this process in Germany, where Hitler was just such a figure.

On a much smaller scale, at work I could see many examples of men trying to uphold the traditional father role and getting into difficulties with other family members as they did so. More than a few child abuses had to do with this, so too cases of domestic violence.

At the end of the 1980s, I felt I had made some progress in understanding the social aspect of the process of psychosocial assessment. I could see, in a general way, that character developed in response to changing circumstances, and that the circumstances followed recurrent patterns. No recurrence was exactly the same as the earlier ones, but these concepts had predictive value in assessment. Also, in the diagnostic phase (Turner, 2002), one could draw conclusions as to how well an individual was adapting.

However, all this, though an advance, seemed not fully adequate. It seemed to rely too exclusively on the basic methods of assessing intrapsychic experience and extending them toward the social realm.

This was not enough. What seemed necessary was a general theory of psychosocial assessment. I envisioned it extending from the small and intrapsychic to the broadly political economic, with an unbroken conceptual chain occupying all the intervening space. At first the deficiency seemed only moderately important, but as I encountered more and more complex issues at work and gave them more careful thought, there seemed to be a gap that I needed to fill.

For the time being, I did not know how to fill this gap.

References

Adorno, T. W. (1975). *The stars down to Earth* (Soziologische Schriften II) (Sociological writings II, Second half). Frankfurt am Main: S. Fischer Verlag.

Adorno, T. W. (1994). *The stars down to Earth and other essays on the irrational in culture.* London and New York: Taylor and Frances.

Baran, P. A., & Sweezy, P. M. (1966). *Monopoly capital: An essay on the American economic and social order.* New York: Monthly Review Press.

Barker-Benfield, G. J. (1976). *The horrors of the half-known life: Male attitudes toward women and sexuality in nineteenth-century America.* New York: Harper & Row.

Blank, H. (2007). *Virgin: The untouched history.* New York: Bloomsbury USA.

Devore, W., & Schlesinger, E. (1981). *Ethnic-sensitive social work practice.* St. Louis: C.V. Mosby.

Elders, M. J., & Kilgore, B. (1997, June 26). The dreaded m-word. *Nerve.* Retrieved from http://www.nerve.com/content/the-dreaded-m-word

Freud, S. (1908). Charakter und analerotik (Character and anal eroticism). In S. Freud, *Studienausgabe* (Study issue), Zwang, paranoia, und perversion (Vol. 7). Frankfurt Am Main: S. Fischer Verlag.

Freud, S. (1991). Character and anal erotism. In F. R. Kets de Vries Manfred & S. Perzow (Eds.), *Handbook of character studies: Psychoanalytic explorations*. Madison, CT: International Universities Press.

Gelfand, D. E., & Fandetti, D. V. (1986). The emergent nature of ethnicity: Dilemmas in assessment. *Social Casework, 67,* 542–550.

Gibson, I. (2001). *The erotomaniac: The secret life of Henry Spencer Ashbee*. Cambridge, MA: Da Capo Press.

Glazer, N., & Moynihan, D. P. (1970). *Beyond the melting pot: The negroes, Puerto Ricans, Jews, Italians, and Irish of New York City*. Cambridge, MA: MIT Press.

Greeley, A. M. (1988, July 30). Defections among Hispanics. *America, 159,* 61–62.

Jay, M. (1973). *The dialectical imagination: A history of the Frankfurt School and the Institute of Social Research, 1923–1950*. Boston: Little, Brown.

Jeffcote, Sir N., & Tindall, V. R. (1987). *Jeffcote's principles of gynaecology* (5th ed.). London: Butterworth's.

Krestan, J.-A. (1996). Czech families. In M. Mcgoldrick, J. K. Pearce, & J. Giordano (Eds.), *Ethnicity and family therapy* (pp. 688–695). New York: Guilford Press.

Marcus, S. (1964). *The other Victorians: A study of sexuality and pornography in mid-nineteenth century England*. New York: Basic Books.

Marx, K. (1972). Manifest der Kommunistischen Partei (The Communist manifesto). In K. Marx & F. Engels (Eds.), *Collected works* (Band 4, pp. 459–493). Berlin: Dietz Verlag.

McGoldrick, M., Pearce, J. K., & Giordano, J. (Eds.). (1982). *Ethnicity and family therapy*. New York: Guilford Press.

Miller, K. A. (1985). *Emigrants and exiles: Ireland and the Irish exodus to North America*. New York: Oxford University Press.

Mills, C. W. (1967). *The sociological imagination*. New York: Oxford University Press.

Moberg, V. (1951). *The emigrants*. New York: Simon & Schuster.

Novak, M. (1971–1972). *The rise of the unmeltable ethnics: The new political force of the seventies*. New York: Macmillan.

Poster, M. (1978). *Critical theory of the family*. New York: Seabury Press.

Reich, W. (1949). *Character analysis*. New York: Noonday Press.

Seton Watson, H. (1989). Eastern Europe between the wars, 1918–1941. New York: Harper & Row.

Shaw, W. (1971). *Shaw's textbook of gynaecology* (9th ed.). London: J. A. Churchill.

Steinberg, S. (1981). *The ethnic myth: Race, ethnicity, and class in America*. New York: Atheneum.

Swift, J. (1933). A modest proposal for preventing the children of Ireland from being a burden to their parents or country. In W. A. Eddy (Ed.), *Satires and personal writings by Jonathan Swift* (pp. 19–32). New York: Oxford University Press.

Szczepanowski, R. (1997). Much to offer: Conference cites church's challenge from growing Hispanic population. *Catholic New York, 17,* p. 6.

Tar, Z. (1985). *The Frankfurt School: The critical theories of Max Horkheimer and Theodor W. Adorno.* New York: Schocken Books.

Thurow, R. (2005, June 13). The promise: Married at 11, A teen in Niger returns to school: After long, difficult deliveries, many girls need surgery; Father's changed outlook; Outcasts in their own villages. *Wall Street Journal,* p. A1.

Turner, Francis J. (2002). *Diagnosis in social work: New imperatives.* Binghamton, New York: Haworth Press.

Walter. (1966). *My secret life* (Vol. 1–11). New York: Grove Press.

Weber, M. (1972). *Wirtschaft und gesellschaft: Grundriss der verstehenden soziologie* (*Economy and society: Outline of interpretive sociology*). Tübingen: J.C.B. Mohr.

Wiggershaus, R. (1988). *Die Frankfurter schule: Geschichte, theoretische entwicklung, politische bedeutung* (*The Frankfurt School: History, theoretical, political importance*). München: Deutscher Taschenbuch Verlag.

Woodham-Smith, C. (1989). *The great hunger: Ireland 1845–1849.* New York: Old Town Books.

Questions for Discussion

1. How does the author's shift to social work in a hospital change his practice? What practice experience has he previously had that proves useful in this setting?

2. Describe the author's relationship with the doctors and nurses in the hospital? As a social worker, how does the author relate to their hierarchies?

3. The author discusses his first encounters with the crack epidemic and AIDS in this chapter. How well do you think he responded?

4. Have you worked with someone who had AIDS, abused drugs, or was homeless? What were your feelings when you first met them?

5. In the mid-1980s, parents often brought their adolescent girls to the hospital emergency room for "virginity clearance." What do you think of the hospital's response to these requests?

6. Why, according to the author, is "ethnicity" an unsatisfactory explanation of people's behavior?

7. How have changes in the economy altered the father's role? How might these changes contribute to domestic violence? Do you think these changes have any implications for modern American politics?

CHAPTER SEVEN

CHANGES IN THE EMERGENCY ROOM: TOWARD BETTER PSYCHOSOCIAL ASSESSMENTS (1989–1999)

IN THE LATE spring of 1988, the emergency room (ER) moved back to the general location that we had left in 1984, but in a newly constructed building. Now it was about twice the size of the temporary ER, and a few times larger than the old one. It had a separate pediatric area, with its own waiting room. My office was in the adult waiting room but next to the common triage booth. There was space for two, and in 1991 or 1992, a new social worker joined me to cover the morning shift. The patient population of the ER increased steadily, and the new location quickly became crowded.

The patient demography also changed. The number of elderly patients gradually decreased and, with them, the elderly Europeans. I cannot recall the last time I spoke German with a patient. It may have been a very old Alsatian man who explained that in both world wars he had served in military intelligence, the first time for the Germans and the second time for the United States, to which he had emigrated in the 1930s.

Or it may have been a charming and interesting, though rather depressed woman, whose parents, affluent owners of a garment factory in Eastern Poland, had sent her to a boarding school in Germany to participate in what they saw as a higher culture. She spoke excellent German, though with a Yiddish accent, and, when she visited the ER, we recited Goethe's beautiful lines together:

Über allen Gipfeln, ist Ruh' [All over the summits, peace]
Über allen Wipfeln, spürest du [Over all the pine tops, you sense]
Kaum einen Hauch. . . . [Barely a whisper]

She explained to me that in 1945, as a young adult and recently liberated from the concentration camp at Bergen-Belsen, she felt much emotional distress and had consulted a psychiatrist, who told her that there were two general kinds of psychiatric illness, and she had the less grave one. He reassured her that she was not "*geistig krank,*" that is, sick in the "spirit,"[1] implying some fundamental personality flaw. Instead, her distress came from her horrifying experience of the concentration camp—terrible, but external to her.

She had taken this insight to heart, and it had sustained her through the years. A few minutes later, I returned to her, and she said, *sotto voce,* that the patient in the next cubicle was indeed geistig krank. In fact, the other patient did seem clearly psychotic.

In place of the elderly people, new populations moved in. Probably the majority were Dominicans, who now moved to the Bronx. Formerly, they had clustered on the west side of Manhattan and in some other areas of the city (Hendricks, 1974). Also, there were immigrants from Eastern Europe, especially from Albania itself and other Albanian-speaking areas of the former Yugoslavia; from Africa; more immigrants from the English-speaking Caribbean, including people of Indian origin from Trinidad and Guyana; and many more.

We also began to see the first Mexicans, who previously had sold flowers, seeming naïve and uncertain. About 1990, for example, I worked on an abuse case in which the mother, about 19 years of age, and her baby, lived with her father and his newer wife and their five small children. When I interviewed the mother and asked how they sustained themselves, she said they sold flowers on the street. I asked where they sold them and, to my amazement, learned that although they lived in walking distance from the Grand Concourse, they did not know enough to go there. The concourse is the showiest street in the Bronx, and the clientele there might have been marginally more affluent and disposed to buy flowers. Apparently, they did not know this and stayed, instead, on the much poorer street where they lived.

The demography of the staff also changed radically. Previously, most had been American-born, the nurses mostly Irish and Italian American, and the physicians Jewish American. Fairly suddenly, in 1988 and 1989, the number of nurses from other countries rapidly increased. Most were from the Philippines. A Filipino nursing administrator from Montefiore Medical Center made visits to the Philippines and returned with airplane loads of nurses. Some nurses came from other countries, in the Caribbean and Asia.

More gradually, many of the medical residents came to be immigrants, or the children of immigrants, in particular, from India, Korea, and China.

In the preceding chapter, I described the attitudes of many internal medicine residents somewhat unfavorably, but as the 1980s gave way to the 1990s, they became more sympathetically oriented toward patients. It became less necessary for me to advocate for vulnerable patients who would be unsafe at home. Partly, this resulted from establishment of a residency program in emergency medicine in the

ER, but, over and above that, young doctors now seemed to be people cut from a rather different pattern. The rise of health maintenance organizations (HMOs) had made medicine less lucrative than it was a decade before, and those who chose it as a career seemed to have correspondingly different motives.

The presence of the other social worker made for some differences in our response to the elderly population. My colleague was a man in his late fifties who had grown up in the Midwest, where his father owned a haberdashery in a small town. He had gone on to run a bookstore as an adult; he once told me that from his youth he had learned to make sales. His great strength was in getting patients admitted directly from the ER to nursing homes, thus averting admissions. Armed with the necessary documentation, called a Patient Review Instrument, or PRI, he would call, or even personally visit, local nursing homes and often was able to get patients accepted. I used to say he was a door-to-door salesman of nursing home patients. He had faults, in particular, that he seldom wrote chart notes, but he did have this one pre-eminent strength.

In 1988 or 1989, we finally came to have attending psychiatrists assigned to the ER. This somewhat diminished my work, though the increase in volume more than compensated for this relief. I still worked with suicidal teenagers, although, as I have said, they became somewhat less prevalent.

At first, the psychiatric area was only an isolation room. However, a few years into the 1990s, a former storage area to the rear of the adult medical area became an actual psychiatric ER, complete with locking doors on patient rooms and on the various parts of the psychiatric area.

Many types of cases gradually changed. The sense of shame at experiencing rape seemed to diminish. I had always asked female rape victims if they felt comfortable talking with a male social worker. In the early to mid-1990s, I began to notice that most of them said they didn't care. Battered women, too, seemed more ready to express straightforward anger toward the men who had hurt them, rather than the ambivalence I encountered in my first years in the ER. More often, too, they were not financially dependent on the batterer. Though this was not exactly conventional feminism in operation, some traditional conceptions of womanliness seemed to have changed to a more contemporary outlook.

Pediatric cases also changed gradually. The suicidal girls, as I noted earlier, became less distinctive. Requests for virginity clearance diminished, though slowly. In place of these presenting problems, parents more frequently brought girls whose sexual conduct was actually known and acknowledged, though not necessarily accepted.

Often girls had issues of pregnancy. Sometimes they came knowing they were pregnant. Sometimes it transpired, on evaluation of symptoms, that their digestive complaints, for example, were really morning sickness. This, then, led to questions of what to do, whether to keep the pregnancy or to abort, and of relationships with parents. Sometimes the parents knew their daughters were pregnant; sometimes they didn't know. Sometimes the patients were able to tell their parents, and sometimes they couldn't. In these instances, the patients usually wanted abortions, and I referred them. If the parents were present, we had to maintain confidentiality if the patients requested it, often a delicate matter.

Child abuses continued at about the same rate. However, parents seemed to be more conscious that physically punishing their children was considered inappropriate. If I recall correctly, really extreme physical abuses slightly diminished over time. There were exceptions, however.

One was the Mexican baby I mentioned earlier. Another, a few years later, was quite striking, as one of the handful of cases I have encountered that involved shake injuries. A shake injury occurs when an adult grasps the child's trunk, or, more usually, the arms or shoulders, and vigorously shakes the child back and forth. The younger the child, the more the danger, inasmuch as before the infant is six months old the head is proportionally larger compared with the rest of the body. The shaking makes the brain move violently back and forth inside the skull, with resulting damage. This can lead to serious impairment of brain functioning. Sometimes the injuries can be fatal.

A father brought one of his twin infant daughters to the ER, saying she was lethargic. As the medical evaluation began, the physicians discussed potential reasons for the very obvious lethargy. One was a shake injury. I decided to interview the father, who was alone with the patient in an ER. Although I had seen relatively few perpetrators of shake injuries over the years and was not sure if my distinctive perception of them meant anything in the statistical sense, it was clear that this father was shortish, broad, and muscular, and showed a blunted effect, like all the others I had encountered.

He explained that the mother had left the house for work early in the morning, leaving him to care for the babies. He went on to describe how this infant had cried, how he could not console her for quite some time, and how then she had become minimally responsive.

I went to the physicians' charting room and said, "The father did it." They asked me how I knew, and I said the father had told me: "He described a clear abuse incident, except that he left out the part when he shook her."

A computed tomography (CT) scan showed several areas of bleeding in the patient's brain, and more searching analysis of these findings showed the bleeds to be of varying ages, indicating multiple incidents of injury. I reported the situation to the State Central Registry, of course, and asked the family to bring the twin for an examination. When examined, she seemed well. On the following day, however, a CT scan of her brain showed the same kind of injuries.

At first the mother did not want to believe the father had hurt the children. Then she decided it must have happened just the one time. Finally, she was able to acknowledge that he must have repeatedly shaken the twins. Fortunately, her family proved very supportive, and relatives were able to care for the children when they were discharged.

THE SPREAD OF HMOs created pressures to deny care and imposed added complexities to servicing patients. I recall very well a physically vigorous, but quite demented older man whose daughter brought him to the ER, saying she could not manage him and that he had threatened her daughter. A representative of the HMO was in the ER and pressed the staff not to admit him. I slipped away and called the patient's granddaughter, who told me in detail how he had come at her with a knife. Then I returned to the discussion and pointed out that if, in fact, the patient's daughter were to take him back to her home, and thus place her child in unacceptable danger, I, and all the other mandated reporters involved, would be under a legal obligation to report her for neglect to the New York State Central Registry for Child Abuse and Neglect. I told the HMO representative that if she was a licensed professional (I think she was a registered nurse), she too would be mandated to make a report, and that if she failed to do so she could be prosecuted for a Class A misdemeanor. They admitted the patient.

IN 1992 I decided to supplement my income with a second, part-time job and began to spend one or two mornings a week working for the Kingsbridge Heights Long-Term Home Health Care Program. This was a Lombardy Program, named after a state senator, Tarky Lombardy, who had proposed it in the New York state legislature. Financed by Medicaid, and sometimes called "The Nursing Home Without Walls," it provides fairly intensive nursing care and up to 42 hours weekly home health aide service. Most of its patients are elderly, somewhat frail, but able to be alone for much of the time. Often they are diabetic.

Usually, I would make visits on Monday mornings, when I was fresh, and then get to the ER in the afternoon. On good days, when the patients lived close together, I could finish five or six visits by early afternoon. I worked with some of the patients for many years; in one or two cases, for most of the time I worked for the program, which I left at the end of 2001. Some stood out, in various ways.

One was a man of about 50 years of age when I began with him in 1993. He had once been a promising college student, but then he went into a diabetic coma and emerged with serious brain damage. One of its effects was a sort of approximation of Gilles de la Tourette's syndrome, and a readiness to anger. After a while, he got used to me and showed a kind of warmth and amiability. When I came to see him, he would sidle up to me and, smiling confidentially, would greet me: "What's the bullshit, motherfucker?!" or, more simply, would mutter, that "motherfucker got his ass shot off!" He lived with his mother, who had a fixed delusion that tenants in the adjacent apartment of their Housing Authority building were operating a garment factory.

She herself had worked in a garment factory in the past, and, naming some specific piece of equipment, would ask me, "Can't you hear the . . . ?" She would look puzzled when I said I couldn't. On the fairly frequent occasions when the mother's somewhat haphazard administration of her son's medications landed him in the ER, I helped the staff understand that this unfortunate pair did not know they were inappropriate.

Another was a very pleasant woman, nearly blind from diabetes. One of my earlier triumphs was to move her from the large project building, where she had lived for years and where some of her neighbors were unpleasant, to a very pleasant project built specifically for older adults. There was a senior center in the building. She thrived in this new place, which was very homey, and where the residents socialized freely. One resident was a formidable old woman who sat in the lobby with various followers and kept track of who came and went.

As the New York State Department of Health introduced more and more Medicaid HMOs, I warned all my patients to avoid them, because joining them would interfere with their home care services. Once, when I was visiting, a patient told me a representative of United Health Care (UHC) had been pestering her to sign up. This person actually visited while I was there. The patient said, "I don't do nothing without asking my social worker."

The UHC representative was dressed in overly flashy clothes, and her hair had gotten more attention than necessary. I explained how there were no advantages whatsoever in the patient's joining her HMO. I also pointed out that I had just read in the *Wall Street Journal* that UHC was in some financial straits. Affecting concern, I said, "I hope *you'll* be OK." She retreated rapidly.

Patients often asked what I thought about these HMOs, whose sales forces prowled clinics and other medical facilities, trying to beguile the ill-informed. I recall very well riding in the subway once, next to two of these people, who were totting up the numbers of people they had signed up that day. I realized they got paid by the head.

In response, I usually asked what they would do if someone, instead of offering an HMO, were to proffer "a white powder that would solve all your problems." Patients could relate to this.

Among the New York State Department of Health's efforts to get people to join HMOs was a two-page letter, sent, in 1995, to all Medicaid recipients. It explained the policy regarding HMOs. The letter was only in English, and almost invincibly complex. Many patients asked me to interpret it, which I was able to do only after careful reading. In recent years, New York state has made HMO participation almost universally compulsory for Medicaid recipients. This serves only to impede use of medical care, and, of course, to enrich the insurance industry.

Another patient was a conspicuous exception to the customary meticulous household cleanliness of Puerto Rican housewives. I worked with her for five or six years. I will call her Mrs. Maysonet. The project apartment was filthy, crawled with innumerable cockroaches. The linoleum was cheap, thin, and torn, but for a long time she resisted replacing it because laying it had been the last act of one of her sons, before his death of AIDS. She shared her home with a cat, two Chihuahuas, and various transient people whose roles only sometimes received satisfactory explanation. I could not escape the suspicion that the apartment was probably the scene of drug storage or sales.

Several times in the first year or so that I visited I found, as I arrived in the morning, some of the furniture broken and the apartment in disarray. What had happened? The patient responded with vague confusion.

Mrs. Maysonet had a granddaughter, who was a substance abuser, homeless, lived in the shelter system, and had AIDS in addition to another chronic illness. She also had a young son, and one day I discovered that she had left the boy, then about three years of age, with Mrs. Maysonet overnight. He had slept in her bed. Given that the patient was in her seventies and frail, and that the apartment was unhealthy for anybody, including a child, I told Mrs. Maysonet that this must not happen again. She told me she didn't like to be alone at night, and that that was why the boy had been there. His mother returned while I was in the home. I told her that she must not leave her son with the patient and that I would report her if I found out that she did it again.

I did not see the boy for a year or two, by which time he had just completed kindergarten and seemed quite disturbed. Mrs. Maysonet and Ana proudly exhibited his diploma and report card, even though the latter showed a rather poor record of achievement, especially in interpersonal areas. The notation from his teacher seemed to indicate anxiety about him and commented unfavorably about his attendance.

He approached me as I sat with the patient on a davenport, and objected to my sitting there. I told him that I was talking with the patient. He then assumed a menacing manner, clenched his little fist, and said: "I'm gonna kick your butt." His mother hit him for this, with the report card. Later, as I was about to leave, he hit my hand with his fist and asked, hopefully, "Did that hurt?"

Over the years, this patient had many aides, few of whom stayed long. It was not pleasant to be in the patient's apartment. I myself always sat on a straight chair, held my coat in my lap, and shook any possible roaches off it before putting it on. Mrs. Maysonet used pieces of newspaper to absorb the droppings of her pets and could not contemplate use of kitty litter. Also, there were bits of food littering the living room, because she liked to give the animals treats from her own plate. Mostly, she gave them morsels that they didn't want, picked at, and abandoned to the hordes of roaches. There would be short periods of time when I could convince her that there are two kinds of food: the kind for people and roaches and the kind for dogs and cats. She would giggle at this, briefly comply, but then, quite soon, there would again be bits of pancake or toast on the furniture and floor.

Several of her aides tried to persuade her to allow more thorough cleaning, joined me in my exhortations about cleanliness, but left in frustration. On one occasion I was pointing out a number of areas of the living room and kitchen that cried out for attention, and went toward a framed print of *The Last Supper*, pointing at some flecks of roach-droppings on its surface. The aide shrieked at me not to touch it—"¡No lo toque!" When I looked behind it from the side, I saw slumbering roaches, in their hundreds, resting in layers behind it.

Eventually, Mrs. Maysonet had an aide—I will call her Luz—whose determination, at least for a while, exceeded the patient's passive aggression. She was less than five feet tall, but she had the probably manic energy of several people. At first she thought the filth resulted from her predecessors' laxity and indolence. She expressed indignation and sympathy for the patient's having to live in such squalor—"La pobre doña . . .," and determined to do what she felt right. Thus, she insisted on buying several bug bombs, dressed Mrs. Maysonet to go for a walk, and put her in the hall. Then she put the bug bombs on the living room floor, and, before running from the apartment herself, set them all off. She described coming back later and sweeping up vast volumes of dead roaches.

One day, the nurses called me in great anxiety. Mrs. Maysonet was an insulin-dependent diabetic but had always refused to inject herself, choosing, instead, to pay a neighbor down the hall to do it. Allegedly, this person had received nursing training in Puerto Rico. But then the neighbor moved back to the island. The nurse could not visit every day to inject Mrs. Maysonet's insulin and asked me to persuade Mrs. Maysonet to administer her own medication.

Mrs. Maysonet was fearful and said she just couldn't do it. I told her that the only alternative would be for her to enter a nursing home, where there would always be nurses to give the insulin. But what about her animals, she asked? I told her bluntly that there would be no place for them in the nursing home. I asked Luz to get one of the pre-filled syringes, and handed it to her. With much persuasion, and wastage of one syringe, Mrs. Maysonet was able to clean the skin of her thigh with alcohol and inject herself. Luz and I cheered and Mrs. Maysonet bubbled feebly with satisfaction. She was able, from then on, to manage this for herself.

I often arrived to find that visitors had come to stay with Mrs. Maysonet. Some of them were apparently relatives visiting from Puerto Rico, though even they were quite diverse. Some seemed more or less normal. Some only looked physically fragile. Others were dubious and even sinister. On one occasion, in the summer of 1997, I arrived in the patient's apartment to find her wearing a white T-shirt with red and green lettering, spelling out the incongruous words: "Italian Bitch."

I asked her where she had gotten this garment, and she said her granddaughter, Ana, had left it in the apartment. Where had Ana gotten it? At a church, she said. I asked which ecclesiastical institution had been responsible for distributing the shirt. Mrs. Maysonet responded with her usual vagueness.

Then I noticed that two more unfamiliar people were present, a man in his twenties and a young woman of about 19 years of age sitting on the davenport and watching television. The woman's only visible garment was a T-shirt, but it was long enough to cover her privates. She was rather pretty.

The man was immensely muscular, and his arms heavily tattooed. He was fully clothed but wore a T-shirt with the sleeves cut off. The musculature and the tattoos suggested past imprisonment. The two regarded me with evident suspicion, apprehension, and even barely concealed alarm. This subsided only gradually after I identified myself, by name and function. I asked the patient if they were family members, and she said the man was her nephew. The woman's relationship was not specified; she sat demurely beside the patient's nephew on the davenport, idly stroking his back and leg.

Allegedly they were the patient's great-nephew and -niece, but it appeared that they were cousins, not siblings, and also seemed to be lovers. They said they were visiting from Puerto Rico. I decided it would be very imprudent to annoy or alarm this man, and so I asked some empty-headed questions about what they planned to do during their visit. Did they want to see the Empire State Building?

He gave me a dismissive look and clearly concluded that I represented no threat to his probably illicit activities. Later, the aide covertly told me that these visitors had been with Mrs. Maysonet for some weeks. She also confirmed that the man had been a convict in Puerto Rico. With exquisite delicacy, she explained that she believed him to be involved in some form of commerce.

I was concerned for Mrs. Maysonet's safety with this pair in her home, but there were no clear grounds to involve the police. I visited more frequently, especially after the patient had intimated to the visiting nurse that she felt uncomfortable with her two relatives being there. It was difficult to decide how to intervene, or if overt intervention would help at all. I could have tried to involve Adult Protective Services (APS), but I was sure the patient herself would not be able to cooperate with APS, even if I could convince the agency that my suspicions were sufficient to justify their getting involved. Attempts to address the situation on that basis seemed more likely to further endanger her. Fortunately, the young woman told me on my second visit that they were looking for a place of their own. This proved to be true.

Later, after they had left, Mrs. Maysonet admitted to me that she had been afraid of these relatives. She explained that the young man was a member of the family of her deceased husband's sons by another woman. The young woman was a descendent of one of the patient's siblings, hence a niece or great-niece, and she and the patient shared a surname. Mrs. Maysonet worried that her relative was living with a substance abuser. This was her first clear acknowledgment that the man was a substance abuser. I commented that it was also unfortunate that the patient herself had had to put up with such housemates. Mrs. Maysonet expressed limp agreement.

Home care paperwork was somewhat onerous. I did it at home and computerized the forms we had to use. In the later years, however, the required wording of the notes I had to submit became much more formulaic. For a time, I used rubber stamps with standard wording, and filled in additional information in longhand.

I enjoyed the home care work while I was actually doing visits, though I really would have preferred other uses for the time. Being out in the field and walking from visit to visit was pleasant. It had been some years since I had done field visiting, and the Bronx had become much less desolate. The arson had subsided, and deterioration of buildings had slowed. Many had been renovated. Among the vacant lots, new buildings had gone up, and more were coming. I found also, that renewing my familiarity with the many communities of the borough gave me a clearer sense of my ER patients' circumstances.

IN 1989, OUR long-time director of social service at Montefiore Medical Center was dismissed. Though the reasons given for this were sketchy, there were disquieting comments at a meeting between the social work staff and a higher administrator, who implied that, as a profession, we were behind the times. He explained that his wife was a social worker and that, sometimes, in glancing through her copies of *Social Work*, he noted the NASW Press's advertisements in the journal. The offerings on medical social work, he thought, were scanty, and apparently dated.

The new director arrived fairly soon. The announcement of his appointment included a glowing comment that he was about to earn his master's in business administration (MBA). We were at the peak of that period when MBAs had a prestige that now seems to have faded a bit. Certainly, the fantasy that human service agencies will improve with use of methods developed in the world of commerce is no longer so prevalent.

I began to take a more active role in the union, Local 1199 of the Service Employees International Union and, after a few years, became a delegate. The hours I worked limited what I could do, but, in addition to the usual grievances and representation of members, I tried to use the union as a means to maintain a professional presence in a difficult time that culminated in the—fortunately temporary—elimination of the social work department, and inclusion of social workers in administrative hierarchies headed by other disciplines.

THROUGHOUT THE 1990S, I continued to supervise students and gradually became more structured in my approach. I tried to meet with incoming students in the spring or summer before they began so as to give them a general orientation to the ER and to my way of approaching my and their roles. I presented the ER as an excellent opportunity to become really good at psychosocial assessment and diagnosis, because it was not a place where long-term work took place. I also took to giving them a bibliography of useful texts that I thought would be a good basis for what they would be doing in the setting. This bibliography was voluntary, and I committed myself to refrain from initiating any discussion of the readings.

The basic reading list included Manuel Puig: *Heartbreak Tango*, a translation of *Boquitas Pintadas* (Puig, 1968–1976); Bertha Capen Reynolds: *Social Work and Social Living, Explorations in Philosophy and Practice* (Reynolds, 1942; Max Weber: "Bureaucracy" (Gerth & Mills, 1958); Sigmund Freud: *The Ego and the Id* (S. Freud, 1923/1961); Anna Freud: *The Ego and Mechanisms of Defense* (A. Freud, 1946). I also suggested Stephen Spielberg's *Sugarland Express* (1974), a movie that I think depicts people who are typical of many social work agency clients and patients. The Puig book is a novel that I described as follows: "Besides being entertaining, it gives a sense of the visual, experiential and sensuous element in everyday human experience and, therefore, in social work practice."

For students who were more advanced and who had had at least the first courses in human behavior, I offered a more advanced reading list.

The readings were generally psychodynamic. I could not expect students to grapple with my own developing thoughts on the social theory before their internship. Also, the psychodynamic emphasis seemed to offer conceptual tools that would go on from what most students had gotten in their course work. The only exception was the Weber article, but it was an obvious choice, being so straightforward and consistent with previous bureaucratic experiences many students would have had.

Though the readings included little social theory, I found myself giving this aspect of psychosocial assessment more emphasis in case discussions. This came from my own increasing knowledge and command of theory. Moreover, it moved somewhat parallel to developments in the social work field in general.

~ . ~ . ~

IN THE 1990s, social workers began to discuss cultural sensitivity and cultural competence. The discussion flourished, and, in 1996, NASW included the following in its *Code of Ethics*:

1.05 Cultural Competence and Social Diversity

(a) Social workers should understand culture and its function in human behavior and society, recognizing the strengths that exist in all cultures.

(b) Social workers should have a knowledge base of their clients' cultures and be able to demonstrate competence in the provision of services that are sensitive to clients' cultures and to differences among people and cultural groups.

(c) Social workers should obtain education about and seek to understand the nature of social diversity and oppression with respect to race, ethnicity, national origin, color, sex, sexual orientation, age, marital status, political belief, religion, and mental or physical disability. (NASW, 2000, p. 9)

This is the core statement on this issue in the *Code of Ethics,* and it reflects much of the social work profession's impulse to pursue democratic goals in work with our clientele. At the same time, we notice that there is no definition of the key term "culture." Still, there are some suggestive phrases in this text. "Knowledge base" implies that there is a body of facts to master about the groups one works with, whether defined by "race, ethnicity, national origin, color, sex, sexual orientation, age, marital status, political belief, religion, and mental or physical disability." I read some of the anthropological literature that sought a definition of culture, in particular Kroeber's report of a comprehensive evaluation of definitions then in use (Kroeber & Kluckhohn, 1963). The most useful treatment of the subject that I found at the time was Geza Róheim's *The Origin and Function of Culture* (Róheim, 1971). As the social work profession approaches the question, however, understanding culture is much like understanding ethnicity. Mostly, it is a matter of knowing information and bringing a degree of sympathy to the encounter with people whose way of life is unfamiliar or unusual.

One obvious problem comes up when the cultural practices of groups are oppressive to their members or involve invidious comparisons or frank hostility to other groups. The NASW *Code of Ethics* (2000) addressed this in section 6.04 Social and Political Action:

> (c) Social workers should promote conditions that encourage respect for cultural and social diversity within the United States and globally. Social workers should promote policies and practices that demonstrate respect for difference, support the expansion of cultural knowledge and resources, advocate for programs and institutions that demonstrate cultural competence, and promote policies that safeguard the rights of and confirm equity and social justice for all people. (NASW, p. 27)

This offers only very general guidance to the social worker working with members of a group that believes in, for example, the right of husbands to corporally punish their wives, the right of parents to deny their children education, or aggressive violence against gays. "Equity and social justice" covers this, of course, but avoids the question of how, as a profession, we should deal practically with these issues when people "sincerely" hold antidemocratic values. Obviously, the culturally competent social worker needs to be familiar with the specifics of clients' values, expectations, customs, family and community institutions, and so forth. Presumably, the ability to address such issues in some effective manner would be an example of cultural competence. But the code offers little guidance when cultures are in conflict, either internally or with the values of a democratic society.

More fundamentally, however, is the essentially nontheoretical character of the concept, such as it is, that underlies this ethical requirement. In the ER, I learned more about these matters every day. But I found culture a moving target, changing as I encountered it. And the conflicts around culture were frequent. Sometimes they involved conflict between patients' values and the values, and sometimes the legal requirements, of the broader society.

I think back on a number of exemplary experiences. One came very early, when I was working for the Bureau of Child Welfare. I interpreted an interview between one of my colleagues and a distraught man from the Dominican Republic who had stabbed his young son in the abdomen, causing an injury that required surgery and a temporary colostomy.

We asked him to explain what had happened in the incident. Tearfully, he explained that he had never intended to injure his child, that it was really his wife's fault. He had concluded that she was unfaithful to him, that he had taken a knife to stab her, that she had dodged, and this brought the toddler into the path of the knife. He was horrified at what had happened, had taken the boy up, and brought him to the local hospital—"*Lo cogí a mí, y corrí p'al Lincoln.*"

As he recounted this, he gave every evidence of intense distress, and he gave us a hopeful look, as if expecting some sympathy, not only for his grief, but also for his actions in the situation. We explained gently that wife-stabbing, whatever the provocation, is never permissible in the United States of America and that he must bear the consequences of his act. He sighed, seemed a little confused, but did not really argue.

Many years later, I encountered a much more complex case with quite involved cultural implications.[2] Very early in 1991, a 12-year-old girl came to the ER with her foster mother. Earlier in the day she and the two younger children in the putative sibling group had gone to the foster care agency's pediatrician for a physical examination, having gone into care a few weeks earlier. The doctor had felt a lump in her belly and sent her in for further evaluation.

The lump proved to be a pregnancy. We learned that the child had lived in the home of a man from a developing country who was in the United States completing training in a prestigious profession. He and his ailing wife had two young children. To care for his wife and children, he imported our patient, having bought her from her parents in his native town for a herd of goats. Then the wife had died, and our patient was left to care for the children and, it appeared, to serve the man's erotic needs. Of course, we reported our findings to Central Registry.

The children had come to school appearing so neglected that the school had reported the family to the New York State Central Registry for Child Abuse and

Maltreatment. The first CPS worker, unfortunately, was a compatriot of the man, and did little. Apparently, he came from a family of some standing in their native land. Her successor, however, a native of the Bronx, removed the children, and it was then discovered that the patient was not really a member of the family.

The child spoke poor English and, at first, had difficulty understanding that she was pregnant. The foster mother, who impressed me very favorably, had met the man, and wrinkled her nose with disgust in describing him, in a manner strongly suggestive of a normal woman's response to a male psychopath.

At the case conference the following day, I ventured the opinion that we should consult an anthropologist so as to inform ourselves as to the customs of the country from which the child and the man originated. It seemed almost certain that he would try to put those who would be working with them off balance by claiming that his relationship with the child was legitimate under their customs. No one else seemed interested in the task. I accepted it, and my student at the time asked to pursue the question. Eventually, she found an anthropologist at the American Museum of Natural History, who was familiar with the relevant part of the world, and assured us that although the man, who was probably from a prominent family in the area, would most likely be able to get away with exploiting the child, this would not be normative or even acceptable behavior. Also, the anthropologist thought the child, should she return to her native country, would be marginalized and probably would only find work as a prostitute. In fact, the man did attempt to claim the child as his wife under local custom. I have read the opinion of the New York state court that made short work of the arguments his lawyers had advanced.

More and more, I came to see multiculturalism as a confused, poorly conceived, and frequently ill-informed combination of sentimentality and guilt. It has clear ties to the 18th century notion of "the noble savage." Confronted with many realities of life, it has little of use to contribute. For example, most of us are aware of practices like genital mutilation, in particular the so-called "female circumcision," which is designed to preserve the "virginity" of girls and young women. Obviously, this is an extreme example of the concern for sexual purity that we find in many cultures, including various ones in the United States.

NASW refers to "the strengths that exist in all culture," but does not mention the obvious fact that some cultural practices are ill-adapted to life in the contemporary United States at the very least. Some too, are oppressive, antihuman, and opposed to social work's democratic values. In particular, they often perpetuate elite control within the group over women, children, and disfavored subgroups (Okin, 1997).

The strengths and weaknesses of the various cultures are not peculiar to ones that are newcomers in the United States. Much of the dominant American culture, of course, can be oppressive and antidemocratic. We should be as critical of this as we are of the cultures of other areas. For example, female genital mutilation in the form of clitoridectomy was a widespread practice in the United States in the 19th century and was a treatment for hysteria. It was the psychosurgery of the time (Barker-Benfield, 1976).

Pollitt (1997) also pointed out the considerable overlap between cultures that are supposed to be "advanced, or "Western" and ones that are—according to one's viewpoint—"backward" or "communal" or indigenous in some pure sense:

> That cultural-rights movements have centered on gender is a telling fact about them. It's related to the way in which nationalism tends to identify the nation with the bodies of its women: they are the ones urged into "traditional" dress, conceptualized as the producers of babies for the fatherland and keepers of the hearth for the men at the front, punished for sleeping with outsiders, raped by the nation's enemies and so forth. But it's also partly due to the fact that gender and family are retrograde areas of most majority cultures, too: these are accommodations majority cultures have often been willing to make. How far would an Algerian immigrant get, I wonder, if he refused to pay the interest on his Visa bill on the grounds that Islam forbids interest on borrowed money? Or a Russian who argued that the cradle-to-grave social security provided by the former Soviet Union was part of his cultural tradition and should also be extended to him in Brooklyn? Everyone understands that money is much too important to be handed out in this whimsical fashion. Women and children are another story. (p. 29)

Acceptance of any particular cultural practice should not be automatic. We need to assess its compatibility with the democratic values to which we as social workers are professionally committed. Social work, after all, has always been part of the ongoing growth of democratic values and institutions, from the Women's Suffrage Movement to the Civil Rights Movement to feminism and gay rights. There is a serious concern that the impulse toward cultural sensitivity may legitimate efforts to give groups rights over their members that would transcend the individual's constitutional and legal rights as a participant in the society.[3] But this raises questions that are essentially insoluble. How are we to know who is the authentic representative of the group? Who can tell us what are really the group's authentic values and practices?

I myself have experienced many situations in which a range of encounters with members of a group produced a similar range of—often contradictory—accounts of their culture.

Multicultural thinking is not absent from the social work literature. Some of it is simply sentimental. Some of it dresses sentimentality in an uninformed nostalgia for what is supposed to have been traditional, and more generally warm, fuzzy, touchy-feely.[4] Also, it often tries to evoke guilt feelings among people from the supposedly dominant Western/Northern cultures of the world. For example:

> Various investigators have attempted to classify societies according to whether they are founded upon libertarian or communitarian values. These investigators suggest that Euro-American (Western) cultures are predominantly individualist; cultures beyond Western frontiers, on the other hand, are characterized by communalism. (Owusu-Bempah, 2003–2004)

This sharp and presumptively unchanging distinction between the West or North and the less developed world is only superficially valid. After all, the West was like this too until pretty recently. Peasant society in Europe was like the communal cultures this author celebrates. The change away from "communitarian values" is a general, worldwide experience. It is an inescapable part[5] of the development of human society.[6]

The more I saw of social work's approach to culture, the more it seemed well-intentioned but inadequate. Most of its deficiencies arise out of its theoretical failure or, better said, its failure to be theoretical at all. I continued to work on what I hoped would be a more sound social theory.

〜 · 〜 · 〜

IN THE 1990s, it began to occur to me that I was relying too purely on historical and thus empirical literature to formulate this theory. Inspired by a remark I found in one of Robert Redfield's studies, I began to look at the classics of sociology—Weber, Durkheim, Tönnies. Durkheim came first, mostly because I decided to improve my French at the same time. I had studied French in school and college but had never become fluent. Hence, I bought his *Les Formes Élémentaire de la Vie Réligieuse* (Durkheim, 1960), and, to read it, set aside the time I spent on the bus riding home. This was a peaceful and comfortable time, and I made steady, if slow, progress. Later I read another, less known essay, *Représentations Individuelles et Représentations Collectives* (Durkheim, 1898), because it began to be clear that his concept of collective representations was a way to make sense of the distinctions between the various ways social work clients experienced the world. For example, this began to offer concepts for theorizing the radical disparity between peasant experience and modern experience. I also began to look at Ferdinand Tönnies *Gemeinschaft und Gesellschaft* (Tönnies, 1935),[7] which really is about the transition from the peasant community to modern society.[8]

Beginning with the concept of character, and linking it with new elements of theory and an understanding of historical family structures, I was now able to extend the theoretical reach much farther across the gap between what I call the small and the large. Human beings have to adapt to whatever material reality they inhabit, but their patterns of adaptation will vary according to the pattern and features of that reality. Wilhelm Reich (1949), in his *Character Analysis,* defined character in this way:

> The character armor developed as the chronic result of the world; the continuing actual conflicts between instinct and outer world give it its strength and continued reason for existence. It is the sum total of those influences of the outer world on instinctual life which, by reason of their similarity, form a historical unit. . . . The place where the armor is formed is the ego, that part of the personality which forms the boundary between instinctual life and outer world. We can call it, therefore, the character of the ego. (p. 146)[9]

According to the material circumstances in which the developing human organism forms a personality, the ego may have any of various types of character. I found that Zaretsky's and Poster's distinctions among historical family patterns corresponded to a range of character types. With the exception of the aristocratic family, most of the family forms they described existed parallel with each other for extended historical periods. At least to some extent, they still exist. For example, it is only in the last 50 years or so that the vast expanses of peasant society in India, China, Africa, and other parts of the underdeveloped world have partly given way to modernity.

Looking at the range of character manifestations, we can see, for example, that the circumstances of early and late bourgeois families tended to engender variations on the theme of anality, which Freud defined simply, in this way:

> The persons I want to describe are conspicuous in showing a regular juxtaposition of the following characteristics: they are especially *orderly, parsimony, and obstinate.* Each of these words covers a small group of

mutually related character traits. "Orderly" comprehends not only bodily cleanliness but also conscientiousness in fulfilling small obligations, and reliability. The opposite would be: disorderly, negligent. Parsimony may rise to the level of avarice; obstinacy may become defiance, connected with rage and vindictiveness. The two latter characteristics—parsimony and obstinacy—hang together more closely than the third, orderliness; they also are the more constant part of the whole complex. However, it seems to me that there is no dispute that all three belong together in some way. (S. Freud, 1908/1959, p. 25)[10]

Freud, of course, came from a late bourgeois family himself and developed his theories through work with such families. This definition of anality, with its implications for the development of the superego, reflects this experience.

By contrast, the early bourgeois family, though somewhat similar, had been significantly more relaxed. Here are some examples of the life of preindustrial artisans:

> The contrast between capitalist and precapitalist work patterns is most striking in respect to the working year. The medieval calendar was filled with holidays. Official—that is, church—holidays included not only long "vacations" at Christmas, Easter, and midsummer but also numerous saints' and rest days. These were spent both in sober churchgoing and in feasting, drinking and merry-making. In addition to official celebrations, there were often weeks' worth of ales—to mark important life events (bride ales or wake ales) as well as less momentous occasions (scot ale, lamb ale, and hock ale). All told, holiday leisure time in medieval England took up probably about one-third of the year. And the English were apparently working harder than their neighbors. The *ancien régime* in France is reported to have guaranteed fifty-two Sundays, ninety rest days, and thirty-eight holidays. In Spain, travelers noted that holidays totaled five months per year. (Schor, 1991, pp. 46–47)

This changed with the introduction of the factory system, at first in England, in the 18th century. The historian E. P. Thompson (1963) describes this process, as artisanal weavers, who worked at home with the whole family forming the productive unit, had to become factory operatives:

> Weaving had offered an employment to the whole family, even when spinning was withdrawn from the home. The young children winding bobbins, older children watching for faults, picking over the cloth, or helping to throw the shuttle in the broad-loom; adolescents working a

second or third loom; the wife taking a turn at weaving in and among her domestic employments. The family was together, and however poor meals were, at least they could sit down at chosen times. A whole pattern of family and community life had grown up around the loom-shops; work did not prevent conversation or singing. The spinning-mills—which offered employment only for their children—and then the power-loom sheds, which generally employed only the wives or adolescents—were resisted until poverty broke down all defences. These places were held to be "immoral"—places of sexual licence, bad language, cruelty, violent accidents, and alien manners. (pp. 306–307)

Elsewhere, Schor (1991) cited the key issue linking the factory work process to anality:

> . . . two important points about capitalism and work. First, employers used *time* itself to regulate labor. In medieval Europe, consciousness of time was vague. The unit of labor time was the "day." It was tied to the sun, and as I have noted, tended to be approximate. Modern time consciousness, which includes habituation to clocks, economy of time, and the ownership of time, became an important weapon which employers used against their employees. . . . As employers consolidated control over their workforces, the day was increasingly split into two kinds of time: "owner's time, the time of *work*"; and "their own time, a time (in theory) for *leisure*." Eventually, workers came to perceive time, not as the milieu in which they lived their life, but "as an objective force within which [they] were imprisoned." (pp. 49–50)

This "objective force" is another way of describing the inner compulsion that comes with anal character.

But in these societies, the majority were always peasants. Both historically and in the transition to modernity, their experience was different from the minorities of aristocrats and urban dwellers. And peasant life presents great uniformity wherever it exists:

> It is abundantly clear that, although the content of peasant society—the cultural details—are infinite, the forms are astonishingly similar. Peasants in Mexico face economic problems very like those confronting the Hindu farmer; the Peruvian villager looks upon illness, and reacts to it, in a way that would be familiar to the Egyptian *fellahin*; the Chinese village family is rent by inheritance squabbles in the same fashion as its Italian counterpart. (Foster, 1962, p. 45)

The more I learned the history of the material life that affected the development of personality, and which thus defines much of the process of psychosocial assessment, the more I discovered that the history of peasant life was a crucial element, and an element that had received far too little attention. The social work profession had given it little attention for many years.[11] Even historians have only turned to it in the last few decades.

However, peasants have been the majority of humanity for the last two or three millennia, and the peasant heritage is somewhere in everybody's past. The only question is how long ago one's forebears moved from the peasantry into other areas of society. Many of the immigrants who flocked to the United States of America in the peak years of immigration from 1880 to 1923 were peasants from the more backward areas of Europe. Some of those coming in the present day are not far from the peasant experience, though usually, nowadays, peasant life has already undergone some changes in the countries of origin.

The inattention[12] to the widespread peasant origins of so many Americans has several roots, one of the more important being that peasants, until recently, were generally illiterate and left no records of their own. However, recent historians have found ways around this problem, in particular the French *Annales* school.[13] Some prominent members of this group are Emmanuel Le Roy Ladurie (Ladurie, 1975, 1979a, 1979b), Georges Duby (Duby, 1976, 1988 [see pages 10–33 and pp. 129–128]) and Fernand Braudel (Braudel, 1969, 1977, 1979a, 1979b, 1979c). Others who have followed them are Eugen Weber (1976), and Judith Devlin (1987).

Only one writer of this general tendency, Philippe Ariès (1962), has achieved some notice in American social work circles, though the critical literature responding to him has not (Ozment, 2001). These writers, though they deal with far-off times and places, perform a sort of psychosocial assessment of the people and communities they investigate. Their findings are not only relevant in illuminating the peasant past, but they offer a different perspective on what really is psychosocial assessment.[14]

Peasant life tended to create material circumstances conducive to development of orality, but on a level of scarcity, not of abundance. Foster (1967) offered an anthropological description of the basic peasant outlook:

> The model of cognitive orientation that seems to me best to account for peasant behavior is the "Image of Limited Good." By "Image of Limited Good," I mean that broad areas of peasant behavior are patterned in such fashion as to suggest that peasants view their social, economic, and natural universes—their total environment—as one in which all of the desired things in life such as land, wealth, health, friendship and love,

manliness and honor, respect and status, power and influence, security and safety, *exist in finite quantity* and *are always in short supply,* as far as the peasant is concerned. Not only do these and all other "good things" exist in finite and limited quantities but in addition *there is no way directly within peasant power to increase the available quantities.* It is as if the obvious fact of land shortage in a densely populated area applied to all other desired things: not enough to go around. "Good," like land, is seen as inherent in nature, there to be divided and redivided, if necessary, but not to be augmented. (p. 304)

Orality is part of any human being's experience, but for it to be a dominant characterological feature implies that the personality develops in a context in which supplies of nurturance are an issue, whether positively or negatively. Obviously, the image of limited good in the peasant context implies that the negative side predominates, and expresses itself in a basic fatalism, though peasants did try to use magical means to influence events. There are still other ways, of course, in which orality can manifest itself.

> All positive and negative emphasis on taking and receiving indicates an oral origin. Unusually pronounced oral satisfaction results in remarkable self-assurance and optimism that may persist throughout life if frustration following this satisfaction has not created a state of vengefulness coupled with continuous demanding. Exceptional oral deprivation, on the other hand, determines a pessimistic (depressive) or sadistic (redress-demanding) attitude. If a person remains fixated in the world of oral wishes, he will, in his general behavior, present a disinclination to take care of himself and require others to look after him. In conformity with the contrasting aims of the two substages of oral eroticism, this demand for care may be expressed through extreme passivity or through a highly active oral-sadistic behavior. (Fenichel, 1945, pp. 488–489)

In traditional peasant life, as part of the reality basis of the image of limited good, the availability of food was chronically problematic. There would be times when nourishment was abundant. And then there would sometimes be lean years. Also, in many climates, there was a season in every year when people had to depend on whatever supplies they had been able to lay in during the growing season.

What Fenichel called the "pessimistic (depressive)" characteristic corresponds to the typical fatalism of the peasant. The peasant realistically felt at the mercy of forces, like the weather, disease, blight that felt immediately tangible, powerful, but under his control only to the extent that the magical influences he would try to invoke proved hospitable.[15] The "highly active oral-sadistic behavior" corresponds to the episodic peasant rebellions that once occurred. These rebellions were almost always ineffectual, mostly because they were dependent on fantasies of a benevolent authority that ought to support them, and because they were attempts to prevent changes to traditions of peasant life, rather than attempts to embrace modernity and guide its development so as to minimize its harmful aspects.[16]

Peasant agriculture operated on a low technological level, with meager returns, and the constant danger of famine or other natural disasters. Hence, peasants were unable to practice the kind of prudence, forethought, and deferral of gratification typical of people whose life circumstances engender anal character:

> Consider, first the attitude toward work. It is said again and again that people in poor communities do not care to work long and hard. Presumably they prefer to be idle instead. Thus, the "leisure" associated with such idleness is valued more highly than the increase in production that could be had from more work. The inference that follows is that these people value this kind of idleness too highly. But what is not reckoned is their lack of vigor and stamina to work hard and long and the low marginal return to additional work.... While particular class or caste arrangements affect choices and the mobility of labor and the adaptive capacity of an economy to changing economic conditions, it does not follow that people who belong to a class or caste which does farm work have a penchant for being idle. It could be that the preferences and motives for working are essentially the same for a wide array of agricultural communities. If so, traditional agriculture is not a consequence of particular farm people having preferences of loafers but what appears to be loafing is a consequence of the low marginal productivity of labor. (Schultz, 1964, pp. 26–27)

This is the core of the basis of peasant oral character. The conditions that might encourage anality were absent. Fenichel's comment on "disinclination to take care of himself" is the statement of a person from a society where anality was dominant and failures of anality were easily seen as pathological. But for the peasant there was no reason to defer gratification. In fact, the peasant had every reason to consume quickly, because it was not possible for him to preserve much food, and it was more prudent to store wealth as adipose tissue, as a hedge against the next famine or epidemic.[17]

In social work practice, we frequently encounter an enduring consequence of this past reality in the manner in which mothers from more traditional backgrounds overfeed their children and exclaim with delight over a particularly fat baby. There was a time when that made sense, if any infant was at risk for intestinal infections caused by contaminated water or food. In work with Hispanic families from recent rural backgrounds, I learned that it was a compliment to describe a baby as "¡bién gordo!" (that is, "nice and fat").

Though the productivity of peasant agriculture was low, peasant farmers were slow to change their methods, for fear that any departure from the tried and true might lead to disaster:

> The particular economic equilibrium represented by traditional agriculture is fundamentally based on the state of the arts underlying the supply of reproducible factors of production, the state of preference and motives underlying the demand for sources of income, and the period of time during which these two states remain constant. In the case of the state of the arts the following *ex post* specifications are essential. The agricultural factors that farmers employ have been used by them and their forebears for a long time and none of these factors meanwhile has been altered significantly as a consequence of learning from experience. Nor have any new agricultural factors been introduced. Thus what is known by farmers about the factors they use has been known by farm people in the community for one or more generations. For a long time nothing new has been learned either from trial and error or from other sources. (Schultz, 1964, pp. 30–31)[18]

Hence, peasant life changed extremely slowly. Aron Gurevich's study of *Medieval Popular Culture* (Gurevich, 1988), shows features that persisted into the 19th and even the 20th centuries, even in advanced countries like France or Italy.[19]

However, change did come, and sometimes it was sudden and traumatic. One of the earlier examples, which had a major influence in the history of the United States, was the Irish potato famine. As the famine began in 1845, Ireland was a peasant society that had already experienced some of the modernizing effects of the market, but which retained many fairly traditional features. In a few years, the unfortunate country experienced a drastic loss of population to starvation, disease, and immigration. Those who moved to urban centers in England, Canada, and the United States had to adapt to work situations that required at least the semblance of anality (Miller, 1985; Woodham-Smith, 1989).

The experience of Irish peasants, as Miller (1985) described it, is just one example of populations making transitions from one set of circumstances to another. Thus people find themselves in situations that demand multiple kinds of character, or at the very least, behavior that is characteristic of multiple kinds of character.[20] Moving from one country to another has almost always been an event that creates this kind of experience. In the ER, I encountered many patients and families who were experiencing these demands in the present day.

The change from the peasant village to the city implied a radical change in developmental experience. Poster (1978) showed that the peasant family was different from either bourgeois family form:

> Peasants lived in close proximity to other villagers, and there were numerous relatives close at hand. Second, the family (parents and children) was not a particularly significant social group. The ties of dependence with the village were so strong that survival was not possible at the household level. Third, daily interactions involved the whole village or large parts of it, and the family was not closed off from society as a private world. Hence the impression of statistical similarity with bourgeois families is controverted by the force of collective dependence. European peasant families of the old regime were not nuclear families. Although their numbers were small, the family was intermeshed in a wide circle of sociability. In fact, the basic unit of early modern peasant life was not the conjugal family at all but the village. The village was the peasant's "family." (pp. 184–185)

Or, as Pirenne (1933) put it: "The village community farmed as a unit, in the field, herds, grazing. The whole unit acted as one, perforce" (p. 64). This implies that the oedipal experiences typical of the bourgeois family would not be common in the peasant village. Productive activity, and most forms of social interaction, followed patterns of custom, less than purposive intent, so the traditional peasant had little conscious ego or superego. Custom and taboo, reinforced by the village community, regulated id forces.[21] In more modern societies, by contrast, specific people, usually parents, personify the reality principle. The developing person internalizes them as ego ideals.

Oedipal conflict is the basis on which the superego grows in the early and late bourgeois family and its successors. Hence, the superego was not the primary regulator of peasant behavior.[22] In peasant society, the primary reality principle was the whole natural and human environment. Children in the peasant village had many significant others, not just parents, as ego ideals. Hence, the ego mirrored village customs and did not arise out of the developing child's relationships with particular individuals—that is, mothers and fathers. This ego was weak, but in a context in which that did not matter. Also, in the context of feudal relationships—which, in much of the European countryside, prevailed into the 19th century[23]—the true father figure was the lord, or seignior. Peasants, both men and women, were somewhat equal to each other under his rule, rather as if they were children. The seignior would have had a feudal superior, and then, of course, there was the king, or other ruler of the country. Patriarchy was integral to feudalism, but as an aspect of the whole society, which was a sort of family, with one father for all.[24] And, of course, the king ruled by divine right. The whole feudal social order was what it was because, as the feudal elites saw it, that was God's plan.[25] When feudalism drew to an end, patriarchal institutions devolved into the family.

The experience of growing up in a peasant village also meant that peasants had only a superficial relationship to ideologies that posit the existence of one god, who is a father—that is, to patriarchal monotheism. This may sound strange to those raised to believe that European Christianity is ancient and that popular participation in the churches was essentially similar to what it is today, or at least in one's grandparents' time. To be sure, it is ancient in one way, in that one can trace its history back to classical times.[26] However, its influence only very gradually extended itself. The feudal aristocracy became fairly consistently christianized by about the year 1000. Some centuries later, the urban bourgeoisies became christianized. Only in the late 19th century did many areas of rural Europe come to a patriarchal monotheist outlook, which gradually supplanted *mythopoeic* thought.[27]

Like secular learning and values, too, patriarchal monotheism came from the cities. The pattern of these urban influences varied. In countries like Ireland, the church influence was overwhelming. In France, by contrast, the republican state was a powerful opponent of ecclesiastical power and patriarchal monotheism.

To be sure, there had been churches in the villages for centuries, but they had been as much a feature of government as of spirituality. Instead, peasant spirituality was a syncretic mixture of patriarchal monotheist ideology—in most of Europe this meant an overlay of Christianity—and older, essentially pagan beliefs.[28] Cults of saints, who often were unknown to the church, and whose origins lay in paganism, were popular well into the 19th century.[29]

The cult of the saints was an integral part of medieval religious life. The saints' role was all the greater in that the notion of a miracle-working patron, to whom one could turn for aid and whose relics were located nearby in a church or cathedral, found a much easier path to the consciousness of the common people than did the idea of a distant, invisible, and awe-inspiring God. Attitudes towards God lacked that "intimacy" and "sincerity" that united the faithful with the local saint (Gurevich, 1988).

Given that peasants lived at the mercy of natural forces, the magical approach to reality seemed more immediately relevant to daily life. Offerings to the saints often enough seemed sufficiently effective to sustain belief in their efficacy. This was the religion and science of the peasant, and this mythopoeic thinking is the precursor not only of the science we know, but of patriarchal monotheism too. And it is not dead. In the United States, social workers often encounter survivals of these practices in the form of ritual healing among many populations. The Santería of Caribbean Hispanics is one example that is common in New York City (González-Wippler, 1975). Anyone who works with these populations needs to have some knowledge of it. Durkheim (1960) showed that most features of modern society have origins in some form of historical religious experience:

> We have established, along the way, that the fundamental categories of thought, and, consequently, of science, have religious origins. We have seen that the same applies to magic and, as a result, to the diverse techniques of science which are derived from it. On the other hand, we have known for a long time, that, up to a relatively advanced moment of evolution, the rules of morality and law have been difficult to distinguish from ritual prescriptions. Hence, one may say, to sum up, that almost all major social institutions of society are born out of religion. In other words, in order for the principal aspects of collective life to have started off only as various aspects of religious life, the religious life must obviously be the eminent form and like a shortened expression of the entire collective life. If religion has engendered everything essential in society, the idea of society is the soul of religion. (pp. 598–599)[30]

The change, among great masses of people, from mythopoesis to patriarchal monotheism and modern scientific thought is a complex, not yet complete process. I will discuss it in more detail in the next chapter.

～ . ～ . ～

These insights helped me comprehend the social roots of many family conflicts that patients brought to the ER. For example, intergenerational conflicts were very common, around a range of issues, from adolescent sexuality (very intense), to consumption, and use of family financial resources.

It would be typical to find the adult generation committing itself to the process of working and earning a living in a forced and compulsive manner. Often, the reality demands of underpaid labor in oppressive workplaces made this at least a functional adaptation.

In many instances, this brittle and poorly integrated anality came to pervade the personality and dominate relations among the generations. Younger family members frequently manifested a kind of orality distinctive to life in the United States: the orality oriented to consumption and pleasure. In the ER, I encountered many conflicts between parents and children in which this dynamic was clear. Moreover, parental suffering in the workplace created a sense of virtue expressed in resentment of the children's irresponsibility in oral areas—" I work so hard and look at what she does. . . . All I want her/him to do is go to school and get an education. . . . He hangs with the wrong crowd."

Of course, much of the thrust of consumer culture has been to create such intergenerational conflict. This has gone on for many decades. It occurs not just in families recently arrived from more archaic cultural circumstances. Stuart Ewen has traced the origins of this phenomenon in the United States to the early 20th century. As far back as the 1920s, when early consumptionist families had become numerous, the advertising industry began to redefine the father's role and the relations between parents and children. This was an intentional ideological campaign:

> The evolution of American industry had moved to a point where the canonization of youth provided a two-pronged support for its institutions. First it undercut a patriarchal family, insofar as that family had located industrial knowledge within its own community. As work became increasingly appended to the machine, the elevation of certain characteristics of youth gave affirmation to a concrete and often devastating change in the process of production. Likewise, the elevation of youth and the reality of youthful endurance, made *youngness* a desirable and salable commodity. People's anxieties over the turn in production were now focused toward a safe solution. Youth could be bought, or so the ads claimed. Once again, the loci of social unrest were being confronted in the marketplace. (Ewen, 1976, p. 149)[31]

And Ewen added:

> To businessmen, the reconstituted family would be one which maintained its reproductive function, but which had abandoned the dogma of parental authority, except insofar as that *authority* could be controlled and provide a conduit to the process of goods consumption. (p. 139)

So the consumer market and its demands have a long history of undermining parental authority and supporting children in their struggle to get their parents to buy. But consumption, as orality, does not stop at the cash register. It forms character like any other set of material circumstances. The images used in advertising are often explicitly sexual, for example, and encourage the consumer to value himself or herself in sexual terms. For adolescents, advertising, mostly implicitly, legitimizes sexual expression. Thus, when parents attempt to maintain the restrained sexual values that correspond to their often somewhat insecure anality, they find that their children can appeal to other strongly propagated oral values.

One can criticize the manipulative aspect of consumer culture, as Ewen clearly did, but, at the same time, the orality of the consumer culture does offer a rather ambiguous kind of freedom and liberation. Many social workers are ambivalent about having to intervene in situations in which parents and children are in conflict around these issues. The conflicts can involve issues as minor as decisions about which sneakers to buy, and more significant ones like the adolescent desire for sexual experience.

Reality is a key factor in such situations, too, and I found that it can work to support one or the other side in these intergenerational conflicts. Parents, for example, can fend off demands for sneakers by claiming insufficient funds. But in the case of adolescent sexuality, reality usually works against the parental effort to maintain control.

This is true for a great many families in the United States.[32] If we look at immigrant populations in particular, we find that one of the primary reasons they gave for coming to the United States was to make a better life for their children. In many cases, their image of the better life included greater material abundance, which means that even in confronting the consumer culture, the parental argument starts out with a handicap. Education too, creates dilemmas for those parents who were members of the struggling middle classes in their countries of origin. They arrive with a hope that their children will have greater educational advantages in the United States. This is a modern and contemporary concern. At one time, immigrant families could take their female children out of school at the point of puberty and watch them carefully until they married; they usually married as adolescents. This is impossible now, of course, partly because compulsory school attendance laws make it illegal, but also because the parents really want their daughters to get an education. Of course, the schools are generally coeducational, and the resulting social opportunities constantly threaten values of sexual restraint that parents frequently want to uphold. Some parents modify their thinking to accommodate these realities, as González-López's (2004) research indicates.[33]

This dilemma is not peculiar to immigrants, of course, but coping with it is typically harder for newcomers, who often are confused by many other demands of American society and less familiar with it than their children.

Between developing theory and the experiences I was accumulating in the ER, and in my home care work, I found what felt like greater clarity in the concepts of psychosocial assessment and diagnosis. However, there was much more to do, before the conceptual range from intrapsychic to social was complete.

References

Ariès, P. (1962). *Centuries of childhood: A social history of family life* (R. Baldick, Trans.). New York: Random House.

Barker-Benfield, G. J. (1976). *The horrors of the half-known life: Male attitudes toward women and sexuality in nineteenth-century America.* New York: Harper & Row.

Barry, B. (2001). *Culture and equality: An egalitarian critique of multiculturalism.* Cambridge, MA: Harvard University Press.

Braudel, F. (1969). Histoire et Sciences Sociales: La Longue Durée. In *Écrits sur l'Histoire* (pp. 41–83). Paris: Flammarion.

Braudel, F. (1977). *Afterthoughts on material civilization and capitalism* (P. Ranum, Trans.). Baltimore: Johns Hopkins University Press.

Braudel, F. (1979a). *The perspective of the world: Civilization and capitalism 15th–18th century.* New York: Harper & Row.

Braudel, F. (1979b). *The structures of everyday life: Civilization and capitalism 15th–18th century.* New York: Harper & Row.

Braudel, F. (1979c). *The wheels of commerce: Civilization and capitalism 15th–18th century.* New York: Harper & Row.

Canak, W., & Swanson, L. (1998). *Modern Mexico.* Boston: McGraw-Hill.

Devlin, J. (1987). *The superstitious mind: French peasants and the supernatural in the nineteenth century.* New Haven: Yale University Press.

Duby, G. (1976). *Rural economy and country life in the medieval west.* Columbia: University of South Carolina Press.

Duby, G. (1988). *Marriage in the Middle Ages: Of love and other essays* (pp. 10–33). Paris: Flammarion.

Durkheim, E. (1898). Représentations individuelles et représentations collectives (Individual performances and collective representations). *Revue de Metaphysique et de Morale, 6,* 273–302.

Durkheim, É. (1960). *Les gorms élémentaires de la vie réligieuse: Le système totémique en Australie* (*The elementary forms of religious life: The totemic system in Australia*) (3rd ed.). Paris: Quadrige, Presses Universitaires de France.

Ewen, S. (1976). *Captains of consciousness: Advertising and the social roots of the consumer culture.* New York: McGraw-Hill.

Ewen, S. (1988). *All consuming images: The politics of style in contemporary culture.* New York: Basic Books.

Ewen, S., & Ewen, S. (1982). *Channels of desire: Mass images and the shaping of American consciousness.* New York: McGraw-Hill.

Fenichel, O. (1945). *The psychoanalytic theory of neurosis.* New York: W. W. Norton.

Foster, G. M. (1962). *Traditional cultures, and the impact of technological change.* New York: Harper & Row.

Foster, G. M. (1967). Peasant society and the image of limited good. In J. M. Potter, M. N. Díaz, & G. M. Foster (Eds.), *Peasant society: A reader* (pp. 300–323). Boston: Little, Brown.

Freud, A. (1946). *The ego and mechanisms of defense* (C. Baines, Trans.). New York: International Universities Press.

Freud, S. (1959). Charakter und analerotik (Character and anal eroticism). In *The standard edition of the complete psychological works of Sigmund Freud, Vols. 1–26* (Vol. 9, pp. 168–175). London: Hogarth Press. (Original work published 1908)

Freud, S. (1961). The ego and the id. In *The standard edition of the complete psychological works of Sigmund Freud, Vols. 1–23* (Vol. 19, pp. 3–66). London: Hogarth Press. (Original work published 1923)

Fuller, T. (2007, December 27). In Laos, Chinese motorcycles change lives. *New York Times,* p. A7.

Gerth, H., & Mills, C. W. (1958). *From Max Weber: Essays in sociology.* New York: Oxford University Press.

González-López, G. (2004). Fathering Latina sexualities: Mexican men and the virginity of their daughters. *Journal of Marriage and Family, 66,* 1118–1130.

González-Wippler, M. (1975). *Santería: African magic in Latin America.* Garden City, NY: Anchor Press/Doubleday.

Gurevich, A. (1988). *Medieval popular culture: Problems of belief and perception* (J. M. Bak & P. A. Hollingsworth, Trans.). Cambridge: Cambridge University Press.

Hanly, C. (1992). From animism to rationalism. In P. Gay (Ed.), *The problem of truth in applied psychoanalysis* (pp. 155–169). New York: Guilford Press.

Hendricks, G. (1974). *The Dominican diaspora: From the Dominican Republic to New York City—Villagers in transition.* New York: Teachers College Press.

Kondrat, M. E. (2002). Actor-centered social work: Revisioning "person-in-environment" through a critical theory lens. *Social Work, 47,* 435–448.

Kroeber, A. L., & Kluckhohn, C. (1963). *Culture: A critical review of concepts and definitions.* New York: Vintage Books.

Ladurie, E. L. (1975). *Montaillou: Village Occitan de 1294 à 1324.* Paris: Éditions Gallimard.

Ladurie, E. L. (1979a). Amenorrhoea in time of famine: Seventh to twentieth century. In B. Reynolds & S. Reynolds (Trans.), *The territory of the historian* (pp. 255–273). Chicago: University of Chicago Press.

Ladurie, E. L. (1979b). Normandy's woods and fields. In B. Reynolds & S. Reynolds (Trans.), *The territory of the historian* (pp. 133–172). Chicago: University of Chicago Press.

Miller, K. A. (1985). *Emigrants and exiles: Ireland and the Irish exodus to North America.* New York: Oxford University Press.

Munthe, A. (1929). *The story of San Michele.* New York: Carroll and Graf.

National Association of Social Workers. (2000). *Code of ethics of the National Association of Social Workers.* Washington, DC: Author.

Nazzari, M. (1980). The significance of present-day changes in the institution of marriage. *Review of Radical Political Economics, 12*(2), 63–75.

Nussbaum, M. C. (1999). *Sex and social justice.* New York: Oxford University Press.

Okin, S. M. (1997, October/November). Is multiculturalism bad for women? *Boston Review, 22*(4). Retrieved from http://www.bostonreview.net/BR22.5/okin.html

Owusu-Bempah, K. (2003–2004). Cultural values and community support systems: Libertaranism versus communitarianism. *BSU/IUC Journal of Social Work Theory and Practice, 8.* Retrieved from http://www.bemidjistate.edu/academics/publications/social_work_journal/issue08/articles/1_Cultural_Values.htm

Ozment, S. (2001). *Ancestors: The loving family in Old Europe.* Cambridge, MA: Harvard University Press.

Piers, G., & Singer, M. B. (1971). Shame and guilt: A psychoanalytic study. In *Shame and guilt: A psychoanalytic and a cultural study* (pp. 15–55). New York: W. W. Norton.

Pirenne, H. (1933). *Economic and social history of medieval Europe.* New York: Harcourt Brace.

Pollitt, K. (1997). Whose culture? A response to Susan Okin's "Is multiculturalism bad for women?" In J. Cohen & M. Howard (Eds.), *Is multiculturalism bad for women?* (pp. 27–30). Princeton, NJ: Princeton University Press.

Poster, M. (1978). *Critical theory of the family.* New York: Seabury Press.

Puig, M. (1968–1976). *Boquitas pintadas.* Barcelona, Caracas, México: Seix Barral.

Randall, M. M. (Ed.). (1972). *Beyond nationalism: The social thought of Emily Greene Balch.* New York: Twayne Publishers.

Reich, W. (1949). *Character analysis.* New York: Noonday Press.

Reynolds, B. C. (1942). *Learning and teaching in the practice of social work.* Silver Spring, MD: National Association of Social Workers.

Richmond, M. (1917). *Social diagnosis.* New York: Russell Sage Foundation.

Róheim, G. (1971). *The origin and function of culture.* Garden City, NY: Anchor Books.

Rösener, W. (1994). The peasantry of Europe. In J. Le Goff (Series Ed.) & T. M. Barker (Trans.), *The making of Europe.* Oxford: Blackwell.

Schemo, D. J. (2002, September 5). Study finds mothers unaware of children's sexual activity. *New York Times.* Retrieved from http://www.nytimes.com/2002/09/05/us/study-finds-mothers-unaware-of-children-s-sexual-activity.html

Schor, J. B. (1991). *The overworked American: The unexpected decline of leisure.* New York: Basic Books.

Schultz, T. W. (1964). *Transforming traditional agriculture. Studies in comparative economics.* New Haven: Yale University Press.

Shostak, A. B. (1969). *Blue-collar life.* New York: Random House.

Spielberg, S. (Director). (1974). *The Sugarland express* [Motion picture]. United States: Universal Studios.

Thompson, E. P. (1963). *The making of the English working class.* New York: Random House.

Tönnies, F. (1935). *Community and society.* Darmstadt: Wissenschaftliche Buchgesellschaft.

Weber, E. (1976). *Peasants into Frenchmen: The modernization of rural France, 1870–1914.* Stanford: Stanford University Press.

Wells, B. E., & Twenge, J. M. (2005). Changes in young people's sexual behavior and attitudes, 1943–1999: A cross-temporal meta-analysis. *Review of General Psychology, 9,* 249–261.

Woodham-Smith, C. (1989). *The great hunger: Ireland 1845–1849.* New York: Old Town Books.

CHAPTER EIGHT
A THEORY FOR SOCIAL WORK PRACTICE? (1999–2007)

IN 1999, THE emergency room (ER) had become too small for the burgeoning patient population, and the institution embarked on an ambitious expansion and modernization. The adult ER became some three times larger than before, while the completely new pediatric area was some four or five times larger.

During the construction, from November 1999 to October 2001, my colleague and I shared an extremely cramped office, located more or less between the two ERs. But I was able to continue student supervision, with two students in 1999 to 2000, and three in the following year.

Even with greatly enlarged facilities, the patient load increased rapidly and other expansions became necessary. My own workload increased correspondingly, except that, beginning in early 2005, another worker was responsible for inpatient services.

Now there were two ERs with separate administrations, and somewhat separate cultures. The staffs increased in size accordingly. I suddenly found that I was one of the eldest (the third or fourth from the top) working in both areas. I had known many of the senior physicians and nurses since the 1980s. It was generally a pleasure to work with them, and the younger staff mostly followed the example of the more-experienced staff.

Most of the house staff were young enough to be my children. In general, they were talented and committed, continuing the improvement that had begun in the late 1980s and early 1990s. A degree of self-selection was at work, inasmuch as the rise of managed care meant that many physicians in training could not reasonably fantasize about living in flourishing circumstances. By contrast, in the 1980s, when I spent a fair amount of time in the staff lounge, it was littered with free medical journals, which I read. A few of them served the sole purpose of advising physicians on how to spend their incomes. I vividly recall an article with an illustration of an aggressively masculine and handsome man, apparently a doctor, in beautifully tailored sports clothes, standing by a handsome horse, on which a woman, also extremely attractive and beautifully clad, was mounted. She looked pretty expensive herself.

The positive changes were particularly evident in the adult ER, where the majority of the residents were in an emergency medicine program. Thus they wanted to be where they were working and were not internists on a rotation they didn't much like.

∽ . ∽ . ∽

THE ELDERLY AMONG the patient population continued to diminish, even as the pediatric area's patient load rapidly increased. Ethnically, our patients became still more diverse, with immigrants from Central America, Africa, South Asia, the Middle East, and other places joining the other large groups that had already become settled in our vicinity.

The number of patients without medical coverage seemed to take up more of my time, particularly when they needed approval of medications that they could not afford. This issue took sometimes distinctive patterns.

By this time, the adult ER had a "Fast-track" area for patients whose complaints seemed susceptible to fairly quick resolution. Frequently, the staff there would call me to approve prescriptions, and I soon found that when the patient was male with a Spanish surname and needed antibiotics, he was likely a Mexican immigrant, working under substandard conditions in either food service or construction, who had gotten hurt on the job. Hand injuries were especially common. There is a whole world, on which the economy depends, of quasi-clandestine enterprise and employment involving immigrants. One injured Mexican construction worker, I recall, arrived with his Korean foreman. Neither spoke competent English.

In all cases in which patients lacked coverage, I would try to point them toward help in applying for whatever they might be eligible. For many, who were well established in the United States, this had to do with loss of jobs and coverage, jobs with no coverage or with unaffordable coverage, or, frequently, Medicaid HMO coverage that somehow did not work. With patients whose immigration status was at least ambiguous, I discussed potential coverage in relation to documentation without actually asking if they were legal residents.

Though I seldom shared personal information, there were occasions when it seemed appropriate to mention that my great-grandmother probably entered the United States in 1870 without observing any formalities. She sailed from the port of Liverpool and landed at Grosse Île, the Ellis Island of Canada, near Quebec. There is no document of her entry to the United States—but there is her certificate of marriage to my great-grandfather in Aurora, Illinois.

Sometimes these seemingly mundane matters turned into significant interventions. One day Fast Track called me to approve prescriptions for a recent immigrant from North Africa, who had chicken pox. His English was minimal. When I asked the medical staff how they had communicated with him, they said one of the house staff, allegedly an Arabic speaker, had interpreted. The man was covered in pocks and looked miserable and frightened. I used telephone interpretation with a competent and trained Arabic interpreter to speak with him.

I asked initially if he was afraid he had some really dangerous illness. The doctors who had taken care of him had not clearly explained his illness and its degree of seriousness. I reassured him that in the United States of America almost everybody gets chicken pox as a child, and that it is not usually a very serious illness. I explained that I knew from experience that there are many parts of the world where chicken pox is rarer, and not everybody gets it.

The man had been staying with friends but had moved out of their home for fear of infecting their children. Temporarily homeless, he had been lurking in a corner near Yankee Stadium.

After checking with the doctor, I explained that it was more likely he had caught the illness from the children than the other way round. Also, as bad as he looked, he was probably not going to be infectious much longer. He was immensely relieved. I also discovered that the patient was diabetic, a fact that the previous interpreter's interview had not elicited, and, of course, I also approved his prescriptions.

It is worth noting Mary Richmond's comments, long ago but still very apt, on the perils of using an indigenous interpreter, as in this case, the allegedly Arabic-speaking staff member.

> The use of interpreters also presents difficulties. When people who do not speak English have to be interviewed through one, the results are the reverse of satisfactory. As one worker put it, if an interpreter can fulfill his part in an honest, unbiased, and intelligent way he had better be turned into a social worker and do the case work needed himself. Such interpreters are almost non-existent. (Richmond, 1917, p. 75)[1]

Another of my more curious tasks was in reaching the families of patients who had lost the ability to speak, usually because of a stroke. The inpatient neurology worker once asked to borrow the ER's camera—used for documenting abuse injuries—to photograph such a man so that she could go to what she thought was his neighborhood to look for family, friends, or associates. The staff refused to let her take it, so

I took the pictures myself, on the floor. The man was Hispanic, seemed late middle age, was physically intact, and I thought he could understand me when we spoke. A search of his pockets had found nothing. I read his chart, focusing on the Ambulance Call Report, which the ambulance crew had left at triage. They had come upon him just as he was losing the ability to speak, and had gotten a garbled version of his name, which I was able to correct, and of his address. I could see immediately that the address was incorrect, a four digit number on a cross street, in a part of the Bronx where all cross streets have numbers with a maximum of three digits. However, the number was plausible for either of the avenues at the ends of the block where he was found. The sheet also designated the point where they had found him, and that he had smelled of alcohol. It was warm weather, and I envisaged him sitting with friends on the street, drinking beer, and playing dominoes on a piece of cardboard atop a milk crate. I thought about the way he looked, which was only moderately deteriorated, and then tried to imagine his psychosocial circumstances. If he had been living with family, it seemed likely they would have tracked him down already. But if he was a single, older man, it seemed likely that someone was paying some attention to his needs, or else he would have looked worse.

I then wrote a note suggesting that whoever went in search of his associates should hypothesize the existence of a woman (not a relative), probably Puerto Rican, age between 35 and 55 or 60 years living in the area where he had been picked up. I suggested inquiries in local bodegas, as a start. The neurology worker went to the field with someone from Public Relations. People at the first bodega recognized the photograph but said the people in the hardware store next door knew him better. They found the hypothetical woman buying mousetraps in the hardware store. I do not know her age, but as I suspected, she had taken it as a duty to make sure the patient had enough to eat and a clean shirt to put on.

Another such patient was a middle-aged man who arrived in an ambulance, also unable to speak. We searched his pockets, and, though there was no really official identification, a membership card in a club revealed his name. He also had some pieces of paper with telephone numbers. I did not recognize the area code. When I called, those who answered said of course they knew the patient. There were sounds of merriment and revelry in the background. It turned out I had interrupted a wedding party in a tavern in the west of Ireland. Everybody there seemed to know our patient, as I had reached his native village. Some of them knew his family and friends in the United States.

Sometimes the nurse practitioners would ask me to help locate patients we wanted to recall for further treatment. Most of them were either young children with positive cultures for strep throat or teenage girls with chlamydia. Usually, the nurse practitioners were able to reach them with a simple call, but there were cases in which this was impossible. There were several reasons for this: Some resulted from mistakes by our registration staff, others from telephone shut-offs, and others still from patients' using other peoples' telephones because they had none of their own. A few had purposely given false information, probably because they were using somebody else's Medicaid card.

My first step was to try another straightforward call to the number given. This sometimes worked, if only because somebody had gotten home from work. Failing that, I would try to call a neighbor in the building, whose numbers I would get from the Verizon address directory. I tried to match the patients with the neighbor I would call according to ethnicity and age (roughly determined by first name). I came to have a certain respect for those pests, the telemarketers, because I found I had 15 to 20 seconds to establish myself as a legitimate caller and gain the neighbor's cooperation. It was rare for anybody to refuse assistance. The only parts of the Bronx where people were surly or even hung up on me were affluent areas like Riverdale. The call-a-neighbor approach usually worked, and I did it so often that once, when I called, speaking Spanish, and got a child, I asked to speak to a grownup. The person who responded spoke to me in English and said she was a neighbor watching the child for her mother and that some months before I had actually called her for the same reason.

Sometimes it proved impossible to reach a neighbor, and then I would use the OASISnyc.net Web site (http://www.oasisnyc.org) to verify the existence of the building. In extreme cases I would use online aerial photographs to double check. Once, I wrote a note recording my efforts to contact the patient and explained that the building, if it had ever existed, had been demolished so as to construct the Bruckner Expressway.

OUR RESPONSE TO child abuse and neglect became more systematic. The institution's Child Advocacy Center took a large role in centralizing the response to cases of children in jeopardy.

One of the more unusual child maltreatment cases in this period was a baby under a year old, whose mother brought her to the ER and said the child had not eaten in three weeks. Though the child was undernourished, the mother was exaggerating a bit. We asked why she was not feeding the child adequately. She claimed that she had been unable to get public assistance, and that she had no one to accompany her to the Women, Infants, and Children office, where she could have gotten formula. Why did she need a companion on such an errand, given that she was young, apparently healthy and articulate in English? She gave very vague and irrational reasons. We also learned from the Emergency Children's Service (ECS) that she had received initial payments of public assistance. We admitted the child, who began to thrive in the hospital and gradually became more related. One of my students at the time, as a project for a paper, made daily visits to her on the floor and observed her gains in responsiveness over a week or so.

In the end, we discovered that what was going on was a sort of analog of Munchhausen's by Proxy—anorexia by proxy. This was not immediately obvious, as the mother appeared well nourished and perhaps 30 pounds above optimal weight. What we did not know, however, was that she had formerly been obese. A few months later, when I saw her in the Family Court, her clothes hung loosely on her frame. She had become attractively slender and, we learned, was supporting herself as an exotic dancer. Other abuse and neglect cases were intertwined with domestic violence. I arrived one afternoon to find five children in the ER in the care of the police, who had made the initial report to the State Central Registry. One of the inpatient pediatric workers, filling in before my arrival, had just made another.

The police explained that a neighbor had called 911 early in the morning to say that the children's mother, during the night, and apparently after a conflict with her live-in boyfriend, had gone off to a hospital and asked the neighbor to watch the children. The neighbor agreed but called the police when the new day dawned and she, with her own three children, had to keep an appointment with her obstetrician. Some of the children seemed developmentally delayed, and one boy explained some scars at the bottom of his neck as small wounds the boyfriend had inflicted with a knife. I immediately reported this, of course. When I interviewed the boy, he also described an automobile trip with this man, which included what sounded like a drive-by shooting.

Finally, the mother arrived, having gone to another hospital for treatment of some minor injuries and to seek her boyfriend who had gone to the same hospital. Another fact also impressed me: the detectives who had responded were not from the familiar Special Victims Unit, which deals with sexual offenses and child abuses, but from the Major Case Squad, a testimonial to the man's eminence in criminal endeavor.

The ECS worker and I interviewed the mother, who explained that she herself was employed as a home attendant. Her relationship with her boyfriend had gone on for a little over a year. Fairly early in their relationship he had told her of people he had killed. After hearing this, I excused myself to make a fourth report: that the mother acknowledged that, while at work, she had left her children in the care of a confessed murderer.

When I encountered victims of domestic violence, I asked them if their children had been present during the violent incident and if they had seemed upset at seeing their mothers injured. Positive answers to these questions indicated reportable child maltreatment.

Some mothers were apprehensive when I told them I would report the situation. Sometimes they feared that the children's services would take their children, and they were skeptical of my assurances that if they were cooperative the agency would try to help them. In some cases, there was an ambivalence about the man in question.

One woman came to the ER with her baby and with another woman. Her husband had given her noticeable injuries. They were from a former French colony in Africa. As usual, I explained her legal options, and she firmly said that although she wanted a divorce, she did not want to proceed legally against the man. God, not she, would be the one to punish him. She was distressed when I explained I had a legal obligation to report him, inasmuch as the child had witnessed the assault and had, she said, been upset.

She visited me for another conversation a few days later. Apparently, the ECS worker had visited and asked her to cooperate with the Administration for Children's Services' investigation. She had expressed her reluctance to take legal steps, citing her religious scruples. The worker had said, "I don't care about your religion." She took this remark as dismissive and contemptuous, when, probably, he had meant, instead, that it was not appropriate to his job to engage in religious disputation.

This situation raised cultural issues, of course, but not the ones one would consider typical. The god she spoke of was not an autochthonous African deity, but the god of Catholic Christianity, introduced by European colonialism. Her faith was certainly strong and meaningfully authentic for her, but was it authentic in the sense many multiculturalists have in mind?

∽ • ∽ • ∽

ALTHOUGH I DID not work in psychiatry, in those years, I worked in concert with the psychiatric staff in several types of cases. One was the kind of pediatric patient who came to the ER with a complaint, from parents or, often, the school, of disruptive behavior. Psychiatry would often decide, especially with adolescents, that admission to a psychiatric hospital would not best serve them. Often they had previous admissions, with diagnoses of oppositional-defiant disorder (ODD) or conduct disorder. For them, the preferred approach involved the Family Court, for a petition alleging each to be a person in need of supervision, and also the Administration for Children's Services, to arrange the placement.

None of these processes moved forward as quickly as the often desperate parents wanted. Having some of these young people in their homes was often frustrating and sometimes frightening. If they were only oppositionally defiant they were often ungovernable, truant, frequent runaways. If they had a conduct disorder, their aggression toward others, including, sometimes, family members, could be a clear danger. The ER could not arrange immediate relief of these overwhelming problems, but I tried to help parents understand that if they persisted, they would eventually be able to get help from the Family Court.

I would explain—in colloquial language—that Section 732 of the Family Court Act provides for judicial intervention if the child in question "is an habitual truant or is incorrigible, ungovernable, or habitually disobedient and beyond the lawful control of his or her parents, guardian or lawful custodian." However, Section 735 requires extensive efforts at "diversion" before filing of a petition, to ensure that all possible efforts to avert judicial intervention and placement are exhausted. On occasion, it would be possible to send a letter to the court, detailing the efforts parents had made to address the problems through counseling, therapy, and involvement with other agencies and suggest that this ought to suffice to demonstrate that they had done all they could short of petitioning the court. On other occasions, I would explain the diversion process to the parents and encourage them to follow through with it despite the time and frustration involved. I would also try to help them understand the reason for the diversion requirement, including the fact that some parents are actually crazier than their children, and that diversion was designed to weed out families who really could resolve their problems in other ways.

This was sometimes cold comfort for those parents who had to contend with adolescent children who were budding psychopaths. I recall, for example, a mother whose daughter, at 12 or 13 years of age, besides chronically running away and acting out sexually in dangerous ways, also stole from everybody in the household. She even raided her little brother's piggy bank. The mother slept with her purse under her pillow.

Another 12-year-old girl was pleasant enough at home, did fairly well when she went to school, and generally did not stand out. However, she had a proclivity for running away for a few days at a time and, while gone, for sex with multiple partners. Her mother came to me for clarification of why some of the psychiatrists thought she was a borderline personality, others that she had ODD, and still others that she was bipolar. The mother had Googled these terms and found herself as confused as when she started. We talked at some length about this, and I showed her the relevant passages in *DSM IV* and explained that there are some psychiatric illnesses that are hard to fit into sharp definitions and that her daughter's behavior partly fitted into the listed characteristics of all these disorders.

With some of the milder cases—those who generally had diagnoses of ODD—it was sometimes possible to arrange therapeutic follow-up and to set up guidelines for family members to follow in their dealings with each other. One girl, and her mother, with an on-call therapist from an agency, sat with me at a computer while we agreed on wording of a written contract between them. It included lists of opprobrious words they would try to avoid using—"asshole, puta, cabrón," among others. They specified these utterances and committed themselves to asking other family members to agree to the same forms of restraint. As they did so, they became increasingly embarrassed at this exposure of their behavior.

Another kind of case in which I worked with Psychiatry was with parents who refused to sign applications for their children's voluntary admission for inpatient treatment. This became my responsibility because their refusal constituted medical neglect under the law, and I was the primary source of reports in the ER.

However, I always tried to discuss this issue with the parents and to understand the reasons for their reluctance. Quite often, I succeeded in securing their cooperation, though not always happily. There were several reasons for these parental attitudes.

In some cases, the shock of hearing a recommendation for psychiatric admission had so upset them that they needed time and more discussion of the clinical issues. Sometimes the psychiatrists had not sufficiently clarified the situation and the reasoning that went into the recommendation. Sometimes they had done so, but the parents were too upset to hear clearly. On one occasion, the issue was nothing more complicated than the mother's uncertainty as to how she would travel to Harrison, New York, to visit her child in Saint Vincent's Hospital.

Some parents needed clarification about the use of medication. In some cases, they confused psychiatric medications with dangerous drugs sold on the street. Another time, a psychiatrist told a father that they would start the patient on one or another antipsychotic or antidepressant and then would "experiment" until they found the most effective mix of medications. "Oh, you're going to experiment on him," said the father, assuming this meant his child would be a research guinea pig. I was able to clarify this misunderstanding.

On another occasion, the parents were reluctant to accept admission for their suicidal daughter who had a psychotic break. They were people of modest education from one of the poorest and most backward countries in the world, and I thought I might have to explain psychiatry to them in simple terms. To my surprise, I found they were fans of psychiatry, as two older siblings had psychotic breaks too and had done well with hospitalization. Their only objection this time was based on their belief that they could maintain a suicide watch until the patient saw an outpatient psychiatrist. This seemed reasonable. I called the psychiatrists, and we discussed this with the family and arrived at an agreement.

However, some of the parents were themselves extremely bizarre. I recall a couple who objected to hospitalization of the woman's daughter. Her new husband, who was much older, and with whom she barely shared English as a common language, was hostile and threatening in a somewhat vague way. At one point in the interview, he commented on how he could stab me in the eye with a knife. I ignored this and turned the conversation to my basic argument in such cases, which essentially was that they would suffer less ignominy if they signed the Minor Voluntary Application for Admission, than if they forced us to involuntarily hospitalize the patient, which would also mean a report to State Central Registry for medical neglect. I read them the form and interpreted it into Spanish for the mother, and eventually she signed.

Later in the evening, they tried to back out by failing to rendezvous with the patient at the psychiatric hospital. I had to confront them with the necessity of reporting them if they did not cooperate.

∽ • ∽ • ∽

IN THESE YEARS, I supervised several fine students from various schools of social work, but mostly Fordham and Stony Brook. I did more to develop my approach to teaching students how to write chart notes. At the beginning of the fall semester, I would tell them this would be a strong focus of my approach. I also said that I anticipated they would need a lot of help and that I was saying this before seeing their first efforts at note writing. I also made the point that notes had to be in standard English, not because it is inherently "better," or is "good English," but because it is a social convention to use this particular dialect in professional settings. Also, I tried to develop a way of making social work notes distinctively different from medical and nursing notes. Because we addressed ourselves especially to the patient's reality as a person in several situations at once, only one of them being the hospital itself, it was necessary to provide a narrative, brief, concise, but still a narrative of the patient's situation, both intrapsychically and socially. I introduced students to note writing by pointing out that chart notes are a particularly challenging literary form—much more difficult, for example, than papers written for classes. Papers, after all, have only one audience, and usually pose and answer a question or questions. Notes, by contrast, have several audiences, and serve multiple purposes, some of them in varying degrees of conflict.

Among these are documentation of the patient's needs, the situation out of which they arise, and the weaknesses and resources available to the patient. This, in itself, is fairly straightforward but happens in a context in which it frequently justifies courses of action that the social worker thinks the medical and nursing staff should take to best serve the patient's health and safety. Sometimes notes are an argument for a specific view of the patient. Such a view might implicitly challenge some form of prejudice. It might also—and this was a frequent occurrence—present the basis for a report of abuse or neglect. Notes could also serve to document the social worker's intervention, and thus form a protection for the worker. More important still, also in form and content, they put forward the social work profession as a distinctive member of the team. For this reason, I used a minimum of the kind of abbreviations prevalent in medical and nursing notes, which are primarily devices for conveying measurable data. Writing social work notes, essentially, is a clinical skill. Students responded well to this challenge, and most said that I had helped them become better writers.

IN THESE SAME years, my theoretical approach developed, and I made strides in linking what, in earlier chapters, I have called the small and the large, or, in social work terms, the person in the situation, the situation being defined broadly.

As these thoughts developed, I shared more of it with the students and was able to link broader social thought with the material on the intrapsychic element in psychosocial assessment that they got, both in classes and in the bibliography I gave them myself. Because much of my interpretation of the situational aspect of person-in-situation was historical, some of the students would tell me that they had never been interested in their classes in history but now understood why it was important. Our discussions of cases, theoretically linked to the broader social context, certainly helped me develop, and, I hope, similarly helped the students.

Making Sense of Complexities

This seemed fairly obvious. Yes, the person does exist in a set of circles of this general sort. But this kind of conceptualization seemed quite inadequate. True, these concepts did challenge those social workers who still wanted to treat the client as an isolated and disconnected unit. But it was not clear to me what this kind of conceptual tool could offer us in social assessment and, especially, in social diagnosis. How do we systematically understand the relationships between the circles?

Social work practice routinely occurs at points where diverse cultural phenomena meet. The person in the situation is a cultural actor. So is the social worker. The situation is a cultural context. The person brings to the situation memories, conscious or not, of other situations in the personal past. So too the situation sums up the complex experiences of its participants. Each social work practitioner, too, is a person in a situation.

This is complexity, but it is not random. That participant in the situation, who is also a social worker, plays several roles. Similarly, each other participant plays several roles, but, in the same way, each person's potential range of roles, behaviors, thoughts, emotions, and expectations has limits, inclusions, and exclusions. In short, all people, in all situations, participate according to patterns and regularities, whether or not they actually live up to their own or others' expectations. The skilled social work practitioner is aware of these patterns. Professional training is an attempt to create this awareness systematically. Systematic awareness of the patterns and regularities of human experience is a basic component of social work practice skill. This applies just as much to the person's place and functioning in the social realm as in his or her intrapsychic adaptation.

As we began the new century, I thought more of the gap I still saw in my theoretical approach and found a useful theoretical tool in the notion of nonsynchronism, a bridging concept linking concepts of the development of society to the functioning of the individual. For a long time I had been using the concept of character for this purpose, but character extends out from concepts of individual personality, and reaches only part way into the social aspects of person in situation. The concept of nonsynchronism comes from the other direction, from the situation, and reaches part way into the personal aspects. It comes out of an analysis of the form, history, and development of human society.

～ • ～ • ～

"NON-SYNCHRONISM" IS AN unfamiliar, and, admittedly, not especially attractive word.[2] It translates Ungleichzeitigkeit,[3] a concept of the philosopher Ernst Bloch. Bloch's life bridged the nineteenth and twentieth centuries, and he experienced the European authoritarianisms of the time. In 1933, he fled Germany. His range was very broad, and he is one of the most important philosophers of the period.[4] The book in which Bloch put forward the idea of nonsynchronism, is *Erbschaft dieser Zeit* or *Heritage of this Time*, and appeared in the mid-1930s, when Bloch was already in exile. It included many occasional pieces[5] he had written for the more progressive journals and newspapers of the time before the Nazi takeover in Germany.

Others are pieces written in exile. Their purpose was mostly to offer cultural and philosophical explanations for the appeal of Nazism to a large minority of the German population. Nonsynchronism is the central feature of these explanations. He developed the notion conceptually in a philosophical essay embedded in the book.[6]

All human beings have organized notions of the world in which they live. These notions develop as people interact with nature and with one another. The institutions of society arise out of the form and content of these interactions. But those institutions themselves reciprocally influence that form and content. All these phenomena, of course, are varying manifestations of the same combined and uneven development. The concept of the "life-world" is useful in defining this aspect of human experience. It is a conceptually sounder approach to discussion of the differences we see over time and space between cultural groups. The concept comes out of the work of Wilhelm Dilthey, Edmund Husserl, and Ernst Cassirer,[7] among others. The historian Rudolf Vierhaus (1995) explained it in this way:

> With the concept of the "life-world" is meant the—more or less clearly—perceived reality, in which social groups and individuals relate mutually and through their thought and action produce further reality. Everything which creates coherence of meaning and establishes continuity pertains to this. The objectivations of the spirit in language and symbols, in works and institutions, but also the ways and forms of creativity, the relational patterns and life-styles, the interpretations of the world and predominant concepts. To put this another way, the life-world is social reality conditioned by space and time, in which time-honored norms and institutions exist and new ones are created. The human being does not stand opposed to it but is in it as a continually symbolically interpreted world. (pp. 13–14)

Vierhaus wrote as a social historian, but his concepts are directly applicable to the more social aspects of psychosocial assessment. After all, the work of the social historian, like the social worker's, is really a form of psychosocial assessment. For example, Le Roy Ladurie's study, Montaillou (Ladurie, 1975), is an examination and assessment of people in a situation. To be sure, the events he discussed occurred 700 years ago, but the situation is small and limited—an isolated village in the Pyrenees mountains, and his main source is the quite detailed and elaborate protocol of an inquisitorial visit by the local bishop, who meticulously records the attitudes, thoughts and behavior of the people he exhaustively interviewed.[8] Thus, Le Roy Ladurie is able to reconstruct the life-world of the villagers in a vivid and comprehensible form, even though it is so distant in time.

Because everybody inhabits at least one life-world, there are bound to be conflicts, both interpersonal and intrapsychic, between various life-worlds, which represent different developments of what Vierhaus called "the spirit," which finds expression in the various "objectivations" he described.

"Spirit," in this context, is a direct translation of the German Geist. There are perils in this, as it imposes a task on the reader, but there is no English word that fits what the German philosophical tradition understands as Geist/Spirit.[9] In common English, the word has a clearly defined meaning only in theological terminology—that is, "the holy spirit."[10] Otherwise, its meaning is fairly vague. The derivative adjective, spiritual, is still vaguer, as in the fairly common utterance: "I'm not religious, I'm spiritual."

Though it has older origins, *geist*/spirit is most associated with the work of Georg Wilhelm Friedrich Hegel (1970). In his work, it also includes many of the connotations of "mind." To define it very simply, *geist*, or spirit, is the collective project of humanity to understand and cope with natural reality. The life-worlds Vierhaus described are local and transitory patterns of the spirit's adaptation.[11] So are the various forms of social organization and interaction I described in earlier chapters.

Of course, one may define life-worlds broadly or narrowly. The whole experience of peasant culture, or of industrial society, for example, is a life-world. But the manifestation of that experience in, for example, a country or a locality is also a life-world, certainly one with greater commonalities.

Life-worlds have distinctive characteristics. We have already seen that peasant culture is generally oral and the transition to a different one in industrial society involves a turn toward anality. If we define a particular life-world in narrower terms, the characteristics will be more numerous and involve more detailed aspects of community life.

Many of the issues social workers encounter are conflicts between nonsynchronous life-worlds. This is true of conflicts between groups, within families, and within individuals.

The concept of nonsynchronism is an effort at theoretical formulation of the ways we experience complex and ever-changing reality, form perceptions of it that are distorted to some degree by previous experience, and respond in ways that reflect the disjunctures and other problems inherent in this process. Bloch (1961) defined nonsynchronism as "the unovercome vestiges of older economic realities and forms of consciousness" (p. 114).

Bloch has an idiosyncratically literary quality, not typical of German philosophical writing.[12] (He was drawn to Gustav Mahler's advance guard music, to expressionism; and he helped found Dadaism.) His language is often rather colloquial, but with imagery that demands thought. For example, his discussion of nonsynchronism begins with the somewhat enigmatic:

> Not all exist in the same now. Outwardly, they appear to do so, inasmuch as you can see them today. But they do not yet live contemporaneously with the others. They bring much earlier stuff along, and that gets mixed in. According to where one stands in real life, especially according to class, one has one's times. Older times influence older social groups. Even in the here and now, it's easy to go back, or dream back, to older times. (Bloch, 1961, p. 104)

So subjective experience is some of what nonsynchronism is about. But not all. The concept of nonsynchronism implies that things are happening out of phase with each other, hence, that there is an issue of time, a matter of when events occur, what the events are, and what conceptions people bring to participation in them.

"Unovercome" means that nonsynchronous people do not understand and experience these remnants as part of a coherently understood social pattern, that the main tendencies of material development in the society have created newer and competing forms of human relationships, behavior, and social expectations, but that the older ones still retain residual and sometimes powerful influence. Many issues for social workers, as well as their clients and patients, presently reflect their struggles with this problem.

Hence, nonsynchronism is at once a material reality and a cognitive and emotional response to the reality. It occurs because the economic, social, and legal institutions; the established patterns of behavior; and the customs and usages we experience from day to day are developing at varying rates at any point in time. Some are newer than others and represent more modern ways in which people produce and reproduce the life of society. Others are older, but persist, sometimes for a long time, after newer forms have taken the lead in determining the society's basic direction. This is combined and uneven development. The disjunctures between these manifestations are the material expressions of nonsynchronism or, as Bloch (1961) called it, *objective nonsynchronism*.

In the past, the social institutions most people experienced were fairly stable over time. As we have seen in the previous chapter, most people were peasants and lived in cultures where change was gradual.

However, the impact of industry, urbanization, and modernity changed this, making the development of society more rapid, more combined, and more uneven. Modernization included many disruptions of peasant society. Earlier, I described the Irish potato famine as an early and particularly intense example, but there have been many more since then. Some contemporary immigrations result from extreme traumas such as the civil wars and political repressions in the less developed countries.[13] Immigration to the United States has typically created situations that are nonsynchronous to the previous experience of many. But rapid economic and social change can also have a similar effect on people who have always lived in the United States. Within families, for example, nonsynchronism can intensify the differences between generations and genders in their experience of everyday reality.

More often, they experience more than one such manifestation during the same general period of their lives, though often in diverse aspects of day-to-day existence. This is objective nonsynchronism working itself out in human experiential terms, and is subjective nonsynchronism. This is not primarily a simply cognitive issue. We frequently find people experiencing life in fragmented ways, in which their responses to some parts of reality are synchronous and others are nonsynchronous. They will show great emotional investment in their efforts to reconcile these fragments of their personalities. Adorno's concept of the biphasic personality, mentioned in chapter 6, is a moderately mild example. A much more extreme one is in Fadiman's *The Spirit Catches You and You Fall Down* (Fadiman, 1997), which records a Hmong family with an epileptic child's conflicts with the expectations of the medical, child welfare, and legal authorities in California.

This is the core dilemma of social work practice. Social workers, especially those in the United States, encounter clients whose formative life experiences consist of bits and pieces from an amalgam of cultures, societies, and political and economic structures. A client may be a recent immigrant from a mostly peasant society in Mexico, a recent immigrant from a newly industrialized sector in Asia, or an American teenager who has been submerged in the consumptionist, highly sexualized environment of mall culture. Their psychosocial legacy may be traced back to Italy, Ireland, Africa, the American South, or Eastern Europe. The challenge of developing social work theory, and the best social work practice is, then, to recognize the effect of these constituent elements on human consciousness and human behavior, and to do so in the hope that truly skillful interventions will help to universalize a 21st century democracy, both in the family and in our political institutions.

References

Bloch, E. (1961). *Natural law and human dignity*. Frankfurt Am Main: Suhrkamp.
Fadiman, A. (1997). *The spirit catches you and you fall down*. New York: Farrar, Straus, and Giroux.
Geoghegan, V. (1995). *Ernest Bloch*. New York: Routledge.
Hegel, G.W.F. (1970). *Philosophy of nature*. New York: Humanities Press.

Ladurie, L. R. (1975). *Montaillou: The promised land of error.* New York: Random House.
McGoldrick, M., Giordano, J., & Garcia-Preta, N. (Eds.). (2005). *Ethnicity and family therapy* (3rd ed.). New York: Guilford Press.
Richmond, M. (1917). *Social diagnosis.* New York: Russell Sage Foundation.
Trejo, P. (1993). *Summary of Hegel's philosophy of mind.* Retrieved from http://philosophy.eserver.org/hegel-summary.html
Vierhaus, R. (1995). Reconstruction of historical life-worlds: A problem of modern cultural history. In H. Lehmann (Ed.), *Paths to a new cultural history* (pp. 7–28). Göttingen, Germany: Wallstein Verlag.

Questions for Discussion

1. What kinds of psychiatric cases did the author have in the renovated emergency room?

2. Choose one of these cases. Do you agree with what the author did? How would you have handled the case differently?

3. The author says that case notes are harder to write than a student paper. Why does he make this statement? Do you think he is correct?

4. Define nonsychronicity. What does the author mean by the concept? Choose one client. Can you use the concept of nonsychronicity to help explain the client's behavior?

5. During the author's 40 years of social work practice, he devoted a lot of time to developing a fuller theory of social work practice. Write a one-page paper summarizing his theory. How does it help you in your practice?

AFTERWORD
SOCIAL WORK: FORTY YEARS OF CHANGE
Joel Blau

CHRISTOPHER DŸKEMA'S REFLECTIONS trace his 40 years in social work. They chronicle his professional growth—the jobs he had, the cases he learned from, and the steady accumulation of practice wisdom that these experiences provided. Two other themes, however, also leaven his memoir. One, of course, was his lifelong search for a social work theory that could span everything from smaller clinical interventions to grander explanations of the social environment. Dÿkema was critical of the profession's failure on this score, and the story of his life in social work is, in part, a tale of his efforts to develop a social work theory of ever increasing complexity and sophistication. This theme is certainly explicit in the book, and his efforts are sure to provoke discussion.

A second theme in this volume is more implicit. By threading his way through 40 years of social work practice, Dÿkema encapsulates the changes that the profession has undergone during this period. Some of these changes are emphasized; others, to be fully appreciated, need to be more completely teased out.

The transformation of the client population is one particularly clear-cut development. To be sure, this change may be more dramatic in the text, because Dÿkema worked in the Bronx, a New York City borough often cited as one of the most ethnically and racially diverse communities in the United States. When he started working in the 1960s, his clients consisted chiefly of older Europeans—the Irish, Italians, and eastern European Jews, along with African Americans who had emigrated from the South, and some Latinos, most of whom were Puerto Rican. But then the population changed, and the prime driver of that change—the influx of Latinos from South and Central America—reflects a demographic shift that has altered social work practice throughout the United States. Forty years ago, few ads for social work jobs would have listed "Spanish-speaking" as a preferred skill. Now, however, many job listings insist that social workers speak Spanish, and practitioners must deal with a wide range of new problems, including the issue of undocumented immigrants, their transition from largely peasant societies to modern American capitalism, and the cultural distinctions among people from different Latin American countries. Dÿkema criticizes the theoretical inadequacies of ethnic studies in social work and is equally harsh on the pursuit of "cultural competence," its professional analogue. Nevertheless, it was his keen awareness of this demographic shift that impelled his search for better theory in social work. The Bronx may have been his laboratory, but as the consequences of a changing client population has swept the nation, his theory building has become relevant everywhere.

A second trend that Dÿkema highlights is the move toward business-oriented administrators in social agencies. Of course, in a hospital setting like that in which Dÿkema worked, the introduction of diagnostic-related groupings (DRGs) in 1983 marked a critical policy shift. Before DRGs, social workers used their professional judgment to determine when patients could be safely discharged from the hospital. When the Reagan administration implemented the DRGs, however, it began to pay hospitals a fixed sum based on the average number of days for an illness. If the hospital could discharge a patient early, it would make money, but if the patient overstayed, it would incur a loss (Blau, 2010).

The introduction of the profit motive into the calculation of when a patient could leave the hospital eroded the hospital social worker's standing as an autonomous professional and was just one of a number of ways in which social work yielded to business values. Subsequently, many social programs have been privatized so that their services are contracted out to a private nonprofit run on a business model with a human services workforce that is less likely to be unionized (see Fabricant & Burghardt, 1992). As Dÿkema noted, nothing epitomizes this trend more dramatically than the widespread appointment of business and other non–social work managers as their executive directors. Business managers, it was thought, would run these social agencies more efficiently. Lacking social workers' "soft-headedness," they were supposed to be able to do something about poverty, too.

The pursuit of legitimacy is another trend that permeates the last 40 years. Dÿkema mentioned this issue when discussing his failure to obtain his doctorate at Columbia. Dismissing "the crude empiricism" of quantification as the leading research methodology, he contended that social work has averted its gaze from bigger, more interesting, but less quantifiable issues, to count. In this desire to count, social work is mimicking more prestigious social sciences disciplines like economics, political science, and sociology (see O'Connor, 2001). Nevertheless, it is hardly coincidental that this pursuit of numbers coincides with a decline in social activism, as the kinds of political activity in which Dÿkema was once involved—unions, human service organizing, and meaningful political alternatives—fade from view.

The social work profession is surely not the only group to have been affected by this trend; the political demobilization of the whole American electorate is one of the most striking features of the past 40 years. Still, the trend does echo the reaction to Abraham Flexner's 1915 declaration that social work is too interested in social reform to be classified as a profession. In the aftermath of Flexner's declaration, social workers in the 1920s tried to gain legitimacy by turning to psychoanalysis (Ehrenreich, 1985). More recently, as social workers worry about funding for their jobs and their loss of professional status, many practitioners, like those in other professions, have quieted down, and many social work educators have turned to depoliticized, heavily quantitative research.

If these developments are changes that Dÿkema noted, there are others that he underemphasized. The most prominent is, of course, the conservative drift of national politics and its effects on social welfare. As the U.S. economy stagnated in the late 1970s, conservatives seized the opportunity to blame government spending in general and social welfare spending in particular for our economic problems. Social welfare, they said, was quashing the natural productivity of American capitalism. Cut it, and the economy would blossom again (see Murray, 1984; Perelman, 2007).

In subsequent years, virtually every major U.S. social program has either been cut or modified to require work or make it more marketlike. Most states, for example, have tightened the eligibility rules for unemployment benefits; general assistance programs for single adults have been slashed almost everywhere; Bill Clinton, a Democratic president, signed the 1996 welfare reform bill that enforced work rules and placed a five-year lifetime limit on eligibility; food programs have metamorphosed from an entitlement to a neighborhood charity; and the Housing and Urban Development budget has declined about 60 percent from its 1978 peak (see Blau, 1992, 2010; U.S. Department of Housing and Urban Development, 2011). This shredding of the safety net has spawned more poverty, and that poverty is of the most desperate sort. It is one thing to be poor; it is quite another when 40 years later, even the poor are downwardly mobile and poverty may mean homelessness.

For social workers, a resource shortage has been one obvious result of this trend. Social workers help people satisfy their common human needs; they are supposed to help them get welfare, jobs, food, housing, and medical care. But just as even the most determined job seeker cannot will herself or himself into a nonexistent job, a social worker aiding a battered woman cannot access an independent source of income if none exists, any more than a hospital social worker tasked with discharging a client can find affordable housing where none is available. Plainly, with the exception of a brief interlude that Dÿkema describes in the late 1960s when social agencies were fairly generous with clients, poor people have always suffered from a shortage of resources (see Cloward & Piven, 1971, 1974). But this is different. Now, when the mantra of "do more with less" bears down on the profession of social work, it has the full political, economic, and ideological apparatus behind it.

Although sympathetic observers have often noted the effects of these trends on clients, much less attention has been devoted to their consequences for the people who serve them. The first consequence stems from the message embedded in the conservative critique of social welfare: social workers are the enablers of the poor, the profession that caters to and nurtures their dependency. Social workers do not crack down sufficiently; at best, they listen and nudge people toward self-sufficiency. The most cogent response to this critique is to argue that "dependency," or more accurately, poverty, is deeply rooted in the U.S. economy, and that the affluent benefit from low wages and the admonitory message sent by a class of people on public assistance who are even worse off. Yet because this response has been delivered only occasionally, the work of the profession has been denigrated, and many labored to cope with the psychological consequences of this denigration. The wide-ranging attack on the collective bargaining rights of public sector social workers in states like Wisconsin, Ohio, and Indiana has only compounded the injury (see, for example, Moberg, 2011).

Some social workers have tried to immunize themselves against these attacks by going into private practice where, as independent professionals, they retain greater control over their hours and choice of clients. Clinical social workers in private practice could once expect that insurance companies would at least partially reimburse them or their clients on a per-session basis. In purely economic terms, however, most private practitioners are small-business people. As a result, when the HMOs of major insurance companies began to dominate the field of mental health, their takeover squeezed social workers by placing limits on their reimbursement. Hence, even if social workers in private practice are not the primary targets of the attack on the profession, they have still suffered from collateral damage.

The dispersal of social work responsibility has been another, somewhat more subtle, manifestation of the profession's recent troubles. Although it apparently did not occur during Dykema's years at Montefiore, nurses in hospitals and other mental health professionals in community agencies have taken over tasks like discharge planning and psychological counseling that used to be a social work prerogative. The loss of these tasks dilutes the profession's responsibility; it contains more than just a hint that despite the profession's diminished state, those who organize human services continue to see social workers as too political and too expensive.

AFTERWORD

The cumulative effect of this campaign on social work as a profession has been self-doubt, frustration, and burnout. Dÿkema does not seem to have experienced these feelings, because he was relatively secure as the senior emergency worker and found emotional sustenance in his determination to develop a better theory for social work. But although the number of accredited Council on Social Work Education (CSWE) programs has risen from 427 in 1985 to 679 in 2011 (compare Watkins & Pierce, 2005 with CSWE, n.d.), and NASW membership has reached 145,000, the profession struggles to maintain its footing (see http://www.naswdc.org/nasw/default.asp). Dÿkema's memoir of his 40 years in social work, with its emphasis on the need for the profession's theoretical development, testifies to the value of what social workers do, and the skill that the best bring to the cases before them. Still, if social workers are to feel better about themselves, and explain themselves more effectively to the general public, they are going to have to develop nuanced and sophisticated theories about their practice. This theoretical development is not only essential in its own right. In the face on attacks on the profession, it is also the best way for social workers to validate and justify their role.

References

Blau, J. (1992). *The visible poor: Homelessness in the United States.* New York: Oxford University Press.

Blau, J. (with Abramovitz, M.). (2010). *The dynamics of social welfare policy* (3rd ed.). New York: Oxford University Press.

Cloward, R., & Piven, F. F. (1971). *Regulating the poor: The functions of public welfare.* New York: Random House.

Cloward, R., & Piven, F. F. (1974). A strategy to end poverty. In R. Cloward & F. F. Piven, *The politics of turmoil: Poverty, race, class, and the urban crisis* (pp. 89–106). New York: Pantheon Books.

Council on Social Work Education. (n.d.). *Accreditation.* Retrieved from http://www.cswe.org/Accreditation.aspx

Ehrenreich, J. (1985). *The altruistic imagination: A history of social work and social policy in the United States.* Ithaca, NY: Cornell University Press.

Fabricant, M., & Burghardt, S. (1992). *The welfare state crisis and the transformation of social service work.* Armonk, NY: M. E. Sharpe.

Moberg, D. (2011). Capitol offensive. *In These Times, 35*(4), 26–28.

Murray, C. (1984). *Losing ground: American social policy, 1950–1980.* New York: Basic Books.

O'Connor, A. (2001). *Poverty knowledge: Social science, social policy and the poor in twentieth century U.S. history.* Princeton, NJ: Princeton University Press.

Perelman, M. (2007). *The confiscation of American prosperity.* New York: Palgrave Macmillan.

U.S. Department of Housing and Urban Development. (2011). *Investing in people and places, 2011 FY budget.* Retrieved from http://www.hud.gov/budgetsummary2011/message-from-sec.pdf

Watkins, J. M., & Pierce, D. (2005). Social work education: A future of strength or peril. *Advances in Social Work, 6,* 17–23.

QUESTIONS FOR DISCUSSION

1. Identify and interview an experienced social worker. How does the social worker think social work has changed? To what extent do her or his recollections agree with the issues raised in this chapter?

4
ENDNOTES

Chapter 1

1. All names of clients, patients, and coworkers are pseudonyms.

2. I discussed this experience in detail in *The Political Economy of Social Welfare: A Perspective* (Dÿkema, 1977).

Chapter 2

1. Though not, of course, the statistical norm.

2. I did not realize this at first, but my appearance then made many people think I was a plain-clothes police officer. I was about the right age; am, phenotypically, conventionally northwest European; and had a large moustache. Also, I dressed myself, in large part, from Army Navy stores, a form of commerce that existed to sell off the vast residue of military uniforms, and other material left over from World War II and Korea. (For example, I once bought a very useful grenade case to carry a carpenter's rule. When I was in the Boy Scouts, in the 1950s, most of us had Army surplus entrenching tools, little collapsible shovels you also wore on your belt.) Hence, I wore tan Army shirts, and in weather neither summery nor wintry, a green Army fatigue jacket. This, however, was the favored attire of white plain-clothes officers trying to fit in.

More than a few people immediately took me for a policeman. I recall once, on a street in Hunts Point, a studious lad carrying his books home from school shouting "Honky cop!" from a safe distance. Then I found that people who I interviewed were so relieved to learn I was not a police official that they relaxed and became forthcoming.

Once I realized the effect of my appearance, I took it into account in field work. None of this was intentional, initially. I descended from long lines of disdainers of showiness who saw frugality as a high virtue.

3. Later, I heard a rumor, unconfirmed, that it had belonged to a Mr. Weintraub, notorious for defrauding the Municipal Loan Program, which lent money to landlords at a favorable rate, to fix up buildings. Weintraub used the money for this purpose, but used materials so inferior that the City condemned some of his buildings immediately.

4. See Isaac Deutscher's *Lenin's Childhood* (Deutscher, 1970, p. 61).

5. It is instructive to read the historian, Jost Hermand's, account of his stay in a Hitler Youth camp in Poland. Among his reminiscences is this:

"Our KLV camp in Gross-Ottingen, which we were not allowed to leave even once in all those months, was much too isolated for us to get any real insight into prevailing conditions. Consequently, we never found out that there were no longer any Polish schools in this territory, as was also the case in parts of the more easterly and southeasterly Polish territory under German rule; that German had become the only official language in the schools" (Hermand, 1997, p. 52).

6. It had been there for years and was best known as the student's friend, where you could buy used textbooks cheap. It was quite different from its now omnipresent glitzy branches.

7. These were paraprofessionals in the New York City Department of Social Services.

8. WEP was the 1970s' version of the forced labor requited of public assistance recipients. Many of the ones assigned to the BCW had personality defects of greater or lesser seriousness. I suspect that this was because the degree of education and literacy consistent with working in our agency was high enough that truly functional personalities with these qualifications would have been employed and not receiving public benefits. Some of those that we received were clearly psychiatrically ill. One, in particular, stands out in memory because he was overtly psychotic and delusional.

9. Followers of Daniel de Leon (December 14, 1852–May 11, 1914), the theorist and leader, for many years, of the Socialist Labor Party (Herreshoff, 1973; Hillquit, 1971).

10. See Herbert Gans's *Popular Culture and High Culture* (Gans, 1974, chap. 2).

11. I must explain this code word for those who have not encountered Leninism in full bloom. Dogmatism is one of Leninism's key characteristics. In other words, there is an ideal of a pure, unsullied Leninism whose essence lies in canonical texts. At the same time, Leninist organizations confront the practical necessity of adapting everyday political activity to the reality that really revolutionary situations occur very rarely, and that the archetypal Leninist revolution—the Bolshevik Revolution in Russia—happened in a country with characteristics more or less reproduced only in some countries at the margins of capitalist development. Adaptation to other circumstances leads to compromises, including reformist activity, alliances with non-Leninists, and so forth. But then other Leninists accuse the adaptors of losing their revolutionary commitment and selling out. In the ensuing controversies disputes over the texts are frequent, with the critics accusing the adaptors of "revising" the Leninist message. Hence "revisionism."

12. This short book is one of the earliest examples of the accusation of revisionism. Kautsky was a leading figure of the Social Democratic parties of Austria and Germany, and Lenin accused him of "revising" the teachings of Marx. It is worth noting that Marx, in contrast to Lenin, was not at all a dogmatist.

13. Once, having read about the early history of socialism in the United States of America, I went to her and explained that, in September 1887, the expelled socialist members of the single taxer Henry George's dying United Labor Party in New York state formed their own party, the Progressive Labor Party, which briefly existed (Hillquit/1903, 1971). I went to Denise and told her she should say she belonged to the Second Progressive Labor Party. Denise had no sense of humor, of course, and could not relate to this. Thereafter, I

never failed to refer to the contemporary party, founded, if I recall correctly, in 1959, as the "Second Progressive Labor Party."

14. One can, in fact, easily make the argument that practice in other agency contexts requires a greater level of practical agility, and that its greatest deficiency comes from the profession's failure to develop theory at a commensurate level of sophistication.

15. The idea appealed to many others, of course, but Lerner himself never had a significant leadership role, and he moved on to other endeavors.

Chapter 3

1. Freud's adherence to Lamarckianism, for example, and his questionable anthropological speculations.

2. My field instructor at the time, when I told her I was preparing a presentation on the encounter between Marxism and psychoanalysis, expressed surprise and described a visit to the USSR, where psychiatrists decried psychoanalysis, calling it "idealism." She was quite surprised to learn that there are alternative traditions.

3. Their separate characters are briefly these. The man's power is active, progressive, defensive. He is eminently the doer, the creator, the discoverer, the defender. His intellect is for speculation and invention; his energy for adventure, for war, and for conquest, wherever war is just, wherever conquest necessary. But the woman's power is for rule, not for battle—and her intellect is not for invention or creating but for sweet ordering, arrangement, and decision. She sees the qualities of things, their claims and their places. Her great function is Praise; she enters into no contest, but infallibly judges the crown of contest. By her office, and place, she is protected from all danger and temptation. The man, in his rough work in open world, must encounter all peril and trial: to him, therefore, the failure, the offense, the inevitable error: often he must be wounded, or subdued, often misled, and *always* hardened. But he guards the woman from all this; within his house, as ruled by her, unless she herself has sought it, need enter no danger, no temptation, no cause of error or offense. This is the true nature of home—it is the place of Peace; the shelter, not only from all injury, but from all terror, doubt, and division. In so far as it is not this, it is not home; so far as the anxieties of the outer life penetrate into it, and the inconsistently-minded, unknown, unloved, or hostile society of the outer world is allowed by either husband or wife to cross the threshold, it ceases to be home; it is then only a part of that outer world which you have roofed over, and lighted fire in. But so far as it is a sacred place, a vestal temple, a temple of the hearth watched over by Household Gods, before whose faces none may come but those whom they can receive with love—so far as it is this, and roof and fire are types only of a nobler shade and light—shade as of the rock in a weary land, and light as of the Pharos in the stormy sea—so far it vindicates the name and fulfills the praise, of home.

Chapter 4

1. The theodicy question is the perennial issue of how evil can exist if there is only one God who is all-knowing, all-powerful, and all-good.

2. It now is a component of the New York State Office of Children and Family Services.

3. Handlin's book is a popularized history, without citations or bibliography of sources. Much of his material on peasant religion (Handlin, 1951) derives from the introduction to Znaniecki and Thomas's *The Polish Peasant in Europe and America* (Thomas & Znaniecki, 1958).

4. This book is out of print but is available online at Mark Poster's Web site: http://www.hnet.uci.edu/mposter/CTF/

5. Just to name a few that I have found helpful are Eugen Weber's *Peasants into Frenchmen* (Weber, 1976), Judith Devlin's *The Superstitious Mind: French Peasants and the Supernatural in the Nineteenth Century* (Devlin, 1987), and Robert Redfield's *The Primitive World and Its Transformations* (Redfield, 1953), *Peasant Society and Culture* (Redfield, 1956), and Ferdinand Tönnies's *Gemeinschaft und Gesellschaft* (Tönnies, 1935).

Chapter 6

1. Indeed, I recall one resident who had grown up, I think, in Long Island, but whose grandmother lived in the neighborhood and was, for a while, a frequent patient in the emergency room.

2. The National Institutes of Health's encyclopedia—http://www.nlm.nih.gov/medlineplus/ency/article/003646.htm#Definition—defines this term as: "Hematocrit is a blood test that measures the number of red blood cells and the size of red blood cells. It gives a percentage of red blood cells found in whole blood. This test is almost always ordered as part of a complete blood count."

3. This trend is well documented, as in this article from *Catholic New York* (Szczepanowski, 1997) "Much to offer: Conference cites church's challenge from growing Hispanic population."

The number of U.S. Hispanics who identify themselves as Catholic is in decline, according to data from the national Opinion Research Center's general social survey.

The survey, based on information from 1,202 Hispanic respondents, shows that by the mid-1990s the percentage of Hispanics who said they are Catholic was 67 percent, down from 78 percent in the early 1970s.

Father Andrew Greeley, a sociologist, decried the defection rate in an article in the September 27 issue of *America,* a Jesuit journal (Greeley, 1988).

"The equivalent of one out of seven Hispanics has left Catholicism in the last quarter of a century," he said. "If this hemorrhage should continue for the next 25 years, half of all American Hispanics will not be Catholic."

"If there is any reason to believe that the defections will not continue, I am unaware of it," Father Greeley said. "A fifth of those who were raised Catholics are no longer such. The loss is catastrophic."

He said that "most of the defection is to Protestant denominations."

Statistics show that in the early 1970s, 17 percent of U.S. Hispanics were Protestant, and now 23 percent are, he added.

The priest also noted that many people assume Hispanic Catholics are joining fundamentalist and Pentecostal groups, but half of all Hispanic Protestants are members of "moderate or even liberal Protestant denominations."

The research showed that Hispanics who change their religion are better educated, make more money, are somewhat older, and are more likely to be married.

It also showed that Hispanic Protestants go to church more often; pray more frequently; are more likely to oppose abortion, premarital and extramarital sex, and homosexuality; and are happier in their marriages, family life, and personal life.

Father Greeley first noted the erosion in numbers of Hispanic Catholics in a 1988 article (National Opinion Research Center, 1997).

4. Weber (1972) called this phenomenon "die Veralltäglilchung des Charisma," which, literally translated means "the everydayifying of charisma."

5. See Hanne Blank, 2007; Jeffcote & Tindall, 1987, pp. 17–18; and Shaw, 1971, p. 5.

6. The article in Wikipedia on this group is informative, and probably fairly accurate: http://en.wikipedia.org/wiki/Worldwide_Church_of_God

7. This is among the major themes of an important contemporary critique of the interest in ethnicity by Gelfand and Fandetti (1986).

8. Mills (1967), in the *Sociological Imagination*, called this "abstracted empiricism."

9. And some of the contributions are extremely weak, with a sad tendency toward ethnic braggadocio, among other faults. In this brief article on Czech Americans, the author has no hesitation in celebrating a man who has probably done more than any other individual to harm the American diet:

"Many Czechs went on to prominence in the United States. One of the biggest Czech entrepreneurs was Ray Kroc, the founder of the McDonald's fast-food chain. Czech-Americans were prominent in science and scholarship. The first curator of the Smithsonian Museum of Physical Anthropology was Czech." (Krestan, 1996, p. 693)

10. And let us not forget that some 15 years ago, the Surgeon General of the United States of America, Joycelyn Elders, had to leave office because she had spoken in favor of educating youths about masturbation. Later she wrote:

Masturbation: it's not a four-letter word, but the president fired me for saying it. In this so-called "communications age," it remains a sexual taboo of monumental proportions to discuss the safe and universal sexual practice of self-pleasure. No doubt, future generations will be amused at our peculiar taboo, laughing in sociology classes at our backwardness, yet also puzzled by it given our high rates of disease and premature pregnancy. We will look foolish in the light of history.

Yet to study masturbation would be to admit its role in our lives—one that many of us are not comfortable with. Instead, we discourage the practice in our children, dispensing cautionary tales that read like Steven King novellas. These myths were more understandable before Pasteur enlightened the world to the presence of germs in the 1870s; prior to his discovery, no one really knew where diseases came from. Masturbation was blamed for dreaded conditions like syphilis and gonorrhea, as well as for their ramifications: dementia, blindness and infertility, to name a few. It is remarkable that some of these rumors still circulate despite clear evidence that they are unfounded.

A friend, a senior citizen, stopped me after church one Sunday and said, "Please tell the children that masturbation won't hurt them. I spent my entire youth in agony waiting to go blind, because my parents told me that's what would happen if I masturbated. I guess I could have stopped, but going blind seemed the better option." We all want to tell our children the truth about their bodies and sex, but many of us are afraid of the consequences. Parents need to let go of the idea that ignorance maintains innocence and begin teaching age-appropriate facts to children. Informed children know what sexual abuse and harassment are, what normal physical closeness with others is, and what should be reported, and to whom. Rather than tell children that touching themselves is forbidden, parents may gently explain that this is best done in private (Elders & Kilgore, 1997).

11. For example, the indefatigable Walter, whose immense *My Secret Life* I will discuss in a minute, uses this terminology, though toward the end of his massive book, Walter himself does use the word "come" in its modern sense.

12. And further:
Relations within the bourgeois family were regulated by strict sex-role divisions. The husband was the dominant authority over the family, and he provided for the family by work in the factory or market. The wife, considered less rational and less capable, concerned herself exclusively with the home, which she cleaned and decorated, sometimes with the aid of servants, to suit the social status of the husband. The husband was considered an autonomous being, a free citizen, upon whom the wife was dependent. Bourgeois women were relative creatures whose sense of self was derived from their husbands' place in the world. The major interest of the wife for a good part of the marriage concerned the children: she was to raise them with the utmost attention, a degree of care new in family history. Children were reevaluated by the bourgeoisie becoming important beings for the parents. A new degree of intimacy and emotional depth characterized the relations between parents and children of this class. A novel form of maternal love was thought natural to women. Women were not simply to tend to the survival of their children, but to train them for a respectable place in society. More than that, they were encouraged to create a bond between themselves and the children so deep that the child's inner life could be shaped to moral perfection. Thus for a large part of their lives bourgeois women were confined to the home as never before; they were to nurture their children, maintain the home, and cater to their husbands, leaving aside the great transformations of politics and economics going on around them (Poster, 1978).

13. Of these, perhaps the most interesting is J. Marion Sims, a physician who invented the procedure for surgical repair of the vesico-vaginal fistula, a complication of childbirth that leaves an opening between the unfortunate woman's bladder and her vagina, with the result that she cannot control her urine. In his quest for a procedure that would close the fistula, he bought slaves—Anarcha, Lucy, and Betsy—with vesico-vaginal fistulas and experimented on them until he discovered a way—silver wire as sutures—to sew up the opening. Previous attempts to close the fistulas had failed because stitches would become infected. He won acclaim with this procedure and migrated North to New York, where he helped found Women's Hospital. There is a statue of Sims in New York City at Fifth Avenue and 115th Street.

The vesico-vaginal fistula is not a problem in the United States, but it still afflicts women in the developing world.

"We all have our own cultures," explained Chiek Abdou Salam, Tarbiyat's chief, as he took his seat of honor under one of the few shade trees in the village. For the Tuaregs, he says, a girl getting pregnant out of wedlock is an enormous shame for the parents. "So marriage is a solution to the problem." And, he said, "People are very poor, you don't have food and means. If you get your daughter married, then that helps."

[Anafghat] announced bigger ambitions, spurred by another role model. "I want to be like her," she told her father, pointing to a tall woman from Niger making the rounds with the U.S. doctors. Ghaichatou Amoul Kinni was a medical student and a Tuareg, living in the capital city. Anafghat saw that Ghaichatou spoke several languages and wore fashionable clothes. "You see how useful it is to be at school," Anafghat told her father. "I want to live in Niamey, be a doctor, and be an important woman."

Next year, Ms. [Assogra Mohamed Adda] wants her daughter, who is now in sixth grade, to go on to secondary school. Anafghat, she said, has alerted them to the perils of early marriage. "There is no rush to get married," says Ms. Adda, who was wed in her early teens. "Going to school doesn't mean you can't get married later. But if you get married, you can't go to school" (Thurow, 2005).

14. The "family values" of the contemporary religious right are ideological prescriptions that rest on notions that originated in the 19th century late bourgeois family.

15. In the foreword to the edition of *My Secret Life* which I have cited, Gershon Legman suggested that "Walter" was really Henry Spencer Ashbee, a London merchant who published erudite and very expensively produced bibliographies of the pornography available at the time. He left his own large collection to the British Museum Library, which was reluctant to accept it but did so because he insisted it should accompany his very valuable collection of editions of Cervantes' works. A recent book supports the identification of Walter with Ashbee but casts some doubt on the veracity of his accounts of his almost innumerable sexual experiences (Gibson, 2001). By contrast, Marcus thinks Walter/Ashbee is truthful, mostly because his accounts sound quite different from pornography, in that, for example, he describes incidents when he was impotent.

16. There is a passage in *The Communist Manifesto*, which refers to this pattern of sexual exploitation of poor women. When I read it in college I thought it exaggerated, but Walter shows that Marx was quite right:

Our bourgeois, not content that the wives and daughters of their proletarians are
at their disposal, and not to speak of official prostitution (Marx, 1972, p. 479).

17. Woodham-Smith shows how British government policy deliberately condemned millions of Irish peasants to starvation, disease, or emigration (Woodham-Smith, 1989). The conventional English view that Ireland was overpopulated, and that the Irish had too many babies, was of long standing. The resemblances to the vilification of African American women's allegedly over-bountiful fecundity that led up to the 1996 changes in public assistance is no coincidence.

Irish overpopulation was the subject of Jonathan Swift's great satirical work, *A Modest Proposal for Preventing the Children of Ireland from Being a Burden to Their Parents or Country* (Swift, 1933, pp. 19–32). Swift's essay is a sort of 18th-century version of what today might be a think-tank report, from some organization like the Heritage Foundation, the

Manhattan Institute, or the Cato Institute. He puts forward a persuasive argument that the Irish should sell their children as a source of meat.

18. Adorno's work is a study of several months' columns from *The Los Angeles Times* by one Carroll Righter, who, 50 or 60 years ago, was the astrologer to the stars. Written originally in English, it shows how Righter, quite seductively, appeals to anxieties around both anal and oral issues in his readers.

19. The results of their work in Germany appeared in Paris in 1934, in a book of some nine hundred pages called *Studien Uber Autorität und Familie—Studies in Authority and the Family*. The introductory essays by Horkheimer, Adorno, and Fromm are particularly valuable even now.

Chapter 7

1. The German "Geist," obviously a cognate of the English "ghost," usually translates as "spirit." However, it has many more meanings than the English word, and many of them lack the religious implications that spirit often evokes. It also has philosophical implications that will form part of the discussion in the subsequent chapter.

2. Though this whole case, including the names of those involved, became a matter of public record, I have chosen to suppress the names, as elsewhere in this book,

3. Okin (1997) argued:
Because societal cultures play so pervasive and fundamental a role in the lives of members, and because such cultures are threatened with extinction, minority cultures should be protected by special rights: That, in essence, is the case for group rights.

Some proponents of group rights argue that even cultures that "flout the rights of [their individual members] in a liberal society" should be accorded group rights or privileges if their minority status endangers the culture's continued existence. Others do not claim that all minority cultural groups should have special rights, but rather that such groups—even illiberal ones, that violate their individual members' rights, requiring them to conform to group beliefs or norms—have the right to be "let alone" in a liberal society. Both claims seem clearly inconsistent with the basic liberal value of individual freedom, which entails that group rights should not trump the individual rights of their members. (Okin, 1997)

Martha Nussbaum (1999) addressed many of these issues in the several chapters of her *Sex and Social Justice*.

4. One must also be aware of the absurdities of which multiculturalism is capable. A comment by Barry (2001):

Martha Nussbaum tells of a conference she attended at which a French anthropologist gave a paper saying that the eradication of smallpox in India was to be regretted because it had 'eradicated the cult of Sittala Devi, the goddess to whom one used to pray in order to avert smallpox'. Since the goddess had manifestly been less efficacious in warding off smallpox than vaccination turned out to be, one might have concluded that her discrediting was to be welcomed, but the anthropologist concluded that this was 'another example of Western neglect of difference'. The objection was made 'that it is surely better to be healthy rather than ill, to live rather than die'. The answer came back that this is a typical piece of Western essentialist thinking, 'which conceives of things in terms of binary oppositions'.

Well, I think that there is much to be said for *some* binary oppositions, and I do not believe that there is anything inherently western about binary oppositions as such. It is better to be alive than dead. It is better to be free than to be a slave. It is better to be healthy than sick. It is better to be adequately nourished than malnourished. It is better to drink pure water than contaminated water. It is better to have effective sanitation than to live over an open sewer. It is better to have a roof over your head than to sleep in the street. It is better to be well educated than to be illiterate and ignorant. It is better to be able to practise the form of worship prescribed by your religion than to be prevented from doing so. It is better to be able to speak freely and be able to join social and political organizations of your choice than to fear that, if your activities attract the disfavour of the regime, you face arbitrary arrest, torture or 'disappearance' at the hands of bodies organized by or connived at by the state. And so on.

It is, of course, a massive understatement to say that the first alternative in each of these binary oppositions is merely preferable to the second. Rather, the first item in each pair constitutes a basic interest of every human being. Together they make up the preconditions (or at any rate a number of the most important preconditions) for what we may describe as a minimally decent human life. And by saying *human* life I wish to emphasize that I am making a claim with cross-cultural scope.

There are a variety of ways in which we might support the claim that such interests are universal. One would be to argue that there is a universal human nature which gives rise to certain physiological and psychological needs. I see no reason why this argument should not be carried through successfully, but I suggest that it may usefully be supplemented by an appeal to the choices actually made by people in a position to make choices. Thus, with rare exceptions that can normally be explained by highly unusual beliefs or circumstances, people strongly prefer life to death, freedom to slavery, and health to sickness. It is worth observing, incidentally, that the devotees of Sittala Devi were no exception: what motivated her worshippers was the hope that she would protect them from smallpox. It was the anthropologist, not the people involved, who elevated the value of cultural diversity above that of health. (pp. 284–285)

5. Just for example, the *New York Times* reported on modernizing changes in a backward country, Laos:

December 27, 2007
Long Lao Gao Journal
In Laos, Chinese Motorcycles Change Lives
By THOMAS FULLER

LONG LAO GAO, Laos—The pineapples that grow on the steep hills above the Mekong River are especially sweet, the red and orange chilies unusually spicy, and the spring onions and watercress retain the freshness of the mountain dew.

For years, getting this prized produce to market meant that someone had to carry a giant basket on a back-breaking, daylong trek down narrow mountain trails cutting through the jungle.

That is changing, thanks in large part to China.

Villagers ride their cheap Chinese motorcycles, which sell for as little as $440, down a dirt road to the markets of Luang Prabang, a charming city of Buddhist temples along the Mekong that draws flocks of foreign tourists. The trip takes one and a half hours.

"No one had a motorcycle before," said Khamphao Janphasid, 43, a teacher in the local school whose extended family now has three of them. "The only motorcycles that used to be available were Japanese, and poor people couldn't afford them."

Inexpensive Chinese products are flooding China's southern neighbors like Cambodia, Laos, Myanmar and Vietnam. The products are transforming the lives of some of the poorest people in Asia, whose worldly possessions a few years ago typically consisted of not much more than one or two sets of clothes, cooking utensils and a thatch-roofed house built by hand.

The concerns in the West about the safety of Chinese toys and pet food are largely moot for the people in the remote villages here. As the introduction to global capitalism, Chinese products are met with deep appreciation. "Life is better," Mr. Khamphao said, "because prices are cheaper."

Chinese television sets and satellite dishes connect villagers to the world. Stereos fill their houses with music. And the Chinese motorcycles often serve as transportation for families.

The motorcycles, typically with small but adequate 110cc, or cubic centimeter, engines, literally save lives, said Saidoa Wu, the village leader of Long Lao Mai, in a valley at the end of the dirt road, adjacent to Long Lao Gao.

"Now when we have a sick person we can get to the hospital in time," said Mr. Wu, 43.

The improvised bamboo stretchers that villagers here used as recently as a decade ago to carry the gravely ill on foot are history. In a village of 150 families, Mr. Wu counts 44 Chinese motorcycles. There were none five years ago.

Chinese motorbikes fill the streets of Hanoi, Vientiane, Mandalay and other large cities in upland Southeast Asia. Thirty-nine percent of the two million motorcycles sold annually in Vietnam are Chinese brands, according to Honda, which has a 34 percent market share.

Chinese exports to Myanmar, Laos and Vietnam amounted to $8.3 billion in the first eight months of the year, up about 50 percent from the same period in 2006.

About seven years ago, residents here say, Chinese salesmen began arriving with suitcases filled with smuggled watches, tools and small radios; they would close up and move on when the police arrived. More recently, Chinese merchants, who speak only passable Lao, received permission to open permanent stalls in the towns and small cities across the region. In Laos, these are "talad jin," or Chinese markets.

Mr. Khamphao and his neighbors all have $100 Chinese-made television sets connected to Chinese-made satellite dishes and decoders, causing both joy and occasional tension among family members sitting on the bare concrete or dirt floors of their living rooms. "I like watching the news," Mr. Khamphao said. "My children love to watch movies."

A two-hour interview with Mr. Khamphao was interrupted twice: once when his buffalo in the adjoining field gave birth to a healthy calf and a second time when a cable TV channel was showing "Lost in Translation," and the actor Bill Murray sang an off-key rendition of Bryan Ferry's "More Than This."

Mr. Khamphao's children, whose daily lives are largely confined to the mountain village, have picked up the Thai language from television, and they sing along to commercials broadcast from Thailand.

http://www.nytimes.com/2007/12/27/world/asia/27laos.html?_r=1&oref=slogin

Is it likely that community life can remain unchanged with this sudden jump in the ability to travel and experience modern life in the consumer society?

6. Owusu-Bempah (2003–2004) also said:

Following Descartes, Euro-American writers use such terms as the self, self-concept, self-identity and self-esteem interchangeably to refer to personhood. For them, the starting point of personhood, of being a human being, is usually epistemological and psychological. They employ these terms to imply the importance of self-knowledge—the ways in which we think and feel about our physical, social and spiritual worlds and ourselves as individuals. Namely, in Euro-American societies, it is believed that one needs self-knowledge in order to comprehend one's place and future in the world. Self-knowledge is also believed to guide one's aspirations and one's own conduct as well as ones conduct towards others. The Cartesian conception of the human being places the emphasis on the individual, it places the individual at the centre of the universe; it sees the individual as an atomistic entity—the architect of his/her own actions, an authentic self with a private identity. In this conception, the human being is untouchable; she/he transcends both his/her physical and social milieux.

In fact, during the lifetime of the great mathematician and philosopher René Descartes (1596–1650), most Europeans were communitarian peasants, quite similar to the communitarian people of the less developed countries Owusu-Bempah so celebrates. In Descartes' original conception—which Owusu-Bempah presents in caricatured form—the individual was subordinate to god. This was the beginning of the split between patriarchal monotheism and scientific thought.

7. For unclear reasons, it is common, even among English writers, to give the title of this book in German. It means "Community and Society." The word "gemein" means "common," and also "vulgar." The element "schaft" is related to the English suffix "ship", as in "friendship." Hence "Gemeinschaft" means that which is in common in human associations.

"Gesellschaft" derives from the reflexive verb "sich gesellen," meaning to associate oneself in a purposive way. The element of conscious volition is key to this term.

8. Some social work theorists have drawn on this body of classical sociological theory: The divide between micro and macro theory is not unique to social work as a discipline. Over the past century, since sociology became an academic subject, a great deal of sociological thought has gone into developing social-structural explanations for the behavior of human individuals and collectivities. Theorists who have adopted this approach to the study of social phenomena, by and large, have followed a perspective shared by classical social theorists like Emile Durkheim, Karl Marx, and Talcott Parsons, who (though differing considerably in the content of their theories of society) understood social structures and institutions as consisting of social regularities and objective patterns external to individual action, intentions, and meanings, and not reducible to the sum of those meanings or actions. This group of theorists developed macro-social theories in which the major explanatory variables were larger structural phenomena. The behavior of individual actors was understood to be strongly influenced or even determined by the various structures or institutions of society. The human being as active agent, exercising free will and contributing to his or her circumstance, was not a consideration in this perspective. (Kondrat, 2002, p. 435)

9. The original text is as follows:
Der charakterliche Panzer entstand als chronisches Ergebnis des Aufeinanderprallens von Triebansprüchen und versagender Außenwelt und bezieht aus den aktuellen Konflikten zwischen Triebe und Außenwelt seine Kraft und seine fortdauernde Daseinsberechtigung. Er ist der Ausdruck und die Summe jener Einwirkungen der Außenwelt auf das Triebleben, die durch Häufung und qualitative Gleichartigkeit ein historisches Ganzes bildeten.... Die Stätte an der er sich bildet, ist das Ich, gerade jener Teil der Persönlichkeit, der an der Grenze zwischen dem bio-physiologisch Triebhaften und der Außenwelt liegt. Wir bezeichnen ihn daher auch als den *Charakter des Ichs*. (Reich, 1971, p. 175)

10. The original text, which I have translated here, is as follows:
Die Personen, die ich beschreiben will, fallen dadurch auf, daß sie in regelmäßiger Vereinigung die nachstehenden drei Eigenschaften zeigen: sie sind besonders *ordentlich, sparsam* und *eigensinnig*. Jedes dieser Worte deckt eigentlich eine kleine Gruppe oder Reihe von miteinander verwandten Charakterzügen. »Ordentlich« begreift sowohl die körperliche Sauberkeit als auch Gewissenhaftigkeit in kleinen Pflichterfüllungen und Verläßlichkeit; das Gegenteil davon wäre: unordentlich, nachläßig. Die Sparsamkeit kann bis zum Geize gesteigert erscheinen; der Eigensinn geht in Trotz über, an den sich leicht Neigung zur Wut und Rachsucht knüpfen. Die beiden letzteren Eigenschaften—Sparsamkeit und Eigensinn—hängen fester miteinander als mit dem ersten, dem »ordentlich«, zusammen; sie sind auch das konstantere Stück des ganzen Komplexes, doch erscheint es mir unabweisbar, daß irgendwie alle drei zusammengehören. (S. Freud, 1908b/1959, p. 25)

11. One of the forgotten bits of social work history is the interest early social workers took in the sociology of the populations they encountered. In her *Social Diagnosis* (Richmond, 1917), Mary Richmond made frequent references to Emily Balch's *Our Slavic Fellow Citizens*, which seems to have rested on the author's intimate familiarity with communities of Slavic peasants, both in Europe and the United States. See Mercedes Randall's collection of Balch's writings, with biographical information. (Randall, 1972)

12. The sociologist Arthur Shostak (1969) was an exception, and here are two of his comments:

The rural origin of many foreign-born and of many native-born blue-collarites, while commonly overlooked, warrants serious attention. These blue-collarites have spent their childhood or adolescence on the farm (p. 7).

A number of contemporary blue-collar attributes are remarkably like those of rural dwellers and are regularly reinforced by the steady influx intro manual work of people who have left the land. Relevant here are such items as parochialism in religion and politics, the presence of self-sufficient females in quasi-patriarchal homes, the development of large families. (p. 8)

13. The Wikipedia article describing the *Annales* school—http://en.wikipedia.org/wiki/Annales_School—is accurate:

"The *Annales* School (*Annales* is pronounced /a(n)'nal(?)/ in French) is a school of historical writing named after the French scholarly journal *Annales d'histoire économique et sociale* (later called *Annales. Economies, sociétés, civilisations*, then renamed in 1994 as *Annales. Histoire, Sciences Sociales*) where it was first expounded. *Annales* school history is best known for incorporating social scientific methods into history.

The *Annales* was founded and edited by Marc Bloch and Lucien Febvre in 1929, while they were teaching at the University of Strasbourg, France. These authors quickly became associated with the distinctive *Annales* approach, which combined geography, history, and the sociological approaches of the *Année Sociologique* (many members of which were their colleagues at Strasbourg) to produce an approach which rejected the predominant emphasis on politics, diplomacy and war of many 19th century historians. Instead, they pioneered an approach to a study of long-term historical structures (*la longue durée*) over events."

14. Le Roy Ladurie's (1975) *Montaillou*, for example, is a vivid description of the pattern of relationships in a Pyrenean village several hundred years ago. The village, Montaillou, was the last center of a Christian heresy, Catharism, stamped out by a papally ordered crusade. He develops his account by drawing on the protocols, preserved in the Vatican Library, of the inquisition that visited the village and prosecuted those found to be Cathars. To this, he adds information on the material life of the pyrenean peasantry, to make up a complete picture.

15. Gurevich (1988) gave examples of efforts to use magical forces to attain practical ends. This was the science and technology of the times.

16. Rösener (1994) explained this in detail:

Peasant revolts seem to have broken out especially when country folk were convinced that their time-honoured rights were being violated. However, their sense of legality was distinct from the rigid corpus of erudite written law that the Early Modern state was fostering. Peasants invoked ancient, orally transmitted norms and attitudes that reflected their legacy of collective resolution of judicial issues; with the passage of time, values corroborated by their actual experience of life took on the binding quality of customary rights. Traditional unwritten rules, regarded as valid in the great majority of rural areas, applied to the most important categories of peasant life, that is, family, village and society. During the sixteenth century, legal scholars employed by state bureaucracies collected and codified much of the heritage of customary law. While the influence of this judicial tradition was thereby strengthened, the flexibility and adaptability that had distinguished it for so many centuries were no more.

In view of the extraordinary dimensions of the body of European rustic law, it is difficult to make any generally valid statements about the subject. Nevertheless, one can ascertain a basic conviction that was evidently common to all Early Modern peasant revolts: the peasants were absolutely certain that their venerable rights had been infringed by the innovations of ruthless bureaucrats or greedy manorial lords, who had arrogated to themselves the authority of a fair-minded king. Two other features may be discerned: a strong belief in the force of tradition and the ruler's commitment to justice. The conservative stance of ploughmen—emphasized again and again in the literature on the topic—and their deliberate, unremitting insistence upon respect for traditional values are normally considered to have been manifestations of ignorance and backwardness. This is of course, patently wrong. One cannot overlook the basic conditions of rural existence and the unique peasant mentality which results from them. As social anthropologists have recently recognized, the heart of the matter is that peasant society is based upon the power of experience to a degree that no other human collectivity is. The fact that ploughmen hold fast to concrete experience must be seen in the context of the fixed rhythms of country life, the regular sequence of the seasons, command of agrarian skills and well-established patterns of assuring one's livelihood. The changes that occurred in the sixteenth and seventeenth centuries benefited the rural population in some respects but also caused much misfortune and pain. Sixteenth-century agrarian prosperity led to tremendous population growth and an increase in the size of the rural underclass. The Catholic–Protestant Wars were devastating. Years of price inflation followed upon years of pestilence and damaged the agrarian economy. Bureaucratic fiscal pressures engendered hate and bitterness.

When manorial lords sought to raise the level of payments and services, the peasants thought that they could call upon the supreme ruler. The rustic world-view included the image of the king as the protector of his subjects, whose most holy duty was to guarantee peace and justice. The peasant mind could not imagine that the king wished his subjects to be unhappy. He was certainly not responsible; the disastrous innovations merely represented the misdeeds of rapacious bureaucrats. Peasants were totally convinced that the king did not know how bad things were for them because he was being deceived by shameless sycophants at court. Thus uprisings often took place in outlying districts and remote regions, sites that lay at the greatest distance from the seat of government—a milieu in which it was easy for strange rumours to circulate about what was happening at court. The minority of kings and unresolved problems of royal succession likewise tended to encourage misconceptions about the will of the central governmental authority. (pp. 90–91)

Globalization is the current expression of the same modernization process, and there are at least some examples of peoples trying to respond to it in a less reactive manner.

17. Le Roy Ladurie (1979b), in describing rural Normandy in the 16th century gave the following example of the sources of disease. Let us remember that understanding of the importance of pure drinking water came only in the 19th century, and obtaining it is still a serious problem in the less developed countries.

> We may smile perhaps at this popular fancy for the manufacture of alcoholic drinks in the sixteenth century, whether wine or cider. For even setting aside the list just mentioned of secondary and not entirely serious justifications, the increase of cider-growing in Renaissance Normandy, like that of vine-growing in the Paris region, had very solid foundations: drinking wines and ciders of low alcoholic content, and drinking them in massive quantities, (the daily consumption of manual laborers of the Languedoc in about 1500–1560 might be as much as two litres of wine a day) meant that one was absorbing a few low-grade calories (of alcoholic origin) which was all to the good. But first and foremost, it meant that one was drinking a comparatively sterile liquid, a good deal less dangerous, that is to say, than the polluted liquids to which water-drinkers were virtually condemned, when one thinks of the countless sources of bacteria, (manure, sewage, run-off from flax-steeping, waste waters contaminated by mass epidemics) which might, in Normandy, a land of schist and granite, pollute the surface waters supplying the brooks, pools, streams, wells, and even springs. In such circumstances, cider provided one of the most agreeable forms of insurance against death and disease. A team of historians from Normandy had demonstrated, with the aid of graphs, that mortality in the region in the age of Louis XIV, fluctuated in direct relationship with the high price or scarcity of cider. (pp. 140–141)

18. Schultz (1964) further described the manner in which knowledge and skill are passed along the generations in peasant communities:

> Although the knowledge that is a part of the state of the arts is passed on from father to son by word of mouth and by demonstration, this does not mean that what is handed down is not authentic knowledge. In general, farmers who are limited to traditional agricultural factors are more secure in what they know about the factors they use than farmers who are adopting and learning how to use new factors of production. The new types of risk and uncertainty about the yield inherent in factors embodying an advance knowledge are of real concern to farmers. They could be of critical importance to farmers who are producing so little that there is barely enough production for survival. But since traditional agriculture is not introducing new factors, new elements of risk and uncertainty do not appear; they arise only when the transformation gets under way. What matters here is that the state of the arts is in fact known, established, and given in the case of traditional agriculture,

and that the supply price of reproducible factors rises as the quantity of these factors increases. (p. 31)

19. At the end of his book he cited the experience of a traveller in the South of Italy in the earlier 20th century, who encountered people who voiced views of religion and the supernatural that paralleled those Gurevich had found in his studies of rural life centuries earlier. He described the steady clientèle of an apothecary, one Done Bartolo. Many were priests, nuns, and monks from the neighborhood. They seldom mentioned the deity. One was an actual priest who spoke of Jesus and Mary, making clear that Jesus' primary distinction was that he was his mother's son, and criticizing Jesus' insensitivity to her: John 2:4

"Jesus saith unto her, Woman, what have I to do with thee? mine hour is not yet come."

The priest comments "'*Percio ha finito male*, that's why he came to a bad end.'" (Gurevich, 1988, p. 217). The quotation is from Axel Munthe's *The Story of San Michele* (Munthe, 1929).

20. Miller comments on the changes modernity imposed on Irish peasants, but shows that they were not specific to Ireland:

Of course, a worldview oriented toward stasis was not unique to Catholic Ireland, but was similar to those held by other "traditional" peasant and subsistence-based societies which discouraged individualism and had "a basically collective idea of man." Hence, it could be expected that many poor Protestants in rural Ireland would share at least some features of this premodern outlook and also that many Catholics would react to the commercialization of the Irish countryside by altering patterns of belief and behavior to comport with new realities and perceived opportunities. In short, it could be argued that the worldview, which in the late eighteenth and early nineteenth centuries seemed to most observers both pervasive among and confined exclusively to Irish Catholics, was in fact less a reflection of religion or ethnicity, as was commonly believed, than of economic situation and social class. (Miller, 1985, p. 112)

21. See Gerhart Piers and M. Singer (1971, pp. 15–55), "Shame and Guilt: A Psychoanalytic Study." In fact, the peasant village, as an unconscious psychological field, probably most resembled what family therapists call an undifferentiated ego mass, except of course, that it was appropriate to the circumstances. Under contemporary circumstances, it usually marks a pathological failure of the family members to individuate. In some instances, this failure may sometimes be a fragmented survival of peasant experience in the history of the family in question.

22. For a description of the very beginning of this type of personality, see Charles Hanly, "From Animism to Rationalism," (Hanly, 1992, pp. 155–169).

23. Rösener shows that deference to feudal superiors persisted long after formal emancipation of the peasants:

What were the effects of peasant emancipation on the economy and society of the nineteenth century altogether? Certainly, one main consequence of agrarian reform was the incorporation of the rural population and agriculture into the new Liberal political and social order. The creation of a statewide citizenry—the goal of eighteenth-century enlightened despotism—ironically turned out to be an accomplishment of early nineteenth-century bourgeois revolutionaries. . . .

As a matter of principle, the vocation of agriculture was now incorporated into the market economy of liberalism; there were no longer any obstacles to real-estate transfers. Competitive forces would determine who acquired and exploited terrain. As agrarian specialists were wont to argue, the best qualified husbandmen would gain control of the land and poor farmers would fall by the wayside. The tendency towards market-orientated conditions had in fact been under way for quite some time and was especially prevalent in the vicinity of prosperous cities. However, only with the triumph of liberalism was a breakthrough achieved; only then was the economy allowed to operate on its own. Admittedly, certain protagonists of the older way of life—representatives of outmoded political, economic and social forces—managed to survive within the new economic and social order and make their presence felt. For example, the fact that the nobility had lost its legal prerogatives did not prevent it from assuming important leadership posts in the economy, politics and social life of the latter nineteenth and early twentieth centuries. While it is true that noblemen had lost some ground to the propertied middle class by 1900, they still occupied a strong social position, not only in Prussia but also in Bavaria and Austria (Rösener, 1994, pp. 182–183).

24. Remember that Rösener, in a passage quoted earlier, described peasant rebellions as appeals to a ruler—the good father—that the peasants assumed to be benevolent, and only misled by intermediate figures in the social hierarchy.

25. Indeed, this patriarchy of feudalism is the institutional ancestor of fatherly authority in the bourgeois family and its successors. This is a complex issue to which I will return. Muriel Nazzari has studied the feudal roots of that quintessentially bourgeois institution, marriage:

> ... the marriage in which the husband provides the support and the wife provides the services is a non-capitalist relation of production, very similar to the feudal relation of production (Nazzari, 1980, p. 63).

Which she explained thus:

> The feudal relation between a serf or a vassal and his lord was a personal relation of dependence and support. Except in the case of the unfree serfs, whose ties were hereditary, the feudal relation was thought to be entered into freely once in a lifetime, and was traditionally only dissolved by the death of one of the parties. A ceremony, called homage or commendation, marked the beginning of the feudal relation of dependence. By it, a man became the "man" of another man, whether it was a lord who became his king's "man" or a serf who became the manorial lord's "man." In this respect. it was like marriage in that it cut across class lines. A woman whether of a high or a low class, becomes the wife of a man who is usually of the same or a higher class, and who is generally more powerful. She receives her status from her husband and his position in the world. Yet the relationship of personal dependence exists as much in a high-class marriage as in a working-class marriage, as it did in both vassalage and serfdom (Nazzari, 1980, p. 66).

26. Of course, there are other patriarchal monotheist ideologies that are older still. Judaism, which evolved out of the state cult of ancient Judaea, is an obvious example. Mithraism, long defunct, of course, was another.

27. And, in some places, the leap from mythopoeic thought to modern laic ideologies was direct, without a stop in the patriarchal monotheist camp. "Religion provided spells and incantations, often written down and passed on preciously like amulets. These, like its ceremonies, were efficacious and protective" (Weber, 1976, p. 340).

Weber shows that these were important rituals, inside and outside of the Church's activities. The rituals were more important than their setting, and when the Church proved unable or unwilling to perform them, the people, and, often, the civil authorities, would perform them extra-ecclesiastically. Hence, Weber's examples of provincial *Maires* who commandeered the churches so as to cause the church bells to be rung so as to ward off storm clouds, and thus protect the crops. And, of course, the peasant tradition was anterior to the scientific tradition just as it was also anterior to the religious one.

28. "Perhaps it was not merely fortuitous that Catholicism won an easy, bloodless acceptance in Gaelic society or that after the eighth century it was perfunctorily observed; for in a thriving secular culture, Catholicism was but a supportive and corroboratory subsystem—merely one of many props of Irish thought and behavior. Not until conquest swept away the old social structure did religion begin to assume its later preeminence. Nevertheless, there were some basic affinities between intrinsic aspects of Catholicism and those of the secular culture. For example, Catholicism is fundamentally collectivist and analogous to the authoritative Irish family. Individual salvation is primarily a consequence of membership in the baptized community and of adherence to essential dogma and rules of worship and conduct which—the *brehon* laws and proverbs—are regarded as eternal and unalterable wisdom. In certain areas, individuality is appropriate: the church authoritatively requires uniformity of belief and restricts personal interpretations of central doctrine. Even in the realm of behavior, Catholicism provides a framework which—while it intensifies personal responsibility to obey God's laws as interpreted by the church—limits the field of individuality" (Miller, 1985, p. 116).

29. Eugen Weber commented:

God was far away. The saints were near. Both were anthropomorphic. Saints were intercessors. One did not address God directly, but prayed to saints to request his favors, rewarded them if the crop was good or the weather fair even chastised them, as at Haudimont (Meuse), where Saint Urban, accused of permitting the vines to freeze on May 25, his own feastday, was dragged in effigy through the nettles around his church. The greatest saint of all, of course, was the Virgin, an unparalleled source of delivery from harm. The *gwerz* (ballad) made up when a new pilgrimage to her was launched in 1894 at Plounéour-Menez recited only recent and concrete miracles: saving men from falling, drowning, prison, and so on. These were the functions of a saint (Weber, 1976, p. 347).

And he added:

But the chief function of saints on earth was healing, and every malady was the province of a particular saint. The attribution could vary from region to region, with some local patron saint taking over duties another saint performed elsewhere; but it was creation of popular design. The conjunction between saint and illness was determined by associations, some naively evident, others lost in the mists of time. Thus Saint Eutropius healed dropsy (*Eutrope=eau en trop*); Saint Cloud healed boils (*furoncles* are also known as *clous*); Saint Diétrine dealt with herpes and scurvy (*teigne*). Saint Clare (Claire) helped eyes see more clearly, and Saint Loup, by fine contradistinction, healed fright. Berry had its own array of saints destined by alliteration or obscure fiat to heal. For the deaf there was Saint Ouen; for the gouty, Saint Genou; for crabbed and peevish women, Saint Acaire (in reference to *femmes acariâtres*). In Finistère Our Lady of Benodet healed aches, depressions, madness, or simplemindedness—disorders associated with the head. Benodet literally means head of Odet, that is, the mouth of the Odet River. In Veurdre (Allier), not far from Bourbon-l'Archambault, Saint Faustin, whose statue stood in the church, became in popular parlance Saint Foutin, the resort of barren women (Weber, 1976, pp. 347–348).

30. I am indebted to Lindsay Dÿkema, MD for help with this and other translations from the French (Durkheim, 1960, pp. 598–599).

31. Ewen has further explored this phenomenon in subsequent works (Ewen, 1988; Ewen & Ewen, 1982).

32. Consider, for example, this report of research on adolescent sexual behavior, conducted in Minnesota, in which the researchers paired mothers and daughters and compared their various outlooks:

"Half of all mothers of sexually active teenagers mistakenly believe that their children are still virgins, according to a report released here today by a team of researchers at the University of Minnesota Adolescent Health Center."

Moreover:

"The research also found that the mother's frequency of religious observance and prayer had no correlation with whether her children became sexually active."

And:

"The brochure noted that close relationships with mothers seemed to discourage youngsters from sexual activity, although the effect diminished with age and, among girls, disappeared altogether.

'High levels of mother–teen connectedness,' . . . 'were not significantly associated with delays in sexual intercourse among 10th- and 11th-grade girls.'" (Schemo, 2002)

Also, see Wells and Twenge's (2005) study of young peoples' sexual behavior and attitudes from 1943 to 1999:

This meta-analysis showed that young people's sexual behavior and attitudes have become more permissive over the past 50 years, particularly in the case of girls and young women. Between the 1940s and the 1990s, young people consistently reported more sexual activity, a younger age at first intercourse, more approval of premarital sex, and less sexual guilt. These changes were large, with age at first intercourse decreasing by more than 3 years and approval of premarital sex increasing by about 60 percentage points among young women and 40 among young men. Behavioral and attitudinal changes in sexuality were correlated with trends in the larger social environment, including the divorce rate and the number of AIDS cases. In addition, there were significant differences across certain ethnic groups and geographical regions. This meta-analysis is the first, to our knowledge, to summarize data on young people's sexual behavior and attitudes, and it included 530 samples with more than a quarter of a million individual respondents. (p. 258)

33. She found that men who are exposed to disguised or de-emphasized expressions of gender inequalities (i.e., urban patriarchies) are more likely to develop more liberal attitudes toward premarital sex for their daughters. This process is prompted by men's exposure to urban settings, which offers women and men multiple possibilities for education, paid employment, well-informed sex education and training, and women's rights organizations (Amuchástegui, 2001; Figueroa Perea, 1997). In contrast, men raised in small provincial locations, or pueblos, are exposed to deeply ingrained gender inequalities (i.e., rural patriarchies), and thus, they are less likely to embrace progressive values with regard to the virginity of their daughters. Lack of education and paid employment opportunities characterizes the lives of women living in rural and semi-industrialized contexts (Canak & Swanson, 1998), which has reinforced the lack of equality between women and men, and between fathers and their daughters (González-López, 2004).

In other words, modernization that takes people away from the peasant context, will modernize their thinking about gender. She goes on to show that realism comes to dominate in the fathers' thinking:

> I argue that Mexican working-class fathers' migration and settlement journeys shape their views of their daughters' sex lives. The men I interviewed perceive the cities they migrate to and the immigrant barrios where they settle as sexually dangerous for their daughters. Fear is at the core of the sex education that these fathers offer their daughters: fear of pregnancy out of wedlock and its negative consequences (e.g., fear of a daughter not attending and completing college); fear of sexual violence; fear of sexually transmitted diseases; fear of being in an abusive relationship; and fear of crime, gangs, drugs, and violence. While promoting an ethic of sexual moderation and personal care, these fathers protect daughters who are vulnerable to these high-risk living conditions in the neighborhood. Safeguarding a daughter from these dangers becomes a priority after migration. For these fathers, virginity becomes secondary. (González-López, 2004)

And she concluded:

> Thus, fatherhood may become a family emotional process (Nichols & Schwartz, 1991) through which men may begin to resolve and disrupt family patterns that promote gender inequality as they educate a new generation of Mexican American women with regard to sexuality. (González-López 2004)

CHAPTER 8

1. Later, Mary Richmond (1917) quoted a long passage by her colleague, Ida Hall, about work with Italian immigrants, giving graphic examples of the problems an indigenous interpreter can create:

"An instance of the failure of such an attempt concerns a most competent Italian social worker who acted as interpreter in the case of a deserted wife. This wife, when asked if she had men lodgers, replied in the negative, and then the investigator begged for further questions as to the owners of three coats, all in the same stage of decay, which were hanging in a bedroom. Instead of pursuing that subject, however, the interpreter stopped to explain in detail that a Sicilian wife could not keep men boarders in the absence of her husband, as such a course would be regarded as highly improper. The interpreter regarded further questions along that line as insulting and the investigator would not courteously press the point. The information given as to Sicilian etiquette was unimpeachable; but, alas! later developments showed that this particular Sicilian woman had done many things which could not be sanctioned by less rigid codes of conduct." (p. 119)

There is a lot to learn from this example. In particular, there is the tendency of social workers from specific ethnic or otherwise identifiable groups to want to attest to the respectability of clients who are their compatriots. Some of this comes through in a number of the essays in Monica McGoldrick's anthology (McGoldrick et al., 2005).

2. It is not completely new to the English language, as it has a use in advanced electronics, according to the *Oxford English Dictionary*. Some writers on Bloch prefer "nonsimultaneity," which is slightly closer to the German word. However, the first publication of Bloch's essay on the subject, which was in *New German Critique* 11, 1977, translated the title as "Nonsynchronism and the Obligation to Its Dialectics." Moreover, "nonsynchronism" captures more of the dynamism of the relationship between those social phenomena which social workers deal with in encounters with nonsynchronism.

3. The German word, though probably also a neologism, is more immediately understandable and sounds more colloquial. *Ungleichzeitigkeit* is a compound word. There are many of them in German, and people form them frequently to address new communicative needs. Their advantage is in avoiding some of the complex verbal constructions that German grammar can impose.

4. Most of this biographical information comes from Deutsches Historisches Museum (see http://www.dhm.de/). Ernst Bloch was born, on July 8, 1885, in Ludwigshafen, a port and industrial city on the Rhine in southwestern Germany. His father was a railroad official. From 1905 to 1908 he studied at Munich and Würzburg, where he received a doctorate. He did not move into an academic position, perhaps because he was an unconventional thinker and, most likely, because he was a Jew. He then spent the years until the first World War as a private tutor and writer in Berlin and Heidelberg, where he belonged to the circle around Max Weber, which included Georg Lúkacs. During the war he and his wife moved first to Bavaria and then, in 1917 to 1919, as a conscientious objector, to Switzerland.

In the cultural and political turmoil of the German 1920s, Bloch joined the Communist Party. His relationship with it was never fully harmonious—he called Lenin "the Red Tsar" and "Genghis Khan," for example (Geoghegan, 1995, p. 124). Bloch was also among the first to take the threat of Fascism and Nazism seriously, and was an open and vocal opponent of the Nazi Party. This may have diminished his criticisms of the Soviet Union. In the 1920s, he lived in various places and supported himself as a writer.

With the Nazi takeover in 1933, Bloch lost German citizenship, and again moved to Switzerland, then to Austria, Czechoslovakia, Paris, and finally Cambridge, Massachusetts, where he lived from 1938 to 1948. In 1934, his first wife having died, and a second marriage having ended, he married an architect, Karola Piotrkowska.

In the United States, Bloch spent many years writing his primary work, *Das Prinzip Hoffnung*, (*The Principle of Hope*). He returned to Germany in 1948, settled in the German Democratic Republic, and assumed a professorship at the University of Leipzig. In the 1950s he was an open critic of the ruling Socialist Unity Party. In 1957, the régime forced Bloch into retirement.

Bloch and his wife were travelling in the German Federal Republic when the Berlin Wall went up in 1961. He then took up a professorship at the University of Tübingen. Bloch died on August 4, 1977.

5. In Germany, there is a long tradition of what is called *"Feuilleton"* (actually a French word), consisting of essays by intellectuals and public figures. It often is in a separate section of the paper. It resembles the OP-ED pages of American papers, but the writings are longer and more meaty.

6. The title of the essay is *Ungleichzeitigkeit und Pflicht zu Ihrer Dialektik,* or in English, *Non-Synchronism and Duty to its Dialektic* (Bloch, 1961, p. 104). The duty to its dialectic likely refers to one of Bloch's major themes, that all social impulses, even those that are clearly authoritarian and regressive, include some little hidden element of hope and striving for the world to be better.

7. Whom Vierhaus cites a few sentences later and who is a key thinker for the further development of social work theory.

8. The bishop, Jacques Fournier, did bring his torturer along, but prided himself on uncovering heresy through the force of his own personality, rather than by cruder means.

9. Such writers as Wilhelm Dilthey and Ernst Cassirer, who offer social work much useful theory, are comfortable using the word.

10. It is similarly confusing that many German writers, including Freud, use the word *Seele*, an obvious cognate of "soul," to mean something like "personality."

11. Paul Trejo's summary of what Hegel means by "spirit" is useful.
SPIRIT in this context is not mystical or religious in the Sunday School sense. We talk freely of School Spirit, or Community Spirit, or Team Spirit, and that is all that Hegel means by this term. Spirit is an invisible reality which is all-important in social organizations, and is probably best represented by the leader of the social group. It is very subjective, even intra-subjective, but it is also objective, precisely because it is shared by many. It is the synthesis of the subjective and the objective, the self-contained resolution of both, and so is closer to any definition of the absolute than we have yet approached. (Trejo, 1993)

12. German philosophy is notorious for obscure writing. Kant, though indispensably great, is quite dry. In the *Phenomenology*, Hegel clearly wants the reader to parse out his prose as a process of understanding. Nietzsche is an exception, though like Bloch, he is subtle and allusive.

13. In the 1980s, for example, I worked with immigrants from El Salvador, most of whom exhibited some degree of posttraumatic stress disorder.

Index

In this index, *n* denotes endnote.

A

Abraham Jacobi Hospital of Bronx Municipal Hospital Center, 46
abstracted empiricism, 63
abundance *vs.* scarcity, 117–118
abuse. *See* child abuse and neglect
accumulationist stage of capitalism, 87, 89
activism, social, 148
Acton, William, 87, 88–89, 90
adaptation, cultural, 88
addicts and child neglect, 16–17
Administration for Children's Services (ACS), 40
admissions and HMOs, hospital, 101
admissions of elderly patients, hospital, 71–74
adolescents
    pregnancy, 79–80, 99–100
    psychiatric issues and, 135–138
    sexually transmitted diseases, 79–80
    suicidal, 78–79, 99
adoption and long-term foster care, 51–52
Adorno, T. W., 64, 87, 92, 144
advocacy and bureaucracies, 10
agents of the state, social workers as, 19, 45
agriculture, peasant, 119, 120
AIDS, 76–77
Albert Einstein College of Medicine, 67

alienation of labor, 23
ambiguity, tolerance of, 64
American Arbitration Association (AAA), 36
American Federation of Labor-Congress of Industrial Organizations (AFL-CIO), 37
American Federation of State, County, and Municipal Employees (AFSCME), 4
anal character
    achievement and maintenance of, 92, 120–121
    described, 114–116
    factory work process and, 116
    immigration and, 120–121, 123–124
    money, feces, and sperm, 88
Annales school, 117, 165*n*13
Appleton Century Crofts, 12–13
Ariès, P., 117
arrest record, 5
Asylums, 7
ataque, 74
Authoritarian Personality, 64
authoritarianism, 64, 92, 93
authoritative interventions, 28–32, 41
authority, parental, 124–125
authority and social work practice, 24, 28
authority figures, seeking, 93

B

Baran, P. A., 92
Barker-Benfield, G. J., 87, 88, 89, 112
bereavement and ethnic distinctions, 74
Beyond the Melting Pot, 83
biography of author, v–vi
biphasic approach, 92, 144
birth control, 4, 57, 80
birth rates and birth control policies, 4
Blau, J., 148, 149
Bloch, E., 140–141, 142–143, 173–174n4
Boquitas Pintadas, 107
borderline personality disorder, 44, 47
bourgeois family forms, 45–46, 89–90, 114–121, 155n3, 158n12
Bramwell, Gillian, 16
Braudel, F., 117
Breslauer, Nathan, 15–16
Bureau of Child Welfare (BCW), 15, 40
bureaucracies, 9–10, 166
"Bureaucracy," 107, 108
Burghardt, S., 148
business model and bureaucracies, 10, 107, 148

C

Capitalism, the Family, and Personal Life, 45
capitalism and accumulationist stage, 87
capitalism and family forms, 45–46
capitalism and work, 116
case examples
    abduction of child by father, 26–28
    adolescents and psychiatric issues, 136–138
    AIDS, 76–77
    Annie in group home, 56–57
    anorexia by proxy, 134
    child abuse, 82
    child pornography, 20–22, 46
    contracting with adolescents and parents, 137
    crack epidemic, 75–76
    cultural conflicts, 110–111
    dangers of social work practice while ill, 29–32
    Daria in group home, 56, 57–58
    domestic violence and child maltreatment, 134–135
    domestic violence and religion, 135
    elderly manipulative patient, 69–71
    elderly mother of journalist, 72
    emergency room patients, 69–70
    European elderly, 72–74, 97–98
    filthy apartment and unsavory relatives, 103–106
    girl with cerebral palsy, 18
    group home residents, 52–53
    home nursing care, 101–106
    parents, working with, 136–138
    petit mal seizures and substance abuse, 26–27
    removal of violent child, 24–25
    riot in group home, 54–55
    searching for families, friends, patients, 131–133
    shake injuries, 100–101
    suicidal adolescent, 79
    supervisor, Sergei Stravinsky, 32–34
    support of mother's efforts to move, 28–29
    virginity clearance, 81–81
    wrongful charge of child abuse, 29
case notes, 138–139
casework and counseling model of practice, 11
Cassirer, E., 141
Catalyst, A Socialist Journal of the Social Services, 60
Central Labor Council (CLC), 36–39
"changing" neighborhoods, 2
character
    anal (*See* anal character)
    bourgeois family forms and, 114–121
    concept as bridge between theories of intrapsychic functioning and society, 92
    consumption and, 124–125

character (*continued*)
    culture and development of, 114–122
    ego and, 114
    multiple kinds of, 120–121
    oral, 92, 117–123, 124
    strong-farmer, 91
    structure and ethnicity, 87–93
Character Analysis, 87, 114
"charisma, the routinization of," 79
child abuse and neglect
    authoritarianism and, 93
    awareness of, 15
    rates, 100
    reporting, 82–83, 100–101, 134–135
    responses to, 133–135
    substance abuse and, 17
child protection, changes in, 40–41
child removal, procedures for, 24–26
child welfare, community endorsement of, 18–19
children, reasons for having multiple, 4
Christianity in Europe, 122–123, 170*n*17, 28
circumcision, female, 111, 112
client demonstrations of 1968, 11–12
clients, ethics and notification of, 9
clients, relationships with welfare systems of, 8–9
clinical social workers, 150
clitoridectomy, 111, 112
Cloward, R., 150
Code of Ethics of National Association of Social Workers (NASW) (2000), 108, 109–110
Cohen, Barton, 35, 36
Cohen Caucus, 36, 39
collective representations concept, 114
Columbia University student strikes of 1968, 12
commercialization, 91
commodities, people as, 60
communal *vs.* individualist cultures, 113, 163*n*6

community endorsement of child welfare, 18–19
Conboy Trucking Company, 13
Concord Hotel, 37
conflicts between nonsynchronous life worlds, 142
conflicts within families, 123–125
conservative politics and social welfare, 149–151
consumer culture, 124–125
consumption and character formation, 124–125
contraception, 57, 80
controls and tracking tasks, 3
Corbett, Ray, 37
Council on Social Work Education (n. d.), 151
court, testifying in, 83
court intervention with children, 136
crack epidemic, 75–76
critical theory, 92–93
Critical Theory of the Family, 60–61
cult of the saints, 122–123, 170–171*n*29
cultural adaptation, 88
cultural competence, 108–113
cultural rights movement, 112
culture
    addicts, 16
    consumer, 124–125
    development of character and, 114–122
    dominant American, 112
    gender and, 112
    individualist *vs.* communal, 113, 163*n*6
    maladaptive practices and, 109–113
    understanding and defining, 109

D

Das Kapital, 60
de Leonites, 154*n*9
democratic values and subjective individuality, 46, 109, 112

demographic changes of the hospital, 97–99, 130
demonstrations of 1968, client, 11–12
Denise (co-delegate for union), 39–40
depressive characteristics, 118
Devlin, J., 117
Devore, W., 84–85
diagnostic phase, 93
diagnostic-related groupings (DRGs), 148
Dilthey, W., 141
diversion process and adolescents, 136
diversity, social, 108–113
doctoral program, 63–65
doctors, and communication with patients, 75
doctors, attitudes of, 71, 129–30, 129–130
doctors and testifying in court, 83
domestic violence, 77–78, 93, 99, 135
draft evasion, 6–7
Dubious Conceptions, 4
Duby, G., 117
Durkheim, E., 113–114
Durkheim, É., 113, 123
Dÿkema, C. R., 43, 60
Dÿkema, Christopher, biography of, *v–vi*

E
economics and family forms, 45–46
ego, character of the, 114, 121
Ego and Mechanisms of Defense, The, 107
Ego and the Id, The, 107
Ehrenreich, J., 149
elderly patients, 71–74, 101–106
Emergency Children's Service (ECS), 134
Emigrants and Exiles, 87, 90
empirical practice, 64
empiricism, abstracted, 63
Erbscharft dieser Zeit, 140–141
errors and social work practice, 29–32
ethclass, 84
ethics and decisions and laws affecting clients, 9
Ethnic-Sensitive Social Work Practice, 84

ethnicity, social work interest in, 83–85
ethnicity and bereavement differences, 74
Ethnicity and Family Therapy, 85
ethnicity and suicidal adolescents, 78–79
Europe, religion in, 122–123
Ewen, S., 124
experience, subjective, 143

F
Fabricant, M., 148
factory systems, 115–116
Fadiman, A., 144
families, conflict sources within, 123–125
families and reasons for multiple children, 4
families as an institution, 45–46, 59
Family Court Act, 25
family forms
    bourgeois, 45–46, 89–90, 114–121, 155n3, 158n12
    peasant forms, 121
    personality and, 61
    strong-farmer structure, 91
family history, 23–24
family planning, 4, 89
family structure and oppression, 23
fantasies and understandings of the world, 87–89
farmer family, the strong-, 91
fatalism and peasant character, 118–119
fathers, positions of, 48, 91–93, 121–124, 172n33
feces and money, 88
feeding/eating too much, history of, 119–120
Felumero, Roxanne, 15
female circumcision, 111, 112
feminism, 22–23, 41
Fenichel, O., 118
Fenton, Jim, 5
feudalism and patriarchy, 122, 169n25
fiscal crises, 34–35, 38–39
Fiscal Crisis of the State, 19

INDEX

Five Percenter, 53
Flexnor, Abraham, 149
Foster, G. M., 116, 117–118
foster care systems, long term care, adoptions and, 51–52
foster care systems, problems in, 40
foster care systems and group care *vs.* family settings, 59
Frankfurt School, 44, 64, 92–93
Frenkel-Brunswik, E., 64
Freud, A., 107
Freud, S., 88, 107, 114–115
From Max Weber, 9
Fromm, E., 64

G

geist/spirit, 142, 160*n*1, 174*n*11
Gemeinschaft und Gesellschaft, 114, 163–164*n*7
gender and culture, 112
generations and social change, 85
genital mutilation, 111, 112
Gerth, H., 9, 107
Giordano, J., 85
Glazer, N., 83
Goffman, E., 7
Goldstein, Eda, 44
González-López, G, 125
González-Wippler, M., 123
"good, limited," 117–118
Gramsci, Antonio, 39
gratification, delay of, 119–120
grief and ethnic distinctions, 74
group care *vs.* family settings, 59
Gurevich, A, 120, 122–123

H

Handlin, O., 60, 91
health maintenance organizations (HMOs), 99, 101, 102–103
Heartbreak Tango, 107, 108
Hegel, G. W. E., 1427

helping relationships, developing, 56–58
Heritage of this Time, 140–141
Hermand, J., 154*n*5
heroin epidemic, 16–17, 76
Hill, Stanley, 35–36
history of family, 23–24
History of the Russian Revolution, 6
Horkheimer, M., 65, 92
Horrors of the Half-Known Life, 87, 89
Hospital of the Albert Einstein College of Medicine (HAECOM), 67
hospital social work practice, 46–47, 69
Husserl, E., 141

I

id, 121
illness, social work practice during, 29–32
"Image of Limited Good," 117–118
immigration, history of, 86–87, 117, 130–131, 143–144, 147–148
individualist *vs.* communal cultures, 113, 163*n*6
individuality, 46
industrial workers, urban, 86
inheritances, 91
Institut für Sozialforschung, 92
Institute for Social Research, 92
institutions, exiting and new, 141
institutions, total, 7–8
intermarriage among ethnic groups, 84
interpreters, 131, 172–173*n*1
interventions, authoritative, 28–32
interventions, domestic violence, 77–78
interventive appropriateness, 64
Irish immigration, 90–91, 159–160*n*17
Irish potato famine, 86, 91, 120–121

J

Jay, M., 64, 92
Jewish Board of Family and Children's Services (JBFCS), 43
Journal of Progressive Human Services, 60

Journal of Sociology and Social Welfare, 43
judicial intervention with children, 136

K

Kashdan, Mr., 9
Keniston, Kenneth, 5
Kernberg, Otto, 44, 47
Kernberg, Paulina, 46
Kingbridge Welfare Center, 2–3
Kingsbridge Heights Long-Term Home Health Care Program, 101
Kluckhohn, C., 109
Knight, Patrick, 36
Kroeber, A. L., 109
Kronberger, Rachel, 16

L

Ladurie, E. L., 117, 141
"left" outlook, new, 17–18
Left-Wing Communism, an Infantile Disorder, 6
legitimacy in social work, pursuit of, 63, 148–149
Lenin, Vladimir Il'ich, 5–6
Leninism, 6, 154n11, 12
Lerner, Michael, 41
Les Formes Élémentaire de la Vie Réligieuse, 113
Levinson, D. J., 64
life-worlds, 141–144
"limited good," 117–118
literacy and relationships, 90
Lombardy, Tarky, 101
Lombardy Program, 101
Luker, K., 4

M

managed care, 129
mandated reporting, 28, 101
Marcus, S., 87, 88–89, 90
Marolla Place group home, 51

marriage and family forms, 89, 91, 158–59n13, 158n12, 169n25
Marx, Karl, 6, 60
Marxism, 6, 44
Master's in Business Administration (MBA), 107
masturbation, 88, 89, 157n10
MBAs (Master's in Business Administration), 107
McGoldrick, M., 85
Medicaid HMOs, 102–103
medical coverage, absence of, 130
medical residents, attitudes of, 71, 98–99, 129–130
medieval life and religion, 115, 122–123
Medieval Popular Culture, 120
middle class and immigration, 86
Miller, K. A., 87, 90–91, 91, 120
Mills, C. W., 9, 10, 63, 107
Moberg, D., 150
Moberg, V., 91
modernity, 90
money, lack of, 3–4
money and feces, 88
money and relationships, 90
monotheism, 60–61
Montefiore Medical Center, 67, 97–99
Moon, Sun Myung, 50–51
Morgenstern, Martin, 35
Moynihan, D. P., 83
multicultural thinking, 111–113, 160n3
Murray, C., 149
My Secret Life, 90
mythopoeic thought, 122–123

N

National Association of Social Workers (NASW): *Code of Ethics* (2000), 108, 109–110
New American Movement (NAM), 6, 41, 60
"new left" outlook, 17–18
New York City Department of Welfare training, 1–2

Nickerson, Lucius, 3, 9
Nietzsche, F., 39
Nine, Luis, 37
non-synchronism, 140–144
norms, existing and new, 141
note writing, 138–139
Novak, M., 83
nurses, characteristics of, 69

O

object relations theory, 11, 28, 41
objectivations, 141–142
objective force, 116
O'Connor, J., 19, 148
oedipal conflict, 121
Okin, S. M., 111, 160n3
oppression, government as instrument of, 22–23
oppression and cultural practices of groups, 109–111
oral character, 92, 117–123, 124
orgasms, 88
Origin and Function of Culture, The, 109
Other Victorians, The, 87
overfeeding/overeating, history of, 119–120
Owusu-Bempah, K., 113, 163n6
Ozment, S., 117

P

paperwork, 55–56, 106
parental authority, 124–125
parents, working with, 136–138
patriarchal monotheism, 51, 60–61, 122
patriarchy and family forms, 45, 61, 121–122
Pearce. J. K., 85
peasant populations
    agriculture in, 119, 120
    Americans and, 117, 165n12
    change in, 120, 167–168n18
    character structure and, 90
    families in, 60–61, 121

    forms of, 116–117
    immigration and, 86
    life of, 117–123
    moving from rural to urban, 91
    prevalence of, 46
    rebellions and, 119, 165–167n16
    religion and, 60–61
Perelman, M., 149
person-in-situation, 139–140
personality. *See also* character
    contemporary inconsistent demands on, 92
    development of, 118
    family forms and, 45–46, 61
    formation of, 114
    Victorian, 87–90
pessimistic characteristics, 118
physical abuse, 82
Pierce, D., 151
Pirenne, H., 121
Piven, F. F., 150
police and roles in child removal, 24–25
policies, family planning and social, 4
politics and social welfare, conservative, 149–151
politics and social work practice, 149–151
Pollitt, K., 112
Positivist–empiricist approach, 64
Poster, M., 60–61, 89, 114, 121
potato famine, Irish, 86, 91, 120–121
poverty, 119–120, 149–150
pregnancy, adolescent, 79–80, 99–100
prestige within social work practice, 41
Prison Notebooks, 39
professional staff, 10–11
professionalism, elements of, 11
Progressive Labor Party (PLP), 6, 35, 39–40
proletarianization, 46, 89, 92
protestantism in Puerto Rican population, 78–79, 156–157n3
psychiatric patients, 78–79, 135–138
psychoanalysis, 11, 44, 47, 108, 149
psychodynamic theory, 11, 44, 47, 108, 149

psychosocial assessment, general theory of, 93
psychosocial assessment, perspectives on, 117
psychosocial assessment, social aspects of, 93
psychosocial assessment and life-world concept, 141–144
Puig, M., 107, 108

R
race and hospital admissions, 71
rape, 78, 99
reading list for social work students, 107–108
reality, creating new, 141
reality and nonsynchronism, 143
red-diaper babies, 5
Redfield, R., 113
reform of welfare system, 11–12
Reich, W., 87, 114
relationships, money and literacy, 90
religion and domestic violence, 135
religion and family forms, 60–61
religion and medieval life, 115
religion and peasant populations, 122–123
religion and suicidal adolescents, 78–79
removal of children from homes, procedures for, 24–28
Représentations Individuelles et Représentations Collectives, 113
research, hypothesis-testing, 63
research, quantitative, 149
resources, shortage of, 149–150
revisionism, 39, 154n11, 154n12
Reynolds, B. C., 107
Richmond, M., 131
Rise of the Unmeltable Ethnics, The, 83
"Robert," 54
Róheim, G., 109
"routinization of charisma," 79
rural populations, 56, 60–61, 86. *See also* peasant populations
Ruskin, J., 45, 155n3

S
sadistic characteristics, 118–119
Saint Lawrence Avenue group home, 49–51
saints, cult of, 122–123, 170–171n29
Sanford, R. N., 64
scarcity *vs.* abundance, 117–118
Schlesinger, E., 84–85
Schor, J. B., 115, 116
Schultz, T. W., 119, 120
scientific thought, foundation of, 123
Service Employees International Union, 107
Seton Watson, H., 91
sexual abuse, 20–22, 40, 43
sexuality, approaches to client, 57
sexually transmitted diseases and adolescents, 79–80
shake injuries, 100–101
"Smith, Mr.", 53–55
social change, generational, 85
social classes, 91
social diversity, 108–113
Social Service Employees Union (SSEU), 4–5, 34
social theory, 47–48, 108
social welfare and conservative politics, 149–151
Social Work and Social Living, Explorations in Philosophy and Practice, 107
social work practice
　attacks on, 149–151
　authority and, 24, 28–32
　borderline personality disorder and, 47
　complexities of, 140
　core dilemma, 144
　errors in, 29–32
　essence of, 71
　immigration and effects on, 147–148
　interpretation of medical findings, 74–75
　note writing, 138–139

social work practice (*continued*)
    prestige in fields of, 41
    pursuit of legitimacy, 63, 148
    social theory and application to, 4
    values, 112
    views of family as an institution, 59
Socialist Revolution, 19
society as the soul of religion, 123
Spanish-language signage, 67–68
Spartacist League, 6, 35
Special Services for Children, 49
spermatic economy, 88–89, 90
Spielberg, S., 107
spirit, the, 142, 160*n*1, 174*n*11
Spirit Catches You and You Fall Down, The, 144
staff, professional, 10–11
Stars Down to Earth, 87, 92
Steinberg, S., 84, 86
"Stravinsky, Sergei," 32–34
strikes, 1968 Columbia University student, 12
strikes, union, 4–5
strong-farmer family, the, 91
Students for a Democratic Society (SDS), 5–6
subjective experience, 143
subjectivity, 46–47
substance abuse and child neglect, 17
Sugarland Express, 107
Sugarman, Jule, 35
suicidal adolescents, 78–79, 99
superego, development of, 114–115, 121
supervision of social work students, 83, 107, 138–139
Sweezy, P. M., 92

T

Tar, Z., 92
testifying in court, 83
The Uncommitted: A Study of Alienated Youth in American Society, 5

theories of social work practice, need for, 151
Thompson, E. P., 115
time, concepts of, 116
Tonnies, F., 114
total institutions, 7–8
transitional objects, 26
Trotsky, Leon, 6
Trotskyite Workers League, 6, 35, 36
Turner, F. J., 93

U

Unification Church of Sun Myung Moon, 50–51
Union, Social Service Employees, 4–5
unions
    American Arbitration Association (AAA), 36
    American Federation of Labor-Congress of Industrial Organizations (AFL-CIO), 37
    American Federation of State, County, and Municipal Employees (AFSCME), 4, 34–36
    challenges faced by, 4, 34–36, 36–39
    Cohen Caucus, 36, 39
    senior delegate duties, 38
    Service Employees International Union, 107
    social workers and, 150
    strikes, 4–5
unovercome, 143
Uprooted, 60
U.S. Department of Housing and Urban Development (2011), 149

V

van Arsdale, Harry, 36
Victorian character, 87–90
Vierhaus, R., 141
Vietnam War and student strikes, 12
Vigilante, Florence, 44

villages as families, 121
virginity clearance, 80–81, 99
voice, use of, 25
Volunteers in Service to America, 11

W
Walter, 90, 159*n*15
Watkins, J. M., 151
Weber, E., 117
Weber, M., 9, 10, 79, 107
welfare system, community endorsement of, 18–19
welfare system, reform of, 11–12
welfare system in 1960s, 1–2
Wiggershaus, R., 92

Winnicott, D. W., 26
withdrawal babies, 16–17
women in bourgeois families, 45, 155*n*3
Woodham-Smith, C., 91, 120
work attitudes of the poor, 119–120
Work Experience Program (WEP), 33–34, 154*n*8
working class, 91

Y
youth, elevation of, 124

Z
Zaretsky, E., 45, 46, 59, 92, 114